Un EXTRAÑO SENTIMIENTO ME INVADE,
SIENDO ALGUIEN TAN CELOSO DE SU PRIVACIDAD.
ESPERO QUE COMPARTIR ESTA EXPERIENCIA
SEA TAN EXCITANTE PARA USTEDES COMO LO
HA SIDO PARA MI.
ME GUSTARÍA QUE EL LECTOR SE SITUARA
EN LAS CIRCUNSTANCIAS DE CADA MOMENTO.
PORQUE FÚTBOL ES, O ASÍ LO SIENTO,
UN CONTEXTO DE EMOCIONES.

I have a strange feeling embarking on this
journey with you. I am very private, extremely so.

But I hope that sharing this experience will be as
exciting for you as it was for me.

I want the reader to place him or herself in the
circumstances of each moment.

Because football is, or feels at least to me, a context
of emotions.

Also by Guillem Balagué

A Season on the Brink
Pep Guardiola: Another Way of Winning
Messi
Barca: The Illustrated History of FC Barcelona
Cristiano Ronaldo: The Biography

INSIDE POCHETTINO'S SPURS

Guillem Balagué

WEIDENFELD & NICOLSON

First published in Great Britain in 2017 by Weidenfeld & Nicolson
an imprint of The Orion Publishing Group Ltd
Carmelite House, 50 Victoria Embankment
London EC4Y 0DZ

An Hachette UK Company

9 10

A CIP catalogue record for this book is
available from the British Library.

ISBN 978-1-4091-5771-7 (hardback)
ISBN 978-1-4091-5772-4 (trade paperback)

Typeset by Input Data Services Ltd, Somerset

Printed and bound in Great Britain by Clays Ltd, Elcograf S.p.A.

www.orionbooks.co.uk

To all of you at Biggleswade United who show me daily the all-conquering force of togetherness, humour and passion

CONTENTS

CONTENTS

LIST OF ILLUSTRATIONS

Pages 3, 33, 61, 93, 118, 143, 171, 192, 209, 226, 250, 260, 261, 262, 263, 264 and 265 courtesy of Tottenham Hotspur Football Club/Getty Images.

Plate Section One
1. My favourite photo. (Courtesy of Mauricio Pochettino)
2. I played outdoors all the time during my childhood and always loved animals. (Courtesy of Mauricio Pochettino)
3. Here we were playing in the Third Division for Newell's second team. (Courtesy of Mauricio Pochettino)
4. This is the day when Karina set her sights on me. (Courtesy of Mauricio Pochettino)
5. With my father and my brothers Martín and Javier. (Courtesy of Mauricio Pochettino)

6. With Jorge Griffa, the coach who handed me my debut and was in charge of the Newell's youth academy. (Courtesy of Mauricio Pochettino)

7. José Manuel Lara, as majority shareholder, played a key role in that period of Espanyol's history. (Pep Morata Morales/*Mundo Deportivo*)

8. With Toni, Spurs' current goalkeeping coach. (Courtesy of Mauricio Pochettino)

9. We could see them blowing up Sarrià from our flat in September 1997. (Courtesy of Mauricio Pochettino)

10. With Marcelo Bielsa. (Rodolfo Molina/*Mundo Deportivo*)

11. Enjoying success with Espanyol was particularly special. (Carlos Mira/RCD Espanyol)

12. Karina, Sebastiano and Yolanda on the day of the Copa del Rey final at Mestalla. (Courtesy of Mauricio Pochettino)

13. I'm actually crying in this picture. (Courtesy of Mauricio Pochettino)

14. I scored against Marseille in the Coupe de France at the Parc des Princes by heading in a Hugo Leal corner. (Courtesy of Mauricio Pochettino)

15. Diego Maradona invited me to his Boca testimonial versus Argentina. (Courtesy of Mauricio Pochettino)

16. Ronnie had just come over to PSG from Brazil. (Courtesy of Mauricio Pochettino)

17. I am extremely fond of Mikel Arteta, who will go on to be a wonderful coach. (Courtesy of Mauricio Pochettino)

18. With my mother Amalia and my brother Martín on my farm. (Courtesy of Mauricio Pochettino)

19. With my cows on my land in Argentina. (Courtesy of Mauricio Pochettino)

20. This photo of me with Simeone and Batistuta is from the 2002 World Cup in Japan. (Courtesy of Mauricio Pochettino)

21. After the 2002 World Cup, we went to Disneyland with my children and my in-laws. (Courtesy of Mauricio Pochettino)

22. In Bordeaux, France, I discovered the magic of wine. (Courtesy of Mauricio Pochettino)

23. With Zinedine Zidane. (Courtesy of Mauricio Pochettino)

Plate Section Two

arrived in Barcelona we went to the pool. (Courtesy of Mauricio Pochettino)

17. Meeting Sir Alex Ferguson was one of the greatest professional pleasures that I have experienced. (Courtesy of Mauricio Pochettino)

18. José Mourinho and I have always had a very good relationship. (Courtesy of Mauricio Pochettino)

19. In Nice with Daniel Levy on the way to Joe Lewis's yacht during the summer when I decided to join Tottenham. (Courtesy of Mauricio Pochettino)

20. In the car with Miguel, Jesús, Toni and Xavier Elaine, our chiropractor and medical expert. (Courtesy of Mauricio Pochettino)

21. The trip to Argentina with Daniel Levy and the coaching staff brought us closer together. (Courtesy of Mauricio Pochettino)

22. Going for a walk and getting away from everything. Sometimes you come across some real gems while clearing your thoughts. (Courtesy of Mauricio Pochettino)

FOREWORD
by Karina Grippaldi

I'm overjoyed to be writing the foreword to this book about Mauricio Pochettino, his life and his number one passion: football.

We met on a night out when I was a student at the National University of Rosario and he was celebrating a *clásico* win, when Newell's beat Central. It was a fabulous evening. Since then, we've been down all the paths that football has taken us on together and our lives certainly revolve around the beautiful game. We've had many years filled with marvellous experiences and others that haven't been quite so wonderful, but we've certainly learned from all of them.

We've created a united family and we all support one another. We're far from our loved ones back in Argentina, but we're lucky to have fantastic friends. As a family, we all have our own individual dreams, but we adapt and support each other, trusting in one another's decisions.

He is certainly the leader of the family and the one whose strength has taken us on so many adventures. Mauricio is incredibly sensitive. He's a people person who likes hearing stories and listening, thanks to his pleasant and positive disposition.

He enjoys spending time with friends and family, and making the most of the little free time at home that he has to play football, tennis or ping-pong with our two boys, do some gym work with me or simply watch a film while having some *mate*, our loyal hot drinking companion. We enjoy our garden or the local green spaces by going on a walk through the park whenever possible. Such moments help him relax, switch off and recharge his batteries for what lies ahead.

He spends almost all his time at the training ground, where I regularly visit him to deal with little family issues and just to see him for a bit, however briefly it may be.

I think we form a strong team. I like seeing myself as the 'guardian of our intimacy'. It all helps build a balance in our lives and daily existence. Experience tells us that there are no straight lines in football. You can go from glory to criticism, being ignored or slated in an instant, so between us we try to maintain the right distance and equilibrium to accept and enjoy our place in the world.

I very much doubt that I've ever given him advice that has helped him do his job. I think Mauricio has exactly what it takes to do what he does. He's like the ocean in that he's plentiful and strong, he flattens all that lies before him and he is relentless. The wise water covers everything in its way, always finds gaps and embarks on new paths.

He isn't scared and sees every opportunity as a challenge. That's his essence. He sees life as an adventure worth exploring and his motto is 'tranquilidad', calmness.

I, on the other hand, am rainwater. I like to nourish, organise, lay the foundations and seek out stability so that my house is a paradise where you can recharge your batteries and come up with and develop new ideas.

That's how we complement one another.

INTRODUCTION

All of literature, Leo Tolstoy pointed out, comes down to one of two stories: a man goes on a journey or a stranger comes to town. What you hold now comprises both of those two things. First, it recounts a journey, that of the 2016–17 season, Pochettino's third at Spurs. But it is also the story of someone who has been a stranger since he left his home in Murphy as a teenage boy.

This is and isn't a diary of Mauricio's campaign. Allow me to explain. It is a kind of collage. His words, his thoughts, his experiences are in here. Some were said by him in the conversations we had on an almost weekly basis. Others were told to me by the people around him to fill in some gaps: players that he has coached in the past or that he coaches now explained private moments, crucial tactical chats, reasons for hugs. Professional colleagues recollected memories of times past. Friends did the same. Travelling companions uncovered little secrets. And big ones.

Eventually their words have become Pochettino's words, channelled through me and always reviewed, although never censored, by the man himself to ensure they reflected his thoughts and actions. This diary that both is and isn't a diary is something of a literary trick that hopes to give readers a better insight into his ideas and methods, as I have gained over the course of a remarkable season. Sometimes Pochettino did not recognise his voice, feeling that in written form his thoughts sounded too brusque. At others he was surprised by how deeply he had explored his shortcomings, learning process and journey, but the rule was not to look back months later and change the predominant feeling at the time. Eventually we agreed that what came out was unusual (a biography in the first person) but that it best explains this particular moment in his career and life.

My chats with him were very regular and the transcriptions have filled hundreds of pages, but they were not weekly, as originally planned, because at times he distanced himself. Like tides that ebb and flow, so Mauricio could be hard to pin down. There were many reasons for his sudden absences, which you will discover later.

At such moments his assistant Jesús Pérez took on a key role, by telling me how the week was going, what it was like in training and how they negotiated any obstacles on and off the pitch. Miguel d'Agostino, the member of the coaching staff who has known Mauricio for the longest, sent me audio files from his car en-route to training, with stories from Rosario, Barcelona, France, Southampton and London. We sometimes sat down with Toni Jiménez for a chat. Karina, his wife, did a key job as quartermaster, searching through photos and adding essential detail.

So let us start by hearing where he stood at the start of the 2016–17 season and soon after how the life of 'Mauricio the Stranger' has developed since his early days in the fields of Murphy, a village where nothing ever happened, but where parameters were set that have stayed with him ever since. He will, at the same time, embark with us on the journey through the season in the form of a diary that is real, but is also not real. Even though everything is true.

1.

SUMMER AND PRE-SEASON

Tottenham Hotspur came third in 2015–16, a remarkable achievement for a club that has to operate without the hefty budgets available to Arsenal, Chelsea, Liverpool, Manchester City and Manchester United. The final league match of the campaign, however, a 5–1 thrashing at the hands of already-relegated Newcastle, left a bad taste in the mouth of Mauricio Pochettino and his coaching staff. The target for the upcoming season was crystal clear: improvement. The coach and most members of the squad were gearing up for their Champions League debut and Tottenham's second foray into Europe's premier club competition, after a five-year absence. While making plans for the new journey, Pochettino could still hear the roars from a rocking St James' Park home faithful celebrating the Championship-bound side's assortment of goals.

Why did we start our holidays before that match? What did we do wrong? That uncomfortable place is where we are at the moment. It was all my fault. I did something wrong. We have to understand the underlying cause behind that defeat.

*

I got the screen out at half-time, when we were 2–0 down. But it wasn't a matter of altering the position of our defensive line or which players played where. 'What's happening here has nothing to do with tactics. We aren't battling. You aren't yourselves on the pitch!' I repeated that several times.

But it was to no avail.

Where was the individual commitment that gave us that special feeling of belonging to the group? I get very annoyed when I cannot find the way to motivate, to generate the passion necessary to enjoy this game.

Was it my fault?

*

At the end of the game, I headed into an empty dressing room. The players gradually came in, but I swiftly had to head off to see to my media commitments with radio and television. I came back 45 minutes later, by which point they had all showered and got changed, so I couldn't say anything. What was I to do?

We went back down to London together, but there was no way to get the players on their own. I didn't even try. Everyone had serious expressions on their faces. They certainly all had their own ideas in their heads and had reached their own conclusions. We were not avoiding one another, but nobody was smiling. We felt embarrassed when we crossed paths, and if we saw a fan we kept our heads down.

Players want first and foremost to win, of course, because they're the ones who are on the pitch, and there's nowhere to hide. But sometimes they live their own reality – without realising it, they become trapped in a bubble. A player's entourage protects him and often blocks out other worlds out there, only allowing him to see his own. Of course, a footballer must look after himself and put up walls in order to ensure that external factors don't have an overbearing impact, but in order to perform well he needs a balance of self-esteem, ego, his own reality and other realities outside those walls. Excessive self-criticism is crushing, as is ignorance of the wider world.

It becomes a serious matter when there's a mental disconnect with the basic principles of the game – if the footballer's aim isn't a shared one, but purely individual, and he forgets the required order in this sport: that the individual shines more when at the service of the team and the structure that supports him.

I was thinking about all of that as we landed back in London from Newcastle. I got in the car and headed home. The first thing that I did when I got there was open a bottle of wine and stuff myself with unhealthy food. I think I let my frustration out on myself. I ate the lot: crisps, snacks ... If we had pizza, some of that as well. No salad. The wine was Argentinian: a Malbec. Whenever I am slightly down, I like to smell Argentinian wine. It makes me happy and takes me back to my country, to recognisable places, to when I was a boy, the redolence of the countryside where I lived until the age of eight, in that house with an orchard and horses ... If I am challenged to some blind wine tasting, I quickly suss out which one is Argentinian, particularly Malbec.

Today I started this diary.

*

Not even 24 hours have passed since the game. I've just received a message from Harry Kane saying thank you for the season and that it was a good year despite the final match ... You could see that he felt ashamed at the end of the game.

I'm not going to reply. He doesn't expect it either.

*

I've started the summer in Qatar. I received an invitation from one of the directors at Aspetar Hospital in Doha, Dr Hakim Chalabi, a good friend of mine who was my doctor at Paris Saint-Germain. It's a three-day trip with Jesús Pérez, my assistant and right-hand man, and my son Sebastiano, who specialises in sports science. We've had a great time and they've explained to us how they're preparing for the World Cup in Qatar.

Everybody was impressed by our campaign. There was talk that we'd played the best football, had the most shots on goal, conceded the fewest goals and the rest, but I couldn't brush off the embarrassment of what had happened on the final day.

I'm experiencing another type of deeper pain. My father-in-law is unwell. He went to Barcelona to continue his treatment, and when we saw him, my wife Karina and I could tell that he wasn't right. He wasn't the same person whom we knew and had enjoyed spending time with two years ago, the last time we saw him.

*

I've just sent good luck messages to the players at Euro 2016, which has just kicked off. While I was writing to them I thought about how at Newcastle we had stopped doing what we'd been practising for two years. Finishing third is certainly not the same as finishing second, even though some seem to think it is. Arsenal leapfrogged us in the end. I didn't recognise my own team.

I should've seen it coming. I should've sensed that some of them were already on holiday and others were thinking about the Euros. In reality, we did sense it and we did see it. I should've stopped that negative spiral, but how?

Sending them good-luck messages hurts. I'll do it before every game, but it hurts.

How can anyone think that finishing third is the same as finishing second?

*

You learn from everything.

I played football and volleyball between the ages of eight and ten. I liked football the most, but lots of girls played volleyball, so . . . We'd play in an indoor gym and when we went to local villages, the girls would come with us for their own matches. I really loved playing volleyball, especially in away games.

I also did judo. The teacher was a strong Japanese man with a very dark character. His son was a year older than me, strong from practising martial arts almost from birth, and also the goalkeeper of a rival team that I came up against during a tournament in Murphy. I was our best player. I went up for a corner and started to position myself to receive the ball, which was delivered with real venom. I began to jump and what ensued left its mark on me for ever.

That son of a . . . of a goalkeeper came up to me and pulled my shorts down to try to put me off. Imagine the fans! And the parents! I was ten years old! It pissed me off so much . . . I cried and cried because I felt so powerless on the pitch. Everyone was looking at me.

6

People who were there and people who weren't. The whole world! Or that is how it felt. It was the most humiliating moment of my life. The most insufferable part was the fact that I didn't have the balls to react . . . I should've grabbed him by the neck and punched his lights out!

Of course it was a lesson. It's useful for when someone beats you in a game, gets the better of you in a duel or you get nutmegged. It makes you fight against your destiny and gives you strength. You retrieve energy from places you thought previously empty. That helped me be even stronger, braver and more passionate.

The next time that something like that happened, I gave the guy a punch. That was in the Argentinian first division. We were playing San Lorenzo and Francisco Oscar Lamolina was the referee. One of the opposition strikers tackled me from behind. I just stood my ground and he shoved his head in my face. He insulted me and I certainly didn't hold back. I could see him working the saliva. He spat at me and his gob went into my mouth! Of course, at that moment of indignation I went to clobber him. As I was approaching his face, I was regretting it. In the end I only made a light connection, so the referee, who could see that I was sorry and what the guy had done, said to me, 'You idiot, what the hell are you doing? I'm going to bloody send you off! Actually, I'm not going to because I saw what the other guy did and I'd have to send you both off!' Both of us stayed on the pitch! That is how it often works in the first division in Argentina! What a wonderful decision.

Lamolina later told me that he would've done the same.

*

I don't know exactly why I'm writing all this. Nor the reason behind the order – or lack thereof – in which I tell the stories. I don't know what to talk about, or if it's suitable for a diary. Maybe it's a good time to reflect on where I come from and try to piece together the puzzle of what I've been and what I am. If that's the aim, I imagine I should start from the start. It's a good time to begin this because I've suddenly found myself with time on my hands that I wasn't expecting. We went on a family holiday to the Bahamas for a week, but it rained every single day. What was supposed to be a week of sunbathing turned into anything but I watched football while we were waiting for the weather to clear up. It was my saviour. I was in a lovely house and the television had cable, meaning every game in the Euros and Copa América was broadcast live. Football comforted me. My wife was rather irritated, of course. My sons were delighted to watch it with me. Three against one – not much of a balance.

We ended up cutting short our trip to the Bahamas. We'd have come back sooner, but I couldn't find any flights. So we made a swift return to London, and then headed to Barcelona to enjoy a week of sunbathing by the pool at our family apartment. And all the while, I've been making notes and filling up blank pages between flights, rain, matches and breaks.

In particular, I've been thinking about Murphy and Newell's, where I made my first steps in football. But before that, I need to go back to my bedroom at my parents' house when I was a teenager. I was asleep when negotiations for my transfer to Newell's Old Boys began in the early hours.

There were two boys from Murphy three or four years older than me who played for Rosario Central. One of them, David Bisconti, went on to play in the first division and for the national team. The guys wanted me to join them at Central. One day I trained with them and the club wanted to sign me straight away, but I was 13 and still finishing the academic year in Murphy, the town in Santa Fe where I was born, some 160 kilometres from Rosario. I couldn't sign until the end of the school year in December or January, so they suggested I went to training with them once or twice a week while I still played in Murphy. Dele Alli did a similar thing when we signed him: he trained with us, but played for League One outfit MK Dons where he came from. In my case I was in a team that were three or four years older than me, but held my own well. I thought I would end up at Central.

This is how the days went: I studied agriculture at a local school around 20 kilometres from my house. I would wake up at 6 a.m. to get the bus and around 5 p.m., after I finished school, I would embark on the three-hour journey to Rosario. Sometimes my dad would take me, but mostly I went on the bus, spending those three hours sleeping or talking to people. That journey used to get on my nerves as the bus stopped everywhere – just like a milkman! I eventually had to change schools to one where I only had to go in the morning and did not have to rush to go to training.

When I got to the facilities at Rosario Central, I would train and then spend the night at their digs. I would work again in the morning and then go home. At the weekend I played in my home town on Saturdays and Sundays. It all started again on Mondays.

On one of those Mondays, Marcelo Bielsa and Jorge Griffa from Newell's Old Boys, Central's city rivals, set up a trial for a group of players in Villa Cañás, a town around 50 kilometres from Murphy. There was a coach in Villa Cañás who knew me and was aware I was a good player, so he asked my father to take me. On that trial day, I left school and got to Murphy around 6 p.m. I was exhausted after a long day at school and having played at the weekend. I didn't fancy going. I told my father and he told me not to worry, so we didn't go to the trial.

At breakfast on Tuesday morning, my father told me what had happened the previous night.

It turns out that after the trial Bielsa and Griffa, who were travelling all over the country in search of fledgling talent, were having a hearty meal with the coach who knew me and they asked him if there were any other interesting prospects in the area. He replied, 'Yes, the best of the lot didn't come because he's at Central.' They looked at each other as if to say, 'no way'. 'Where does he live?' they asked. And they set off to meet me.

It was one o'clock in the morning in the middle of winter.

They reached the service station in Murphy and asked the very few passers-by around at that time of night until they found the house. They knocked on the door and my mother got up. They told her who they were, but she refused to open up, opting to fetch my father instead. She woke him up, and because he had heard about them, he invited them in for a coffee. Bielsa later told me that after chatting for five or ten minutes and explaining why they were there, they didn't know what to say or talk about, so they decided to ask my father, 'Could we see the boy?' Despite the early hour, my proud parents said yes and they came to my bedroom to take a look.

They saw me sleeping and Griffa asked, 'May I see his legs?' My mother pulled the covers off me and they both said, 'He looks like a footballer. Look at those legs!' Of course! What were they going to say to my parents? Although my small bedroom was full of people admiring my legs, I slept like a log and had no idea about it until my old man spilled the beans the following morning.

From that point, they started calling my father to convince him to take me to training. I didn't want to go. I was happy at Central. My grandfather, who had a friend who had played for Newell's, was the one who convinced me. So I went to meet Bielsa and Griffa. I travelled by bus, because my father was busy working the land. Again, it took me three nervous hours to get to Rosario. Some club representatives were waiting for me at the station and they took me to the training ground. They asked me to change into the kit that I'd brought with me (shorts, shirt, socks, boots), unlike now at Spurs where you turn up and they give you everything. I was introduced to Bielsa, who said to me, 'Go and warm up with the group and join the game. Where do you play?'

'Centre-back,' I answered.

'But aren't you a striker?'

'Well, in my town I play up front, but I don't like it, I'm a defender.'

'OK, that's where you'll play, in defence.'

The game kicked off and five minutes in, after touching the ball three or four times, they said to me, 'Come off, someone else is coming on.' I thought, 'What is going on here?'

'Come here, kid, sit down.' Bielsa was next to me, sitting on a ball. 'Look, in January we're playing in a tournament in Mar del Plata and we want you to go with your age group, those born in '72.'

'Well, I don't know, I have to speak to my parents . . .'

'Sure, speak to your parents,' Marcelo replied, 'and let us know. Now, go and get showered.' I'd only played five minutes and I so wanted to keep being involved, even more so at Newell's ground – it's like coming from a small village in rural England and visiting the Tottenham training ground. 'No, no, take a shower and someone will take you to the offices by the stadium.'

I was taken there and Griffa was waiting for me: 'OK, son, here is your ticket. Go home and we'll talk. I hope you come with us to play in the tournament, it'd be really great, an experience ...' That's how it was. I'd gone to Rosario in the morning to be with them and in the afternoon I was travelling back to my home town.

My parents were happy for me to join Newell's for that tournament, so I returned a few days later and the club treasurer Vicente Tasca put me up for a couple of nights. His son was also going to be in the team. I trained with my new colleagues and we set off for Mar del Plata. We reached the final against Olimpia from Paraguay and it was all-square at 2–2 after 90 minutes. In the second half of extra-time, the goalkeeper passed the ball to me on the edge of our area, I kept going and going and going, I exchanged passes with a teammate and then I went to put a cross in ... And it went in! Goal! We won 3–2 and clinched the tournament! We got back to Rosario and when I got off the coach, Bielsa and Griffa were waiting for me. 'So now what? Are you going to stay with us?'

'Yes, I'm going to sign.' And so I did. I was a Racing fan because of my father, but over time I was drawn to Newell's. That's the story. Incredible.

And interesting. Bielsa needed only five minutes. I never asked him what he saw, but I think I understand his thought process. When Jesús Pérez, Miki D'Agostino or Toni Jiménez and I watch a game now, we see who we need and who we don't. We realise immediately. It's a question of attitude and energy. Do they transmit those traits or not? A guy like Bielsa, who was ahead of his time, just like Griffa, could see the lot in five minutes.

My career and story would've been completely different if I'd signed for Central. Or, who knows, maybe we'd have made Central as big as Newell's. You always have to think big, don't you?

*

Griffa, who was Newell's director of football, became my father figure while I was in Rosario, especially between the ages of fourteen and seventeen. I had a stronger relationship with him than I had with Bielsa, who was initially the reserve-team coach. José Yudica was in charge of the first team when I made my debut as a 17-year-old. Soon after, Marcelo was promoted to first-team coach and we won the league. Under Bielsa we reached the Copa Libertadores final the following season but lost to Telê Santana's São Paulo on penalties. It was a sensational achievement for a modest team like ours. The philosophy was very similar to the current one at Tottenham.

The squad was a mix of young players, like Fernando Gamboa, Eduardo Berizzo and me, and more experienced heads, such as 'Tata' Martino, Juan Manuel Llop and Norberto Scoponi. In that era, players didn't leave Argentina, so it was harder for youngsters like us to get the nod, unless the man in charge was someone like Bielsa, who was just starting out as a coach and hadn't been a top-level player. He had his own ideas about it all.

The team's style of play also bore many similarities with Spurs': it was intense, fast-paced with a high press and plenty of mechanical movement. We looked to dominate physically and our game was about suffocating our opponents, making them uncomfortable when we did not have the ball. We all needed to believe in the coach for it to work. The team was full of players who had responsibilities. We weren't just soldiers. We were all part of the decision-making process. Playing as a left-sided centre-back, I developed under Bielsa, whose audacious and brave philosophy dared to challenge the norm at the time.

He was given the nickname 'Loco', although I never liked it. I know it's a tribute to his different way of thinking, but I consider a move away from common patterns as being exceptional rather than crazy. These days who has the intellectual ability to see things in a different light? I now understand him better than ever, more so than when I was a footballer. I'd love to sit down with him for some *mate* and a chat again. Although we do not agree on everything, he was certainly an inspiration when I decided to become a coach.

*

I'm lucky enough to have a wife who understands me and understands football. Karina sometimes complains, and so she must if she thinks we are headed down the wrong path, but she is aware of the fact that football has made me who I am and who we are as a family. It's what we wanted and what we chose to be. The ball has to be our travelling companion.

Meeting my wife transformed my life. During a period of change, when everything at Newell's was happening at such a fast pace, she gave me a platform of stability and calmness. In my late teenage years, having won the title, it would have been normal to get caught up in the moment. There were countless sources of temptation and we Newell's boys felt like we owned the city.

*

In 1993 *El Indio* Solari was Newell's coach. He was a very special guy and one day he got us all in for a meeting and said, 'Lads, what would you think if we signed Maradona?' Maradona was at Sevilla. I cracked up.

'Maradona at Newell's? Impossible!'

El Indio responded, 'It could be a possibility. What would you think?'

'What do you mean, what would we think? If Maradona comes here, we'll die of excitement!'

El Gringo Giusti was involved in the deal alongside fellow well-known agent *Tota* Rodríguez. The contract was signed nine months before the 1994 World Cup. *El Gringo* Giusti contacted many of the players saying, 'Here is Diego's number. He'd love you to call him.' I was with Karina in my flat on the 13th floor in Córdoba, opposite the National Flag Memorial, but I had my doubts. 'Should I call him or not? How can I phone Maradona? Bloody hell!' I told Karina that when I moved to Rosario as a youngster, I lived in a very small apartment. There was a picture next to the bed, the only one that I had in the whole flat, and it was Maradona in 1986 lifting the World Cup. I always went to sleep with Maradona looking down on me. And now I had to ring him.

In the end, I said to myself, 'I'll call him.'

I nervously heard a 'Hello?'

'Yes, Diego, it's Mauricio Pochettino, I'm going to be your teammate.'

'*Poche!*' I almost fainted when he called me *Poche*. 'How are you doing, *Poche*? It's so great to hear from you! I'm very grateful to you for phoning me, with me soon heading over there . . .' I was speechless!

Diego arrived in Rosario and had his unveiling the following day. We all went to Newell's stadium to wait for the big moment. There were about 40,000 people there. The ground was full and it was a dream-come-true. We looked at him thinking, 'No way is Maradona here with us.'

We didn't have a gym at Newell's, so we went to one on Calle Mendoza. Maradona would go there in the morning to use the treadmill and boost his strength. He trained very hard and then he'd join the group in the afternoon. It was a pleasure to train with him. He only wanted to be on the ball. He wasn't about running. He was all about the game. He'd warm up on his own by grabbing a ball before even doing up his laces and kicking it about. It's difficult to explain exactly what he would do, from the noise the ball made when his foot connected with it to his incredible control and the swerve that he could put on it. Afterwards, he'd eat some type of porridge and he'd go back to the gym on his own in the evening.

I was lucky enough to room with him before games. Individual rooms were certainly not the norm. Try telling that to today's players.

I didn't sleep for the first few nights, I just looked at him, but after a while the notion that it was Maradona wore off. He was just my teammate. On one occasion, we were lying on the bed watching football. I don't remember which game it was, but as all players do, we started criticising players. 'Look at that shot, he's rubbish!' One player dribbled past one, then another, but then lost it, and I found myself saying, 'Who does that guy think he is? Maradona?' I immediately covered my mouth, but he was already pissing himself with laughter.

Remote controls didn't really exist back then. The physio was treating me one afternoon when I was lying on the bed next to Maradona at the Embajador Hotel in Buenos Aires. I can't remember what was on the TV, but at one point we looked at each other as if to say, 'What the hell is this nonsense?' And I unintentionally said to him, 'Diego, change that rubbish and put something else on.' Diego got off the bed and started pressing some buttons on the TV. He suddenly stopped, realised and said to me, 'Bloody hell, mate, who do you think you are?

I'm Maradona! You can change the bloody channel yourself!' and he cracked up.

I wouldn't say we are friends, but we are fond of each other. I was at his testimonial match on what was a special day in November 2001 at Boca's ground. We all cried when he made his speech.

It went like this: 'I've been waiting . . . I've been waiting for this game for so long and it's all over. I hope my love for football and your love for me never waver. I've made mistakes and I've paid for them. But my love of the ball is still pure.'

How could we not cry as our idol took his leave?

*

Back in 1991, before Maradona arrived, we headed to Tenerife for a friendly against *El Indio* Solari's side. We went on to Barcelona and played at UE Figueres where Jorge D'Alessandro was in charge. During that tour I discovered the city of Barcelona, which was gearing up for the Olympic Games. Argentina didn't qualify for the football competition, which was incredible because we had a wonderful team. They called us 'the goal and touch crew'.

I fell in love with the city and when the opportunity to join Espanyol arose, I didn't think twice. I had a chance to go to Boca or one of a number of clubs in Mexico. The Catalan side's offer was the least financially attractive and it was the riskiest option because they'd just clinched promotion.

I didn't know much about what was there, but Karina, who was pregnant with Sebastiano, and I chose to head to Barcelona in 1994. That decision had a huge bearing on my career, and my life.

Griffa, who had played for Espanyol and had become a huge influence on me in my formative years, came with us on that initial trip to Europe and he was there when I signed the contract with the Catalan club.

*

We played in the UEFA Cup once and in the Intertoto Cup on a couple of occasions, but in general terms suffering and enjoyment were served up in equal measure at Espanyol. I remember the last derby at Sarrià Stadium in 1997 before it was demolished. It was an uneven contest.

We were in the drop zone, with a new manager and a lengthy injury list, including Toni Jiménez, the current goalkeeping coach at Tottenham. Bobby Robson's Barcelona had to win to keep the pressure on Fabio Capello's Real Madrid, so they started their strongest line-up, including Ronaldo, then FIFA World Player of the Year, and it was my job to mark him. The Brazilian didn't get many touches of the ball. I don't know how I managed it!

Well, I did have a plan. I prepared myself mentally: 'What's the best way to mark Ronaldo? If they pass to him and I give him space to run into, he'll kill me. So, what should I do? Not give him space. If he turns, either I foul him or he'll do me . . .'

You simply had to anticipate Ronaldo's movement. I did not need my coach to tell me. I know I had to use all of the tools at my disposal, those that I call 'basic concepts', the things you learn during your football education.

A topic that the Spurs coaching group discuss nowadays and that worries us is the fact that footballers sometimes lack those 'basic concepts'. We have extraordinary methodology and preparation, so players are well drilled when it comes to tactics. But as for those 'basic concepts', those things that help you be better on the pitch, not so much. I am talking about how to take advantage of situations, how to unsettle someone, how to use non-footballing weapons to beat your opponent, how to utilise your intelligence, how to be smart. They're gradually getting lost. They've stopped being transmitted from generation to generation, from old to young. Even coaches have forgotten how to pass down that knowledge.

The media also contributes to this bout of collective amnesia. An example would be Toby Alderweireld, who I signed for Tottenham and has been one of the best centre-backs in England over the last two years. It makes me laugh the way they pinpoint how he is one of the best because he doesn't commit fouls. A centre-back that doesn't commit fouls! In my time, if you didn't commit fouls, it was because you couldn't play at centre-back. Twenty years ago, if you didn't go in hard and mark your territory, strikers would eat you alive. And when you got a yellow card, at least it was after giving someone a good kick. I'd say to the striker, 'If you're going to get past me or if you're going to nutmeg me, think twice about it, because I'll kill you.' Of course I didn't, but at least he thought that I might.

Now the defender who commits the fewest fouls is the best. You've got to be kidding me! How times change!

*

Before Bielsa's arrival at Espanyol was confirmed, I had the chance to move on, but I stayed, as I was very much looking forward to playing under him. Even though he stayed only six months before he left to take the reins at the national team, our encounter was crucial for me, as he ended up waking me up from a period of lethargy. I was seemingly asleep, hibernating. He knew the Pochettino from Newell's, but the one he met six years later at Espanyol was something else. I was too much in my comfort zone. In fact, I was lost but I did not know it.

We had three training sessions during pre-season under Bielsa. The first was from 7.30 a.m., a 45-minute run at the Sant Cugat High Performance Training Centre with inclines and descents. We had heart-rate monitors and they told us how fast we each had to run. We headed back in, showered, had breakfast, relaxed for an hour and then it was off to the gym for a 90-minute session. We'd shower again and eat lunch. Then it was siesta time and finally training with Bielsa.

We didn't see Marcelo during the morning, so he'd come in for the afternoon session, bursting with energy. It was all about tactical work with him, but there were days when we were shattered. We were doing some drills on one of those scorching hot afternoons and I said to him, 'Marcelo' – calling him by his first name was a bad start – 'Have we got much longer to go?'

'Five minutes.' And we kept working. At the end, a furious Bielsa called me over. 'Look, that's the last thing I expected from you. It confirms to me just what you've become.' He laid into me and I cried. I went home in tears because I felt so embarrassed, as embarrassed as I've ever felt in front of someone. Everything he said was right. I'd been blinded, trapped in my own world. I had stopped doing what had got me there in the first place.

He helped me to move on and later called me when he was in charge of the national team. He handed me my full international debut against Netherlands in 1999. If he hadn't gone to Espanyol, I never would've become a senior international.

*

It was a good move not to leave Espanyol in 1999–2000, despite receiving offers from big clubs. Valencia were one of those clubs, but their coach Héctor Cúper phoned me to give me a series of explanations which, rather than convincing me to go there, seemed to say, 'I don't know if I want you.' I feel quite sensitive about these details. I thought, 'The club makes a written offer and then the coach tells me he doesn't know if I'm going to play or not and doesn't show any enthusiasm whatsoever. Mmm, interesting . . .' That style of approach taught me a lot. In fact, now I understand it even more. There was also talk of Liverpool, but it felt like England was on another planet back then.

I stayed because the club was in a difficult financial position. When I turned Valencia down, I got a call from José Manuel Lara. His family run a publishing house called Planeta and he was the club's major shareholder. 'We know some clubs want you. We aren't doing well financially, but we want to make this a big club and you're key to that. We want you to finish your career at Espanyol.' It was music to my ears. I had a year left on my contract, but they offered me an improved six-year deal, which I accepted. I signed the pre-agreement, but that document was never presented to the federation, as it hinged on the agreement between the club, Lara and Planeta Deportivo, the company linked to the publishing house that wanted to take Espanyol to another level, by buying players and loaning them to the club.

That season we won the Copa del Rey final against Atlético Madrid in Valencia, which was a unique achievement after 60 years without a trophy. That victory has possibly greater significance than any of my other accomplishments.

After winning the cup, the relationship between Planeta and Espanyol broke down and I found myself in the middle. I could've asked for the club to honour the new contract that was offered to me, as it had been signed by the president, but it would've put the club in a tight situation because they could only finance it if Planeta kept helping out, which was no longer the case. So I stayed loyal to the club during the final year of my old contract. So much was written about whether I'd sign a new deal, but in January an offer came in from Paris Saint-Germain. The club asked me to accept it and leave. Which I did.

It meant going from Barcelona, a city that I knew well and felt comfortable in, to Paris, where I had to learn a new language and sharpen my senses. I was at PSG when the club signed Ronaldinho and we had other incredible players like Nicolas Anelka and Mikel Arteta. It all made a huge impact on me. It was a fast-paced bout of personal development. The league was strong, with the likes of Lyon, Marseille, Lille, Girondins de Bordeaux, which were sharing the titles.

While at PSG, Bielsa picked me for the 2002 World Cup squad and took me to Japan, although it was a huge disappointment since, despite being favourites, we got knocked out in the group stage. We had Batistuta, Ayala, Zanetti, Verón, Simeone, Aimar, Crespo ... We lost 1–0 to England, with David Beckham converting a penalty after I supposedly fouled Michael Owen. He had the ball, I stuck a leg out and he dived. Owen was more Argentinian than me at that very moment. I retired from international football at the age of 30 in 2002, although not for that reason – I wanted to focus on club football.

After a year and a half, 70 games and four goals for PSG, I moved on to Bordeaux, despite there being an offer from Villarreal on the table. I love wine and that was part of my thought process. While I was at PSG, I lived in Chambourcy where the training ground was, on the outskirts of Paris. My landlord worked for the club and was also a salesman for a major winery so he sent me bottles of champagne and fine wines. Jean-Louis Triaud, the Bordeaux president, owned a *château* and I was able to fulfil my dream of visiting the different wine regions. I believe Bordeaux has the best wine in the world, but it's also a very special region in terms of the energy it gives off.

Just six months later, in January 2004, I went back to Espanyol, three years after leaving. Well, after I was asked to leave.

*

Those six months from the day I went back to Espanyol until the final game of the season were among my happiest as a player. It was a real mixed bag. Luis Fernández had replaced Javier Clemente as coach, with the team rooted to the bottom of the table and nine points from safety, although there was still half a season left to play. I felt a very intense feeling when I got there. I was welcomed with open arms and was expected to unite a team that was riddled with divisions and problems. I accepted the challenge and was ready for it. That sense of responsibility made me feel important and the experience will always be with me as Luis Fernández allowed me to work very closely with him. He could confide in me and I was part of the coaching staff's decision-making process. We discussed each and every conundrum, which helped me understand many different aspects of the game. I'm very grateful to him for that.

The last match of the campaign was on the horizon. We'd picked up plenty of points and were on the verge of leaving the nightmare prospect of relegation behind. We were at home to John Toshack's Murcia, knowing that victory would guarantee safety. We had a mix of veterans, including the talented Iván de la Peña, and academy products like Raúl Tamudo and Alberto Lopo. Both youngsters got on the scoresheet and we stayed up.

Yes, those were six deeply emotional months.

*

In the summer of 2006, Ernesto Valverde took over at Espanyol and decided that he didn't want me in the squad for the following season because he felt that I controlled the dressing room. In reality, it was completely the opposite. I defended the previous coach, Miguel Ángel Lotina, even in situations when I disagreed with him. There's plenty of proof and many people know that I was always loyal to my coaches. In football there are people who live off confusion and you sometimes don't know who the good and bad apples are.

I talked it over with Valverde. It was hard for me to accept, but I understood over time. When you take over, it's normal to seek out the influential individuals. You ask and you find out, but you may be given incorrect advice. The truth is I couldn't have lasted much longer at Espanyol anyway. I'd already given all that I had to give. I thought that I could contribute in the dressing room by calling upon my experience, but Valverde made the right call.

I saw him some time later and said, 'Thank you so much for not letting me stay on for another year.'

If I hadn't been pushed to hang up my boots, I'd still be struggling out on a pitch somewhere today. That's the honest truth, although of course it was hard to take at the time.

After almost 300 games over 12 years, including two Copas del Rey (one in 2000 and the one we'd just won in 2006), I said goodbye to the club at a very emotional press conference. My family was there, including my 12-year-old son Sebastiano, who was born during my first season at the club. I cried. I think it was because I saw him cry. Or maybe not. I cried because I cried.

I had to leave the room for five minutes to compose myself.

*

I sometimes get involved in *rondos* with the players, but I bestow upon myself the privilege of only having to go in the middle to win the ball back when I want to. Come on, if it's a bad pass, the person who played it has to pay for it. I often play in the football tennis World Cup finals at the Tottenham training ground. You never completely stop being a footballer, even after you hang up your boots.

In 2006 I had offers from Dubai, Qatar and the United States. A few Spanish teams were also interested, but my family and I needed the stability that we could find in Barcelona. Retiring at 34 gave me the chance to start thinking about my future, prepare for life as a coach and try to do other things.

Having said that, the first thing I did was fly to Argentina after many years away, for a trip to Bariloche, which I had owed to myself since my teenage years. I wanted to get away from everything. I didn't want to watch television or see photos from training in newspapers. It was really good for me. Almost two months later, we returned to Barcelona for the children to go back to school. I received several tributes, from friends in Espanyol 3.0, a lobby group that wanted to take over the institution, and from the club, including the presentation of a gold and diamond badge before a game against Celta.

My friend Pepe Gay, a professor at the private Escuela de

Administración de Empresas business school, recommended a masters degree in sports management, which filled up my mornings from Monday to Friday. A new routine was established and I didn't mind it one bit. I didn't miss anything. I was happy that year, very happy.

Something clicked in my head. I came out of the bubble that Bielsa had talked about all those years before and changed the way I viewed things.

I bought myself a small Smart car which I drove everywhere and I spent time with people from all over the world. My football career had ended and I had to open myself up to a new working environment. I did keep going to watch Espanyol every other week and forged a great relationship with former coach Javier Azkargorta. I started getting my coaching badges.

Three years after retiring, I was already coaching in the top tier.

*

People say that I started managing Espanyol women's team, but it's not true. I had to tread carefully because, given my name, if I'd done the hours needed to get my badges with the youth team, the coach would've thought that I was gunning for his job. So we found a solution. Ramón Catalá, who was in charge of the Espanyol Academy and had been my fitness coach, invited me to join Emili Montagut, who coached the women, in training during the evenings and that way Ramón would sign off my placement. So that's what I did. At the start I went once a week, but the girls asked why I didn't show up more often. I ended up going almost every day. I loved it so much and even played football with them as a way of keeping fit.

Spending the evenings with them was a splendid experience. If I'd been able to instil the passion that those girls had in all the teams I've coached, we'd have won the lot. The boys should watch them closely, see how much they put in and their training conditions, yet they enjoy it so much. The way they compete, how they battle, how they react when a teammate plays a bad pass, how much they want to win and how united they are, what an example to all. We'd train at 10 p.m. in Sant Adrià in deepest winter with such little light that you could hardly see anything on the synthetic pitch. That sort of commitment takes something special.

I always say to the Spurs players, 'It's all recorded up here. One day I'll show you the looks on your faces when you go out the door to train, and later I'll show you your faces when you head back to the dressing room. Why don't you make the same face when you get back to the dressing room as when you head out to training? Why not enjoy training? Why don't you love it? Do you only see training as something difficult, an obligation? Do you like football? Or is it just a job for you or a way to earn money? If the answer to this last question is yes, you can't be the best, it's impossible . . .'

When I say that, I often think about those girls.

*

Many people told me that I would be crazy to take over an Espanyol side in crisis, that it would go badly. As a consequence, I would disappear from the map. I was 37 and I'd retired three years earlier. When it was offered to me, my head was telling me not do it and it'd be difficult to save them. Maybe I didn't have enough experience, but I followed my gut. I said to myself, 'Why not?'

Halfway through the season in January 2009, the team languished 18th in the table with only 15 points. I was the third coach that campaign, which was the last one at Montjuïc. The Cornellà-El Prat stadium was set to be completed ahead of the summer and an inaugural fixture against Rafa Benítez's Liverpool was in the offing, but first we had to stave off relegation.

My first game was in the Copa del Rey quarter-finals against Pep Guardiola's Barcelona, with Messi coming off the bench in the second half, yet we held them to a 0–0 stalemate. Not long after in the season we headed to the Camp Nou in the league as the basement boys, yet we beat them with Iván de la Peña bagging a brace. He had never previously scored twice in a game, not even at youth level. We ended up surviving comfortably. We finished tenth on 47 points, thanks to a spectacular second half of the season.

We had some decent campaigns. Twenty players from the academy were handed their debuts during my tenure. I had a showdown with club legend Raúl Tamudo, I made mistakes, we won, we lost and I learned from every second of it. Those five seasons allowed me to develop into a coach that championed a particular style of play and did so at a club that we all at home loved.

In the midst of all that, on my watch, our captain Dani Jarque passed away, aged 26. The blow to the club is still being felt.

*

The decision to come to England had plenty to do with my wife and Jesús Pérez, who had already become my assistant at Espanyol. Of course, I'll always be grateful to Nicola Cortese, the Southampton chairman, for having the courage to bring me in. But, in truth, I did not want to join. Why? First of all because I didn't know a word of English, and second because I'd left Espanyol in November and planned to get my head in order and start studying English from January until June. I even had a teacher lined up. I wanted to devote weekends to the family and then be fresh to take on another challenge in five or six months' time.

I'd watch my son play football at the weekend, I'd take my wife out for dinner on Saturday evenings, we'd go to watch a film on Sundays, I'd watch live football. It would've been the perfect world, but suddenly after finishing one day, I was offered the possibility of going at it again. My head was about to explode.

This is how we made the decision: I was with Jesús and my wife, discussing whether we should say yes or no. It all felt overwhelming for a moment and I said I wouldn't go to England, that's it, goodbye. I went to the bathroom downstairs and silence descended upon the house.

I wasn't scared. I respect everything and everyone, but I don't fear anything. My four years at Espanyol had been so tough and I thought, 'Where do I have to go? Southampton? Where's that? In England? No bloody way!' We'd started tracking all the major leagues and gathering information, but, as I said, I'd already planned the following six months in my head.

I went back into the lounge and both of them were staring at me. My wife said, 'You have to go.'

I looked at Jesús and he said, 'I agree, we have to go!' Of course, he wanted to go because he spoke English! I thought, 'What can I say to a player when I do not understand a word of what is said to me?' Jesús insisted, 'It's an opportunity for you.' My wife agreed. I don't know why she had that vision, but she said that England was a good place for me.

At that moment I decided to accept the offer.

From then on, of course, I started watching game after game. I immersed myself in Southampton, the other teams, the whole Premier League and all the rest.

*

I don't know if two weeks' rest is long enough after a gruelling Premier League season. It's an unknown. To put it another way: holidays are never long enough. It happens to all of us. When you have a perfect week, you want another one. If you have a month off, you'll certainly want another one. In my 17-year playing career, I always said, 'The day when I stop playing football will be the day when I enjoy my holidays again, I'll have unlimited holidays.' Pah. It's hard to do that, isn't it? When you don't know what's happening with your future, those holidays feel very different compared with when you know you have a fixed target ahead of you. When you don't know if you're going to work, if you're going to find a team, holidays stop being that coveted source of relaxation.

I am lucky I work at Spurs, a top club, but it's been a confusing summer with mixed emotions. We start pre-season tomorrow. My blood still boils when I think about the Newcastle game – we need to keep looking for the reasons. Of course, what we achieved and the way we did it didn't go unnoticed. Big European clubs have been looking for and interviewing prospective new coaches. They want excitement and hard work. Not to mention success as soon as possible. One of them rang me, one that wants to change things and win the lot. They got in touch on several occasions, but it isn't time to change. Pep Guardiola is coming to the Premier League with Manchester City, José Mourinho is taking over at Old Trafford, Antonio Conte is going to Chelsea. We'll have to perform really well to be at their level. But we can do it.

*

On Friday 1 July, Jesús, Toni and Miki (Miguel D'Agostino, a former teammate from my Newell's days) started working with the players who weren't on international duty and also with the group of youngsters who, at the end of last season, we'd decided would be given a chance to train with the first team.

25

My team and I love helping young players. It's like planting a tree, watering it and watching it grow. All the fruit that it bears comes from the land and environment that you put in place. There's nothing quite like winning with the team you joined at 13 or 14 and have given your heart and soul to. You then move on to play for the first team with a feeling of identity that offers the team an added extra. It's something that will be stamped on every side I coach. It was instilled in my genes during my time at Newell's, it's what Griffa and Bielsa taught me.

In any case, moving up is not an automatic process. Over a three, four, five or six-month period, the players with potential train with the first team until they are ready. We don't just play footballers from the Under-21s straight away. As with everything, there is a process of adapting to training and gaining acceptance. The first-team players need to feel that the youngster is part of the group, so his time comes when a majority endorse him with both sporting and personal recognition.

Today, Monday 4 July, I joined up with the squad.

*

We worked on improving the squad early on, even before last spring. It's the chairman who takes the final steps when it comes to transfers, especially with regard to financial decisions and we do have our limits in that field. We're kicking off pre-season feeling calm, as we've sealed two signings that will boost the squad: Victor Wanyama from Southampton and Vincent Janssen from AZ Alkmaar. It's now time to see what other options might crop up.

I already know Victor from when Southampton signed him from Celtic three years ago. He has the human attributes we want, as does Janssen, who we need for a position for which we already have a number one. It was a pleasant surprise to find someone like Victor back then, a mature 21-year-old with clear ideas in his head and burning to be part of the group. These things can be detected quickly. You don't go around with a questionnaire to deduce which characteristics a player possesses, but psychology plays a part. On top of that, everything is explained to them, so there's no excuse. There are no surprises, so there can be no complaints.

*

We've based the first few days of training on getting our rhythm back and reconditioning the players, but without going as far as working on our style of play because many members of the squad are still missing. From day six, we'll start applying some of the basic concepts of the game, both in and out of possession, in preparation for the first friendly at the end of the first ten-day training block.

In this period, we've been able to focus on players who are knocking on the first-team door. Two in particular: Josh Onomah, who we ended up convincing to stay, despite him having one foot out of the club after many clubs showed interest – he made his debut for us, age 18, in November 2015 replacing Dele Alli; and Marcus Edwards, another sensationally talented player with the ability to dazzle – he's a little Messi.

We keep trying to get all the layers of the club (chairman, sporting directors, first team, academy heads) to push together in the same direction, so we don't lose anyone we want. John McDermott's job, as head of coaching and development since February this year, has been crucial. Not all the effort is focused on the pitch: the youngsters' parents need to be convinced that their sons are going to get a chance at the club.

Many hours have been invested in the club's structure and in debating the new arrivals' situation over these first two weeks. I have to admit that the working day has been extended since I came in. I love chatting to everyone. We aren't here watching videos all day long. I spend plenty of time speaking to people at the club.

I like going through situations over and over again, so that I can see things from different points of view and consider a range of scenarios before making a final decision: transfers, moving players up and down, deciding if a player isn't cut out for us or has gone off the rails. I make group decisions, rather than unilateral ones.

We try never to rush our steps.

*

Our 12 international players arrived two days before we headed to Australia for the International Champions Cup to face Juventus (26 July) and the Champions League runners-up Atlético Madrid (29

July). We then play Inter Milan in Oslo. It'll be a short but intense pre-season.

Before we left, a decision had to be made about the players that had just touched down. Should we make them train with the others and take them to Australia to play in two friendlies, despite being short on preparation time? That would have meant two days of travelling without training, getting to a hotel, staying there for seven nights, going from summer to winter, not knowing what condition the pitches and facilities would be in and then two more days to travel back. It would have meant they'd start proper pre-season ten or 12 days after the others.

Alternatively we could leave them in London and they could be eased back into training, giving them stability and a calmness after Euro 2016 and their holidays. If so, we would expect them to be in good shape when we got back from Australia. We decided on the latter.

When the club initially suggested the friendlies to me a while back, I explained that the dates seemed fine, but the internationals wouldn't be going. I kept my word. I know the club were concerned about letting the fans down by touring without the big names. It happens: clubs say yes ten months earlier and in the final few days, there is a lot of debate to be had. The most important thing is the players' fitness. It's true that our fans in Australia, and there are many of them, expected to see players like Harry Kane, Hugo Lloris, Dele Alli and co., but they have to understand that footballers aren't machines, they need rest and suitable training regimes to be able to compete for ten months.

We won that battle. I think the players who stayed home were happy, although they do have plenty of homework to do.

*

Jet lag has set in. We spent two days travelling which involved leaving one morning and arriving the following evening.

Yesterday after dinner, I went for a drink with Toni, Miki and Jesús, the hardcore coaching team, at a bar at the Grand Hyatt in Melbourne where we're staying. I mentioned I could see energy levels were down. We were, in fact, all shattered. A man suddenly appeared and he wanted to say hello to me. He was wearing a Tottenham tracksuit top and started thanking me for what we'd been doing at the club. He was a Malaysian lawyer who'd come to see the Juve match with his wife. His family supports Liverpool, but he's a Tottenham fan because he's always liked the club's style of play. He follows us all over the globe. He usually brings his six-year-old son, although he left him at home on this occasion.

He had something different to say. Yes, he was thankful that we've been competing at the highest level, but he started mentioning a heap of things that are often undervalued. Most of the time in football you only see those who win trophies, but this man explained how proud he was of our side. He felt that not having remarkable individuals from yesteryear like Ossie Ardiles, Ricky Villa or Paul Gascoigne made us a strong team and the fans really like the sense of collective belonging that we exude.

He looked back on that tough 2–2 draw with Chelsea at Stamford Bridge which ended our hopes of the title last season. He cried that day, as did his young son. He told me something that stuck in my mind. It wasn't the expected result, but the team showed how much it hurt not to win, which signified a change in history, not just in recent terms, but possibly over the last 30 or 40 years.

Allan Dixon, our first-team manager for non-football activities, was also there and he took down the fan's details because I invited him and his family to the training ground, to see how we work. I want him to speak to the players about those group values that he appreciates so much from a distance, and explain to them what their behaviour on the pitch means to people, young and old, who live in other countries and on other continents. Sometimes these things aren't valued highly enough.

*

I'm in almost daily conversation with the guys we left behind in England. I WhatsApp them a lot. I told Danny Rose that it hurt me to send them messages during the Euros because they disappointed me at Newcastle. He admitted they still feel ashamed of that performance.

We're videoing training sessions both here and in London. The London videos are sent to us in Australia. I've just been watching one from yesterday morning. I copied a part of the session and sent it back to them, congratulating them on their work. Sometimes intensity levels drop when the manager is absent, but these boys are fully aware of how important the process is and they give it their all without anyone needing to watch over them.

Before we look at Juventus-related footage ahead of our game against them, we'll play the video from the Tottenham training ground. As the guys come into the meeting room, they'll see just how hard the others are training back in London.

You should never stop studying the finer details. Eric Dier scored for England and performed well in midfield, although it was a difficult tournament for the team. Manchester United want to sign him to play in that position, although he arrived here as a centre-back. It's not always easy to keep your feet on the ground after representing your country. We'll have to keep tabs on Eric. He's a young and intelligent guy and it's all happening very fast for him. Dele Alli is also experiencing a new situation. Praise can create confusion.

*

It's the night before the Juventus game. We did gym work in the morning and then some activities with local dignitaries at lunchtime. We later visited the Melbourne Cricket Ground, the legendary cricket and Australian football stadium where we're going to play.

Before training, we had the first press conference of the season which, in general terms, went well. The journalists asked me about what had happened at Newcastle and if my anger had waned. I said that it hadn't and I'll only be able to calm myself down when we're all together and I tell the players what I need to say to their faces.

I brought all the players and coaching staff together at the start of our open training session. I stood them in a line facing the stand where all the fans were. At the end of the short talk, we all applauded and greeted the people who had made the effort to be there. It started pouring with rain and some parts of the pitch became waterlogged, but we managed to do some tactical drills to work on some specific patterns of play both in defence and in attack.

At the end of the session, Toni, Jesús, Miki, a club director and I went out for dinner at a fine Melbourne restaurant. We all went for the twelve-course taster menu which had a bit of everything, including kangaroo, and suitable wines. Toni is a fellow wine lover, although I don't think he's always been one. When we were at Espanyol, we developed a tradition of going out for dinner the evening before matches. One day at the Juan Carlos I hotel, they brought over a wine, we sampled it and Toni said, 'No, this one is no good, I don't like it.' We got them to bring us another one, but we made sure they put the first wine in Toni's glass again. He tried it and with a serious expression on his face, stated, 'Yes, this one is good.' We never let him forget that incident.

*

It's the evening of 26 July. We played Juventus, the Italian champions, who put out a star-studded line-up. We lost 2–1 but confidence was flowing, especially in the second half. Érik Lamela scored for us after a powerful run by Wanyama and we put the Italians under real pressure in search of an equaliser. It was the first game for many of the 17- and 18-year-olds, and there were a few pleasant surprises. Twenty-year-old Will Miller, for example, a committed, hardworking player who always gives his all, did well in the first 45 minutes. We found out that he'd been the main actor in *Oliver Twist* (a BBC One adaptation in 2007), *Runaway* (2009) and others. I asked him why he gave up acting and he told me that he wanted to play football. It was tough being a footballer and going to acting school and spending time with his friends, so he's leaving that side for now, maybe to take it up again further down the line. An interesting story.

*

It's 11 p.m. here in Australia on the 27th. Today has been quite relaxed. We trained in the morning and most of us had a nice, long siesta in the afternoon, almost four hours' long.

We are low on energy.

*

29 July. We've just got back to the hotel after the game against Atlético. We lost to a Godín goal, although we had the clearer chances. Janssen played again, as did Lamela and Eriksen.

Let's go home.

*

31

We got back from Australia on Saturday the 30th in the afternoon and found it hard to recover. Everyone had today (Sunday) off to enjoy family time. Back to work tomorrow.

2.

AUGUST

A fter one last pre-season fixture against Inter in Oslo, the curtain was raised on the Premier League. First up was Everton at Goodison Park before home games against a physical Crystal Palace side and a Liverpool team vying for Champions League qualification. The transfer window approached its conclusion with one more player expected to be added to the squad in the final hours.

Monday 1 August. Today was a great day. The players who had travelled to Australia joined up with the internationals who'd stayed in London. Hugo Lloris and Ben Davies, who reported back later because their countries performed so well at Euro 2016, also arrived. There was plenty to sort out. It was a meeting-filled day.

The least pleasurable aspect of it was sending some of the players back to the Under-21s. I sat down with Jesús and John McDermott and we spoke to each of the youngsters one by one to evaluate pre-season and explain the plan going forward. I'm sure some of them felt disappointed, although they seemed motivated to keep battling to break into the first team. Well-channelled frustration can be used to fuel ambition.

*

Today, Tuesday, we performed various types of physical tests on the players who still needed to be examined. As the cardiologist was around, the coaching staff also took advantage and we got our tickers checked out. It turns out that all of us must take greater care of our health. It was a simple equation: stress plus a lack of exercise equals problems.

I turned 44 in March. I came back from Australia overweight and it wasn't just me. We had some mammoth breakfasts over there! Given that the jet lag made it hard to get to sleep, we woke up very early. At 3 a.m. we were up and all we could do was wait for them to open the restaurant. We were already there by seven, with a breakfast of champions on the cards. Each morning, we ate enough to last us for two days: omelettes, toast, butter, jam, croissants, juice, fruit, sometimes even ham and cheese, coffee . . . It was crazy. So logically we all came back with some excess baggage.

We're all going to go on diets and do some exercise, not purely for aesthetic reasons. We'll ease ourselves into it: walks, some jogging and watching what we eat. We'll try to help one another.

With a week to go until the Premier League kicks off, our recruitment isn't yet done and dusted, which means pressure levels are only going to increase.

*

I don't like preparing for talks with too much detail. I think of a list of tactical topics and ask for some videos, but I don't always use them. I don't usually tell my coaching staff what's going to happen in the talk either, or which route I'm going to take. Before going into the meeting room, I go over the content that I've prepared, I ask the people around me for their impressions, a whirlwind of ideas brews. Sometimes things might happen that make you change tack.

That's just exactly what took place during the first pre-season talk. We'd trained well during the week with the whole squad and it was time to speak to everyone as a group. Miki stood up with his computer, as always. I usually stand up next to him by the big screen, but today I sat down to wait for the players to arrive.

Kyle Walker came into the room late. Not good. Something clicked in my head at that moment. I said to myself, 'I'm going to make a speech. But they also need to watch something.' I spoke for half an hour, or so it seemed to me.

*

As we all know, we have our conscious and also unconscious minds. You educate a group, put yourself in your charges' heads at certain moments, help them progress with their way of thinking or of doing things. That is relatively easy when there is no competitive stress. But when the competition starts, if you are not with a high level of activation and preparation, the other bit, the unconscious mind, takes over. It is what I call the 'automatic pilot', a way of behaving and thinking that we have been incorporating from birth and that undoubtedly takes us away from the principal objective and the things we should be doing.

When our title hopes were extinguished after putting in such a colossal effort throughout last season, finishing second turned into an insignificant prize. We lost sight of the fact that it would still be marvellous for our fans, like winning a trophy because it would mean finishing above Arsenal. The group lost its focus and started to get influenced by factors that, until that time, we had left in a room with a triple lock on the door. Up until that game against Chelsea, that insufferable 2–2 stalemate, holidays didn't exist, nobody was focused on personal challenges at Euro 2016, transfers or improved contracts. It all remained locked away until that draw effectively meant the league slipped away from us and that door was flung wide open. Suddenly we were distracted and we forgot just how important it was to win our last two games against Southampton and Newcastle.

Our performance against Newcastle explained everything.

Football is a team sport and if it starts to revolve around individuals, or if your game doesn't cohere and becomes disjointed, a relegated team can put five past you. Newcastle seemed to be geared up for a party, and we joined them in the celebrations.

At the end of the game and after I'd let off some steam in the press conference, Rafa Benítez came over to console me. By then, I was lucid enough to say, 'Rafa, you've gone down. You'll be playing in the second tier next season and we're in the Champions League, without a qualifier. We came third! If you'd said that to me last year when the season started, I'd have said that was our hope. Our dream was to play in the Champions League at Wembley. Rafa, you don't need to say anything to me!'

But I wasn't totally truthful. The disappointment can make you feel like killing your players. And also yourself.

I spent the whole summer thinking that I had to remind them about all that when the moment came. Seeing Walker turn up late to the talk was the trigger I needed to tear into the group.

Part of my talk went something like this: 'Football is a screen that shows you how a group co-exists. Lads, have a look at this video. I got goosebumps watching how in the friendly the other day, Fernando Torres ran after a loose ball in stoppage time, after 93 minutes of slogging it out and travelling for 30 hours the day before, without sleeping well. The guy sprinted to try to score after all that, when his side were winning 1–0. A player who has won everything and with a long trajectory in the game. That is passion. That feeling that you're a footballer and you enjoy it, that's what you need. Not that attitude we had at Newcastle where we showed a face that does not define us as a team. We didn't seem to care and we were distant from what football is and the feeling that brought us together and got us to this point. You should be ashamed.'

And ciao. To hell with it.

*

We had to put that chapter to bed between ourselves and dig out all our feelings. So I said all that and more. I spoke about things that had happened, about respect and life. We all ended up red-faced, but I liked it.

It's important to be honest with your players. Of course, they won't all believe what you say. They might speak to a friend, agent or parent whose vision may not be in line with the coach's. I prefer to open up and although putting your cards on the table isn't always a good idea, in this case I was certain that they were wounded and if they didn't get treated in time, it would be very hard to make a full recovery.

Of course, that talk will have no effect if I don't reinforce it tomorrow, the day after tomorrow and the day after that. In the following days I usually leave regular signs and reminders, in things I say in training or when we cross paths in the corridors of the training ground, so that they go over what was said a week or a month ago. It's the same story when it comes to tactics. If we don't go over everything we've worked on throughout the week on the Friday before a game, or even on the Saturday itself, they forget.

It's a difficult era for managing footballers. These days you have to spell it all out for them if you want them to be comfortable, as if everything were plotted on a map. Managers nowadays are more like architects or highway engineers. You spend the day mapping out and reminding them of the journey because footballers' concentration spans are shorter and shorter. The electronic gadgets surrounding us are to blame for the players constantly needing new sources of stimulation, so we have to aim for variety and try to keep their minds fresh.

It's also true that not everything that happened at the end of last season is linked to the players and I've had plenty of discussions with the coaching staff about this topic. We had a big influence over what happened from the Chelsea game onwards. We're directly responsible for it. Some things got away from us and that's what we're still evaluating now. The next time we find ourselves in a similar situation, we'll certainly know how to manage it better.

*

It's Thursday and we're in Oslo for our last match before the Premier League season kicks off. We've travelled with an almost full squad for the first time, although Clinton N'Jie and Victor Wanyama have had to stay behind because of visa issues. The group is bedding in nicely.

Whenever there is a World Cup or European Championship, it makes for a tricky pre-season. Players report back later than usual and are often burnt out, short of motivation. You've got to try to make them feel comfortable. We don't drop our standards, but we don't bust any balls either. That's why all our friendlies were scheduled to give them Saturday evening and Sunday off, and even Monday afternoon on occasion, so that they could enjoy some family time. After we face Inter Milan tomorrow, Friday, they will have their last full weekend free of competitive action for a long time – especially in the internationals' case.

The training session after yesterday's talk was highly productive. The lads were really focused, so we changed our minds about today's session. Instead of doing tactical drills on the pitch, which is very physically and mentally demanding, we played them videos to run through some improvements, variations and footballing concepts that we want to introduce. I reminded them again that we've got to dig deeper and that it shouldn't be necessary for the coaching team to be constantly pushing them; they need to find the winning mentality within themselves.

We have just arrived at the hotel, which has a lovely location overlooking a bay. I'm told that Javier Zanetti, who is now Inter's vice-president, is waiting to greet us at the stadium.

*

Karina has just phoned me. My father-in-law has passed away. Rest in peace, Manuel Antonio Grippaldi.

He has lost his battle against illness and I've heard the news while abroad. I am far away from Karina again and she has to cope all on her own; Sebastiano is here in Oslo with me.

Football detaches you from everyday life and from pain, too. Word always reaches us late, we almost never have time to say goodbye.

*

I'm having trouble sleeping. Grief has taken hold of everything.

Sometimes we get worked up over stupid things and then, in a flash, your life can burn out like a candle. Here today, gone tomorrow. My wife is always planning twenty things at once. She wants to do everything like yesterday and I always say, 'Whoa, hold your horses. Let's do one thing at a time, because otherwise we won't get anything done.' But when you lose someone close to you, the temptation is to live life to the full.

We flew Manuel Antonio over to Barcelona a month before he died. He had bone cancer, metastases. He deteriorated rapidly in the last few months. It's a big blow for all four of us, but especially for my Karina.

He had lived in Misiones, Argentina – in Eldorado, to be precise. He was a very active person and was football mad. When people like that are no longer able to stay active, they often will themselves to death. It's amazing. It's like . . . they can't go on any more, as if they've nothing left to live for. As recently as six months ago, he still enjoyed playing football, going on bike rides and playing padel, and when he realised he couldn't keep doing all those things, he checked out. I didn't discuss all that with him when he came to Barcelona, because he wasn't his old lucid self. There were times when he was with it, but he was pretty distressed. The treatment helped ease some of his pain and made his final days a bit more bearable.

All of my family, my parents and brothers, live in Argentina, and I can go a month without talking to them, without even exchanging messages. It's not a rare occurrence: my wife and kids talk to my parents more than I do. Sometimes you imagine things, your mind is drawn to the worst-case scenario, and you say to yourself, 'Why don't you just call them today, you fool?' But you get bogged down by things and you don't pick up the phone. Then, if something terrible happens one day, you blame yourself. I miss doing everyday stuff with my wife and kids, and distance only heightens that feeling of missing things that I should not miss. There is a defence mechanism for that: on a daily basis, you repress lots of feelings, locking them away in a drawer. Unfortunately, you have to learn to put up walls to protect yourself from the outside world, otherwise you would become a ticking time bomb.

In this profession, or in fact whenever you are consumed by that passion for what you do, you sacrifice plenty of things. All sorts of stuff. It's not that I envy him, but I find it hard to fathom being like Manuel Pellegrini, who has told me about his need to earmark space and time to read books, play golf and go to the cinema or theatre. Maybe we've got it wrong and working 12 hours a day, as we do, doesn't mean you're any more passionate than someone who does eight-hour days. When you're young, you think that passion is about investing all your time in what you do, but perhaps it's part of growing older and wiser to realise that the key is quality, not quantity.

For the time being, though, football pretty much commands all of my attention. On occasion I snap out of it. When I'm at home, for instance, or when something serious happens. But your mind continues to wander and you find yourself thinking about football even when you're nowhere near the pitch.

*

We beat Inter 6–1. It can be easy to read too much into pre-season results because there are so many ways of interpreting them. Inter came into the game in poor shape. It was our first match with our internationals and we impressed. Four of the goals came in the second half, after we went into the break 2–1 up. You could clearly see that the team have taken the style of play on board, and several media outlets recognised that we made the right call by leaving the players who took part in the Euros behind in London. Though it flattered us a bit, the result confirmed that we can continue to be competitive whoever plays, thanks to our team structure.

The challenge is to keep it up for the whole season.

*

Back to the UK. After two days off, we held one-on-one meetings at the training ground to tell some of the players who haven't been up to scratch during pre-season to shape up. Sometimes a good tournament can distract you. Transfer rumours are also unsettling and it can be helpful to sit down with a player to remind him that he has your confidence. The tune-up process has been accelerated because the season kicks off this coming weekend. Training on Tuesday (when we did a double session) and Wednesday was brimming with tactical content, not to mention collective work and individual fundamentals.

Last night we held a team dinner, which is a ritual I have maintained since my first season at Southampton. Usually, before the season starts, I take the players and coaching staff out for dinner. The first time was soon after I joined the Saints, halfway through the season, and I had to pay with my Spanish card because we didn't have English bank accounts yet. I let the players pick the place this time. In theory, I was supposed to split the bill with Harry Kane, as it was his way of celebrating being the top scorer in the Premier League last season, but I tricked Harry so I could pay the lot. Good food and fine wine – an excellent Nicolás Catena Zapata. A great group night out.

Today, Thursday, we did a recovery session and some video preparation for Saturday's game against Everton.

Earlier this week, the press broke the story that Paul Mitchell – Spurs' head of recruitment, who joined from Southampton, where we worked together – is set to leave. As a main spokesman for the club, I will have to respond to this when asked by the media.

We also had the annual meeting with referees, who always have new things to explain. At the beginning of the season, the rules tend to be applied more harshly, but afterwards they get more lenient. Anyway, after they had delivered their talk to the players, I asked the officials to hang around for just a little while longer, because I wanted to share with them some of my feelings about the end of the last campaign. I played some videos to back up my comments. I never put pressure on referees through the media, I never highlight their mistakes and I'll never lay defeats at their door. But I do like talking things through face-to-face with them and discussing decisions, and even touchline behaviour.

*

Some of the internationals are struggling to reach the level of the rest of the group. I've got to find a way to warn them that they need to do more. It's not a physical issue, it's about mentality.

The rules are clear-cut – even if they're unwritten. And we can't go back on them. Improving attitudes and laying down the blueprint was our biggest task in our first few months at the club.

I pitched up at Tottenham in summer 2014. In our first season, we reached the League Cup final and in May 2015 I signed a new five-year contract. In our second season, with the youngest squad in the Premier League, we went toe to toe with Leicester in the title race. Gary Neville vindicated what we were doing with a glowing analysis in his column in *The Telegraph*, informed by his position as England's assistant manager:

In my role as an England coach, I have noticed the difference in psychology and application when Tottenham players come into the camp. They now arrive prepared for the battle, ready to play, ready to work. They look like they want to partake in the meetings. All the things you would want from responsible players are there. It seems to me that Pochettino has given the

41

younger players the confidence to express themselves, off the pitch as well.

But the route to that point was a steep, winding one.

To use a typically English understatement, my appointment as Tottenham coach wasn't exactly a 'universally popular choice'. The club wasn't sure what road to take and when that happens, the fans are usually torn too. Should the club be buying in the best players or looking to the academy?

Spurs have always been synonymous with a certain way of playing, an entertaining, stylish brand of football. But they have not always been effective. John McDermott summed this up to me with an apt image: the club was perceived as being 'all fur coat and no knickers'. Perennial underachievers, in the previous seven years they had finished 11th, eighth and sixth once, and fifth and fourth twice apiece.

On top of that, not only Tottenham, but English football as a whole was in constant flux: coaches came and went, and so did ideas. Directors of football were in vogue one day and had fallen out of fashion the next.

Amid all this, what our chairman Daniel asked of us was a sense of direction and conviction, for us to instil a process, our process. There is no one-size-fits-all approach; what we do can't be applied by anyone and everyone. Every group, every person with responsibilities and every decision is a world unto itself. What was important wasn't what was done, but how.

We were embarking, then, on a journey without a road map. There is no magic formula. Or if there is, maybe it is buried beneath the heaps of things in our minds – and those of the people at the club, including the squad.

It wasn't a happy place when we arrived. We had to throw open the windows, bring in some fresh air, change the mentality. We were being asked to turn a load of dirty, wrinkled laundry into a pile of clean, neatly folded and ironed clothes, all through a new philosophy. But it takes more than a week or a month to get people to buy into a system based on hard work and endeavour.

The squad we inherited contained all sorts. However, unlike

Southampton, where we found hungry players who didn't want to be relegated, the Tottenham dressing room was full of figures who at some point in their careers had been considered stars but had lost their way. And the team didn't come first.

Two weeks after taking over, I remember saying to Hugo Lloris, 'What am I doing here?' I'd come from a really friendly club, where I often had to force the players to go home. At Southampton, we'd installed a machine called a VertiMax in the gym, which helps to improve strength, speed and endurance. The look on their faces when they saw it! But soon enough, they were smitten.

By contrast, the Spurs players would come in, train and shoot off home again. There was no love affair with the VertiMax.

We wanted to run the rule over the existing squad before making any signings. We had to gauge what the players were made of, one by one. We warned them the first months would be tough physically because we needed them to be fit.

Some of them didn't share our ideas but tried to adapt; others rejected them from day one. A few disrespected us. And there were others from whom we couldn't expect something they simply didn't have in them. Many, though, realised that they had to partake in the process in order to halt the negative spiral. That there was an urgent need for us to show leadership and strength, we could not doubt.

The way that many of them looked at us said it all: they knew that if things didn't work out, as always happens in football, we would carry the can. Little by little, in an almost imperceptible way, day by day, a transformation took place. The strategic design was set up with intelligence and nerve. We only needed one thing. I don't know which shop to buy it from, but it's essential: time!

We gave everyone a shot. We even tested players during games, because we were looking beyond the match in question. Some didn't pass those tests and are no longer with us. The gap was filled by youngsters: inexperienced full-backs, or a centre-forward who had never played a full Premier League season. We also reassured our goalkeeper, Lloris, who was considering leaving and needed to change his way of thinking about life and his profession.

The supporters grew restless in the first few months. That was only to be expected.

*

Me and my backroom staff are barred from the first-team dressing room at the training ground. We share one at the stadium, but the one at Enfield is the squad's sanctuary. They can do and say what they want there without fear of us barging in. Only the physios and kitmen are allowed in. Some secrets do make it out, though. I was told that Emmanuel Adebayor brought in his own water, paid for out of his own pocket. But pretty much all players have their foibles. Despite what was said at the time, I never had any problems with Ade – far from it, we had a fantastic relationship. At first, he came back from holiday in Africa with malaria and, on top of that, he got enmeshed in some family issues that everyone knows about, so he asked me for permission to go to Togo to sort things out. The biggest difficulty for him, as for Roberto Soldado, was Kane's emergence. They were big names and needed the team and club to be built around them. When Harry burst on to the scene, they both felt displaced.

Ade's eccentricities gave us plenty of laughs. Take one day when I left him out of the matchday squad. That afternoon, after training, I was in my office, in a meeting with Daniel and our technical director Franco Baldini. Jesús was there too. We heard a knock on the door. It was Ade. I asked him to wait five minutes. Franco and Daniel were stony-faced, wondering what was going on. Problems! After the meeting, I asked Jesús to fetch him in. He arrived wrapped in a towel and I asked him, 'What's up?'

'Why didn't you tell me yesterday that I wasn't going to be in the squad?' he replied. How could I have done that when there was still one training session to go – what if something had happened? 'Yeah, but you've got to tell me if you're not sure. I've sent my chauffeur home with the car; what am I supposed to do now? Call a taxi? I can't believe it!' Priceless! I'd thought he was angry or put out after being omitted from the squad, because he wanted to play. But his gripe was the fact that his chauffeur had left! He was obviously upset, or so I thought. To be honest, I am not sure. Let's assume it was another show of his great sense of humour.

He's a player of real class but, in the circumstances, continuing to work together wouldn't have been beneficial for either of us. Right up to the day when I told him that he wasn't in my plans, he always thanked me for being honest with him. He rescinded his contract, which had a year to run, and joined Crystal Palace.

*

The other day I read that Dele Alli had said of me, 'You don't want to get on his wrong side.' I found it funny, but we're not policemen and I've never torn into a player in front of the team. There's no rule book. It's just about common sense. Professionalism. Letting natural selection follow its course.

They've got to arrive early for training, greet each other and shake hands. Respect their teammates and opponents. Before 9.45, they have to talk to the sports scientist and tell him how they feel and how they've slept. What they've eaten and how. We have regular nutrition tests, which we know can help recuperation and performance.

We have to cover all the bases, but ultimately, how far players go is up to them. When they leave – or we leave – no one can say they weren't given the opportunity to get better.

We have breakfast together. That's when the first conversations start up, helping to create the right mood to ensure training is enjoyable. Everybody has to be ready by 10.30.

Phones must be on silent in the canteen; they're allowed to send messages, but they have to go outside to make calls. It's no good players using their phones in the physiotherapy room, for example. They need to listen to their bodies and to the physio.

There are not many more rules. The rest is in their hands. They're adults. I've never punished a player for being late. I prefer to talk it over with them. Punishment is the preserve of those who can't wield their power in other ways. That is left for those who think they are bosses. I believe in leadership. Two different things.

*

In our first season, my team and I weren't able to convince everyone that that was the way forward. In fact, there was one game that made me worry for our future.

We were up against Aston Villa. I'll always remember that trip to

Birmingham. It was November and we were down in eighth place, on 14 points. A long way off the European pace. We arrived at the hotel and the coaching staff went for a drink before dinner. The hotel bar was a gloomy place. It was Saturday night in November in Birmingham. Not the most uplifting of scenes. We were on a bad run of results and we said to one another, 'We've got to win tomorrow, guys, it's a must-win, because otherwise . . .' The tension and nerves were palpable. If we didn't win, we knew we'd be getting to know the version of Daniel that everyone spoke of with such fear.

I remember our preparations and everything else vividly. We conceded a goal in the first half. In the 65th minute, Villa striker Christian Benteke was sent off for pushing Ryan Mason. We started to control the match. We brought on Kane for Adebayor. But we were still losing. With seven or eight minutes to go, I turned to face the dugout. I looked at Toni, Jesús and Miki and told them, 'Lads, pack your bags tonight, because tomorrow we're going home.'

Our next attack won us an 84th-minute corner. The ball fell to Nacer Chadli and bam, it was 1–1.

'Bloody hell, get in! Come on, we can do it, we can save our necks!'

Cue a free-kick in the 90th minute. And Kane scores!

After the final whistle, I said to my staff, 'Lads, we've been saved, we've earned ourselves a couple more lives, but now we've got to turn the corner. We can't carry on like this.' The revolution had begun.

That match made us realise that, to succeed at this club, we had to do things our way. That game unshackled us. Before then, we had too many people around us spouting their opinions. All those voices confused me and passed their fears onto me. After the Aston Villa game, I found myself saying, 'I know what I've got to do. I know where to go, I'm sure I'm going to be successful, I have no doubts.' And that was that. I told my people, 'It's over. We're locking the door.'

It had been a necessary period of increasing understanding, of collecting information. From the first months of trying to discover where we were and allowing the benefit of the doubt to everybody involved, we moved to the period of taking decisions.

'Let's go!'

I started to build the team in my image. I resolved not to cave in, whatever happened. Here's hoping luck is on our side, I thought.

Only eight players from that original squad are still here.

From December onwards, results took a major upturn. On New Year's Day, we faced top-of-the-table and eventual Premier League winners Chelsea and beat them 5–3. I'm sure the fans went home thinking that something was happening, something was changing. A month later, we beat Arsenal 2–1, with Kane bagging both goals. Then came the League Cup final, which we lost to Chelsea, before we ended up six points off Champions League qualification and 13 adrift of top spot. A respectable fifth-place finish in our first season, just behind Arsène Wenger's side.

*

13 August. Today we took on Everton in our first game of the season. The noise was back, the excitement. Your could sense it. The starting line-up was: Hugo Lloris; Kyle Walker, Eric Dier, Toby Alderweireld, Jan Vertonghen, Danny Rose; Érik Lamela, Victor Wanyama, Christian Eriksen; Dele Alli, Harry Kane.

During the week, we focused our work on some new things we want to introduce. We're still adjusting the team. It didn't make much sense to give too much detail about the opposition, who have a new coach (Ronald Koeman) still working out his preferred XI. So the key to the first league fixture of the season was to play the game on our terms and try to dominate, whatever the opponents might do.

The first half was somewhat disappointing; for a while we looked to be paying the price for being one of the teams that had the most representatives at the Euros. We conceded in the fifth minute, when we were still settling into the game, and that shaped the match. Everton were able to sit back and spring forward swiftly on the counter. We struggled to adapt and we were ponderous and leggy, our movement sluggish. In our desperation to turn the scoreline around, we panicked, as if we only had five minutes to come back rather than 85. That impatience and lack of conviction meant we started to make mistakes.

Toni came over ten minutes before half-time. 'Hugo is asking to come off.'

'You're bloody kidding me.'

That's football. Even if your preparations are ideal, there are factors for which you can't legislate.

Toni headed off to the dressing room to find out what had happened. When he came back to the dugout, he kept silent. He knew the time wasn't right to talk about it.

At the break, I made use of images – just like I've always done since the Espanyol days – to convey a very clear message. In positional terms, the defensive line had to push up and give us more width. But that was the least of it. We were lacking energy, the passion we need to play our game. I told them as much. 'Come on lads, let's play!' It was as if we were stuck at the end of last season.

Things changed in the second half. Lamela levelled and I breathed easier – I could recognise the team. And we would've won had it not been for their keeper, Maarten Stekelenburg, who made a couple of great saves. A year ago we were on a par with Everton, but today we're disappointed with the result. That is a positive to take.

After the game, I consoled Hugo Lloris, who has sustained a serious muscular injury. I also congratulated Michel Vorm. We're not used to losing our goalkeepers, but when one is out, it's another one's chance to rise to the occasion.

*

We gave the squad Sunday off. We analysed the game on Monday and had one-to-one talks with certain players. There are things we aren't satisfied with – we didn't show up for the first half against Everton. So on Tuesday, I felt the onus was on me to motivate everyone.

We're just getting started again, but we've had to get tough with a few lads who have come back confused from the summer break or international duty. Sometimes their parents or agents tell them things that do not always help – that they need to think more about themselves, that sort of stuff. I have a stock response when I hear a parent or agent say something along those lines: 'If he doesn't work for the team, he won't play.' And I make sure not to laugh or flinch even in the slightest. I think the message is sent out loud and clear.

It's a young squad that has seen a lot of change over the last two years. Some of the players were in League One when we arrived and their status has changed.

I also spoke to Victor Wanyama. We chatted about everything and nothing. Toni was there too. Victor told us about playing for his country last week, about when they lost a home game and a few of the players, who had made mistakes, had to make a run for it after the fans invaded the pitch. We laughed. At the training ground, we put the players through a gruelling test that no one likes (we call it the Gacon test; I must explain more about it one day), but Victor was jokingly telling us that his national side does not need it because they get fit after games by running away from the fans.

*

Today, Wednesday, we trained at Wembley. It was glorious weather for the occasion. I played at the old Wembley with Argentina 16 years ago. Also the 2015 League Cup final was hosted here, and we'll be back for our Champions League home games this year.

Son Heung-min came back to rejoin us after featuring in the Olympics with South Korea. In his homeland, all men must do two years' military service before the age of 28, or something like that. But exemptions are granted to those who, for instance, help the country to major sporting success. For that reason, winning a medal at the Games would have been a big deal for Son, but it wasn't to be.

I had to do military service. It was one of the last years in which it was mandatory in Argentina. A draw was held to determine who was drafted; the last three digits of your ID number dictated your fate. I was stationed in the army. It was while I was a top-flight player with Newell's. I kept going to training, sometimes I was allowed to leave a bit early to make it on time, but I had to wear uniform every day. And I cut my hair, obviously. I went from being a total hunk, with my fashionable long hairstyle, to a number one all over. Not sure it suited me.

*

Roll on the matchday routine at White Hart Lane again. It's like getting a hug from an old friend, made more special because it will be our last season here.

When we're playing at home, like today against Crystal Palace, we never stay together the night before. If it's a three o'clock kick-off, for example, we'll be at the training ground four hours beforehand. I will go over the game plan with the coaches, eat three and a quarter hours before kick-off, have a short meeting, do some last-minute preparations, and then meet up again at the stadium.

Sometimes I reveal the line-up a couple of hours before kick-off. At other times I do it the day before, after we have watched footage of the opposition, but no more than four or five minutes, as the players' attention disappears if it lasts any longer. I have a clear idea of how we will start. We then train with the chosen XI. It depends on the vibe I get from the group and what plans we want to introduce. On match-day, we focus more on the motivational side, or we show some videos of the situations we've worked on in training. Then, an hour and a half before the game, Jesús does a two- or three-minute run-through of the defensive and attacking strategy, so that it's all fresh in their minds. When I get the opposition line-up, I write it up on the board so that the team knows the score. I may give a few individual instructions, but not too many.

Before the warm-up, we do some exercises in the dressing room to preactivate the players, to switch them on, but I don't have to be there at the time. Later, during the warm-up, I go to talk to Sky Sports and then head back to my office, where it's usually just Miki and me on our own, talking, watching a match, listening to music, chatting idly about what happened the previous day or some film we've seen, or exchanging views about the opposition's line-up. I take the opportunity to then have a shower, get changed and fix myself something to eat and drink. We're often joined by Ossie Ardiles, a club ambassador. It's always a pleasure to see him.

That is the time to relax, the calm before the storm. And it goes slowly. Some managers feel at a loss at that moment, when we've got nothing to do. Everything is in place, prepared. It's a 45-minute vacuum. But honestly, it's one of the parts I enjoy the most.

Naturally, you always have to be on your guard. A player can start throwing up or have a stomach ache, or maybe their knee is bothering them and they can't play, so you've got to figure out who's going to replace them. It feels like a sudden invasion, disturbing the harmony of that magical moment.

I've always heard people talk about nerves in the minutes before a match. It's true that when I was a player I had butterflies in my stomach and used to go to the toilet two or three times, but as a coach it's the complete opposite. The closer we get to show time, the calmer I feel. And that sense of calm helps you analyse things more lucidly.

*

After the match against Crystal Palace, I told the press that I was happy with the lads' efforts. We created a lot of chances in the first half; it was just a shame we didn't score. I added that there wasn't much to adjust at half-time.

That wasn't entirely true.

Matches against Palace are always tricky. If you don't get an early goal, they can make you suffer. We had a lot of clear-cut chances, but so did they. At the interval, we asked the central midfielders to take up better positions. We used video to illustrate what we wanted: for them to circulate the ball more efficiently and to occupy space better, so that we'd be able to stop Palace's counter-attacks.

After the interval, we threatened more than them and the team had the edge physically, but still we couldn't score. Searching for solutions, I spoke to Jesús and Miki, but sometimes decisions that seem right at the time can turn sour by the end of the match. Taking a player off when things get complicated can crush them and risks alienating them for the rest of the season. My own experience as a footballer helps. I try not to piss my players off. You've got to learn to be patient.

Finally, in the 83rd minute, we won a corner. We had five players who are strong in the air in the box. Lamela whipped over a great cross and there was Wanyama to head the ball into the net. A relief. Our first three points.

Janssen made his home debut and played the full 90 minutes, being named the man of the match.

Today we appeared to have stepped it up a notch. During the week we'd said that if we could change a couple of things, everything else would come together. If we managed to play with a slightly higher defensive line, that would enable the players ahead of them to push up and press. The more compact we are, the less scope the opposition have to create. We were able to put this into practice in the game, and it worked. We were also more aggressive, particularly at set-pieces and in 50-50 tackles. This win gives us a platform to build on.

The media asked me about Dele Alli. He was in the starting line-up against Everton, but didn't start today because he was feeling ill, due to an upset stomach. He wasn't fit to play more than half an hour and he ended up coming on in the 68th minute. But it's always the same story: when you do something unexpected, it's assumed that there's a serious problem. And the fact is that you can't always divulge what's going on. On top of that, we have a 25-man squad and we've got to rotate. We have four competitions ahead of us, including one that is new for everyone: the Champions League.

Something fascinating is being played out within the group. The likes of Kane and Alli aren't the same players they were a year ago. Just 12 months ago, Kane played in the UEFA Under-21 Championship, whereas now he's coming off the back of going to the senior equivalent as the Premier League's top scorer. Dele Alli, when he first arrived from MK Dons, had a burning need to prove his worth and showed that hunger in every training session, constantly putting his body on the line. But now, a year on, Dele has signed three new contracts, each including a wage hike. It's normal for them to believe, and for their entourage to tell them, that their position in the hierarchy has changed. And it has, because of what they offer us. That's where the coach, who has witnessed their development, has to tread carefully and be intelligent enough to realise that they're no longer the up-and-coming kids of a year back.

This is also a very instructive process for us. A year ago, you could yell at Dele during a session, but now you necessarily have to strike a different tone. You have to deal with them more sensitively, and grant them the odd privilege that would've been impossible before. It is a very delicate balance. But we must be doing something right: so far, my authority has not been challenged in training at Tottenham on even a single occasion.

*

I got a message from Nicola Cortese, the former Southampton chairman. We arranged to have dinner together. It was Nicola who sought me out – when I didn't speak a word of English – to replace the manager who had led them to promotion to the Premier League, and at a time when he was getting good results. He is a man of conviction, let's say. Either that, or he's half-crazy!

It hurts me that the crowd there now treat us like enemies.

*

The win over Crystal Palace has given us some breathing space. Still, we started the week by going over what we did wrong in the match. I had a few individual meetings, including with the full-backs, Walker and Rose.

We play Liverpool tomorrow. We think they are going to try to stop our build-up play and attempt to put the squeeze on us up the flanks, forcing us into mistakes, so we have to work on different ways of bringing the ball out from the back, with decoys so that we can evade their attentions. The positioning of our midfielders is important in this respect; they need to be fully aware of the strategy and ready to receive possession. Since we don't want to go long, we will also devise other ways of bypassing their high press.

Because it's the day before the game, I've already spoken to the media. After preparing for the match, I thought it would be a quiet afternoon, but there was all sorts going on. We posed for a photo with legendary Tottenham coach Keith Burkinshaw. We spent a while chatting with him. Ossie had come down too and he stayed for lunch.

In fact it's been an eventful week. After the Liverpool game, there will still be five days before the transfer window closes. I've been sitting down with players, agents, the chairman, discussing scenarios, possibilities, contracts. And limitations. There are many players out there hoping to move on. I think someone will come in and we have to be on the alert in case there are any interesting developments. I've been told that a Real Madrid player is considering leaving. They say you shouldn't look a gift horse in the mouth, but I get the impression that the people around him are more motivated by money than by anything else. Leaving a club like Madrid or Barça is a very big decision for a player's career; you have to think carefully about when you leave. And why. There are brave souls who leave because they want to play; others think twice. You have to be open to any possibility.

I sat down with Ryan Mason today and our conversation struck a chord with me. Ryan is the sort of player I like having around. When

53

I first arrived at the club, I saw him sitting in the gym, looking sad and oozing pessimism. I don't know why, but I decided to take him on our US tour. He played in a couple of the matches and on one of the journeys between Chicago, Toronto and Seattle, while we were waiting at the airport, we started chatting. I had a hunch about the kid. I enjoyed talking to him and found that he was eager to fight for a place. We spoke again after the tour and I asked him to stay. On one condition: that he would work a lot on his fitness, which had suffered as he had bounced aimlessly from club to club. I wanted to turn him into a Premier League player. I told him he'd train with the squad, as well as with the Under-21s sometimes, and we'd see what happened.

Anyway, Mason stayed, knuckled down and ended up playing against Arsenal at the Emirates in September that first season, when there was still uncertainty in the air. I put him in the starting line-up. In hindsight that may seem normal, but to throw Mason into the fray for his first derby, away from home, and leave big-name players like Paulinho on the bench . . . It was a key decision that no one probably understood before the game, but we knew it was the right one. He ended up playing an important role in that campaign. Last term he got injured while scoring the winner against Sunderland, giving us our first victory of the season in our fifth game. But he really struggled to get back into his stride after that and Mousa Dembélé started to play really well. I spoke to him before he went to Hull and was hoping to convince him to stay, but Ryan wants to play more regularly. He feels like a Premier League footballer and is searching for new challenges. I feel we helped make that happen.

It was hard to say goodbye.

*

The goalkeeping position is certainly the one that has changed the most over the last decade, creating insecurity for those who learned the trade in one way and have had to make considerable changes along the path. It isn't easy. A goalkeeper's level of responsibility nowadays is even more crucial because his decisions can define the type of move that the team put together. We see Hugo Lloris as the best goalkeeper in the world. He picked up an injury against Everton but it's important that his absence doesn't feel like too much of a problem. We need every player and nobody is more important than anyone else. Hugo came out of the team, Michel Vorm came in and that's that. Michel deserves all our recognition as a great goalie, excellent person and extraordinary professional. At the same time, this injury may allow Hugo, who joined up with the group later than the others, to do some extensive fitness work that he didn't have time to do earlier. You have to try to seek out positives from seemingly negative situations.

Then you have the person himself. Hugo is special. When you're injured, you feel alone, even if there are people around you. We've all been through it. That's why it's so important to be in regular contact, both for the player and for us, so that we can share our feelings. We've spoken so much about football and life ever since I took over. Since his injury we've studied his game and looked at other goalkeepers who have a similar footballing philosophy. Players spend more hours at the training ground when they're injured compared with when they're not, so we made the most of his role as captain and team leader to discuss certain areas that we want to improve in future and others that we're going to suggest to the squad. He's a mature person, a moral leader who has real authority, because of his professionalism and because of the way he is. I almost consider him to be part of the coaching staff because he embodies the philosophy that we want to champion in our game when he's on the pitch: possession, attacking mentality, not in fear of a high line, an active and brave goalkeeper who's good on the ball.

*

It was the Champions League draw and given that we were being filmed, our reaction was not as unguarded as it could have been. Maybe it would've been better to watch it in my office without anyone around because it was such an important moment. We started out with Spurs in the Europa League and this year it's the Champions League, so a big step forward. We've always watched the draw to see which team drew which, and this time we were involved in it, in the biggest competition of the lot.

We're going to be up against AS Monaco, CSKA Moscow and Bayer Leverkusen.

*

27 August. Today we were at home to Liverpool who always make tough opponents. They have players who I know well from my Southampton days: Nathaniel Clyne, Adam Lallana and Dejan Lovren, who was my man of the match. As well as a couple more we know very well.

Before the game, we went over what we'd been working on during the week, but just before the clock struck the half-hour mark, Walker felt sick and had to come off. We initially thought about a straight swap and bringing on a full-back, but I decided against it. We brought on a centre-forward and Dier moved to full-back, going on to be one of the best players on the pitch. I didn't understand why, but other guys besides Walker were also not feeling very well and they told us so en route to the dressing room. We went in at the break 1–0 down.

We used half-time to make some adjustments in terms of how we were keeping possession and that gave us control of the game in the second half, particularly in the first 30 minutes. Rose equalised and a draw was a fair result which we were happy with.

Maybe the fixture came too early in the season for us. We've barely got out of first gear so far. We've gone three games unbeaten, but many aspects haven't gone as planned. Many key players aren't performing at the desired level (Kane, Eriksen). We started out with Dier and Wanyama forming a new partnership in midfield. We're still working on the general concepts with the players without delving into too much detail, although that's exactly what you need for this type of game.

Harry hasn't scored yet, but we aren't worried. Last year was tough for him. He went ten games without scoring and went off track. He thought he was a different player and had to do different things to the ones we were suggesting. I sat down with him in the second week of the season, showed him some videos and said to him, 'You're Harry Kane. If Harry Kane doesn't do what Harry Kane does . . .' That was a real eye-opener for him. In the end, he scored against Manchester City which came from a set-piece when he was borderline offside. He then spent another six games not scoring before a hat-trick against Bournemouth started an unstoppable run.

He scored a wonderful goal in the friendly against Inter. He's had his chances in the league, but he hasn't put them away. We do know that he needs a few games to get into the swing of things. He likes playing as a number 10 behind the striker, giving him more space and without having centre-backs on top of him. People disagree and think he should play up top on his own, but I believe that having another forward alongside him is a better option.

To sum up, we're doing well. The team have been doing what we've needed, apart from during the first half against Everton. At the same stage last season we had two points. This year we're on five and the league is even tougher. We're unbeaten, we've conceded one goal from a direct free-kick and another from the penalty spot. We're sixth.

*

A lovely photo of a hug between me and Liverpool midfielder Adam Lallana came out in the press. We chatted a bit. There was always a good connection between the two of us. We speak the same language, the language of football, which we're so passionate about and which transcends any barriers. When I took over at Southampton, my English was atrocious, but we still connected.

I remember that just over three months after arriving, I sat down with Adam after training. Jesús was also there. 'What's up? What's wrong?' He didn't seem at ease, he wasn't fulfilling his potential and he wasn't enjoying his football.

He looked at me and said, 'What do you mean, boss?'

'Do you have any problems at home?' I asked him. The previous manager Nigel Adkins had made him captain at the start of the campaign. One day he saw his name on the board with a 'C' for captain next to it. There was nothing formal about it. He was 24 and his game dipped when he found himself needing to lead the team without being ready for it.

He had been suffering injuries the season we arrived and went in and out of the team with us in charge too. The conversation with Lallana was slow because of the language barrier but I felt I was getting somewhere after a couple of hours. 'I was given the armband and I felt I had to do more than the rest, work more, think of everybody, and at the end I started to do everything but focus on my football.' As the team were fighting to stave off relegation, there was even more pressure on him.

I started to understand the stress, even some of the reasons for so many injuries.

Also, he told me, the chairman called him after every game to tell him: 'We shouldn't have lost, we should've scored, we can't go down . . .'

'What? Stop right there,' I said.

Within the Latin culture, we're used to the chairman speaking to players without going through the coach, but in Lallana's case it seemed illogical to me, especially because the role of manager involves so much more in England. The responsibility has to fall on the manager, rather than on the players. Although I knew Nicola, the chairman, was only trying to help, he'd made the wrong call.

'It's okay,' – I said. 'I understand now. You're under too much pressure. That's why you aren't enjoying it. Let's finish the season but next campaign this will be truly and fully sorted.' After three hours we decided to leave the training centre.

I asked Nicola to stop calling Adam and little by little his performances started to take off. But something else was needed – he had to know where he stood with the team and the captaincy.

Before the start of the following season, we organised a barbecue at the hotel where the coaching staff had been staying. Our guests were what we considered the captains and leaders of the team: Lallana, Kelvin Davis, Rickie Lambert and José Fonte, most of them accompanied by their wife and kids. Nicola, Toni, Miki and Jesús were there with their wives. After we had some food, the men went aside and the players told Lallana, out of the blue, that they wanted him to be the captain, that he honoured the armband, that he represented the essence of the team and the club. It was very emotional. He cried, and some of us too. There was a real connection at that point. He accepted, of course.

*

It is the international break. We've got 16 internationals, so we'll have to make do with only six first-team players this week, including two goalkeepers. We will promote ten kids from the youth ranks. The pace in training will be dictated by the guys who have stayed behind. There is also the added distraction of the transfer market.

Incidentally, before the Liverpool match, Georginio Wijnaldum told

CHILDREN'S MENU

Choose one of each for £5.95

SIDE + DRINK

SIDE

Fries
Make your chips
cheesy for 50p

....

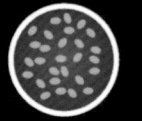

Salad

....

Baked Beans

DRINK

Milk

....

**Children's
Orange or Apple
Juice**

....

Bottled Water

....

Ribena minis
Blackcurrant or
Apple & Mango

....

DEXTERS KITCHEN

MENU

HOW TO ORDER

1. Order at the till
2. Collect your number
3. We'll do the rest!

DRINKS
SOFT DRINKS

SLUSH PUPPiE.

Regular	£2.75
Large	£3.25

Diet Coke, Sprite, Fanta	Regular	£2.85
	Large	£3.00

Coca-Cola	Regular	£2.90
	Large	£3.15

Ribena minis

Blackcurrant or apple & mango	£1.75

WHY NOT ENJOY SOME FRESHLY BAKED COOKIES?

Millie's COOKIES

Buxton Still 750ml or Sparkling 500ml	£2.25
Buxton Still 500ml	£2.00
Appletiser	£2.50
Semi-Skimmed Milk	£1.10

SLURP ICE CREAM SHAKES

Chocolate, or Vanilla	£2.99

SSP_CPRC_DEXTR_MENU_012856

ICE CREAM ★ ★
CANDY SHOP

the press that he would have liked to have joined Tottenham. It must seem like clubs are stealing a march on us because we're not up to the task, that we lose players for not being on the ball, but that's not the case. If we're interested in a player, we monitor and scout them. We need to improve the squad and take the team to the next level, but that would require bringing in the number ones in their position, not the number twos.

I can't stand the last few days of the window. I get fed up with the on-off, will-he, won't-he nature of transfers. I'm going to go to Barcelona, as I've been doing for the last few years. By this stage, the end of August, I've made it perfectly clear what I think and what the team needs; my homework is done. The rest isn't in my hands. And if we can't sign anyone, well then so be it. So I prefer to go away.

As I always try to do in late summer, I take some time off to be with family and friends. Generally I meet my friend Alejandro, the Argentinian consul of Barcelona, and his family. The destination is usually Ibiza, an ideal location if you're in search of good weather and food. It is a sort of tradition, which I tend to stick to. I don't like things done at the last minute.

Daniel is looking to strengthen the squad. He feels he has to offer me something else. I think it's a job he's always enjoyed. Before, responsibility for signings was shared with the manager and the sporting director, or with the people who advised Daniel. Things have been clearer since I joined. We just need to get to know each other a bit better so the process becomes even smoother. Daniel is finalising the arrival of Moussa Sissoko, who had a great Euros, although he underwhelmed for Newcastle.

The deal for Sissoko isn't that expensive when compared to others, especially considering he's played more than forty games a season for seven or eight years. It is not ideal arriving at a club when the season has started, without proper preparation. We know he will find it difficult to adapt to his new surroundings and to our philosophy. He felt the move was very attractive because of the appeal of the Champions League, getting to play alongside his international teammate Hugo Lloris, and because of our way of working and our style of football.

*

1 September. The transfer window has closed and Sissoko's signing was confirmed late last night while I am spending my last hours in Ibiza.

I think Daniel's thought process was, 'he's a good player, but Mauricio will make him better'.

We'll see.

3.

SEPTEMBER

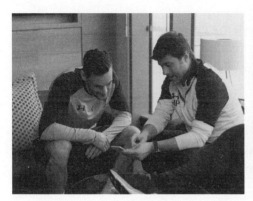

The matches came thick and fast, and it was a matter of looking for the best way to bed in players who'd had varying levels of physical preparation. The team travelled to Stoke straight after the international break, before contesting league games against bottom-half opposition in the shape of Sunderland and Middlesbrough. League One outfit Gillingham were the first hurdle to overcome in the League Cup, while all eyes were focused on the Champions League opener against Monaco at Wembley.

There's a photo from when I was very young, I must've been two or three. I´m sitting in front of a shed that my father had built and the grass is very long. I have a tight grip on a football and am grinning from ear to ear. That's me. That happy kid. I'm 44 now, but I still look at that photo every now and then, in order not to forget that that's who I am, not only the person I see in the mirror today.

As a boy, I used to say that I was born into a middle-class family. In reality, it was nothing of the sort. In Argentina, they call almost everyone middle class. I was working class, where Saturdays and Sundays don't exist. If a pig or cow goes into labour, you have to see to them, whatever day of the week it is. My father used to work alone on 100 hectares of land, which back then produced enough for two or three families to live off, but now it barely feeds one person.

It was a big house, although the sink and the bathroom were outside which was the norm back then. When it was cold, nobody wanted to move away from the fireplace. We had great times sitting in front of a 14-inch battery-powered TV. When my father arrived home in the evening on his tractor or some other machine, we'd take the battery out and stick it in the TV. We had to move the antenna on top of the box in order to pick up the only signal that reached Murphy. I was allowed to watch it for half an hour, which almost always meant a soap, and then it was bedtime.

I remember playing football aged four or five in the fields. There were of course plenty of those around the house. I spent all day kicking a ball around waiting for my old man to come back from working the land. If it rained in the afternoon, it was brilliant, because nobody worked and everyone who was at home would play.

Maybe because my life seemed far away from the places where things happened, when I was little I used to build up images in my head of future events. I don't know if it's natural or something I was taught, but I've done so ever since I can remember. I used to imagine whatever was needed at the time. A girl that I took a liking to, for example. I thought about what I had to do to win her over and it would then go just as I'd dreamt it. Others may call it intuition. Or even an aptitude for reading the future. I am sure it is not that, but I have great faith in this ability which I've always had and can't fully explain. I use it to make decisions and understand our world.

Also, I would sometimes hear a player's name on the TV, such as Beckenbauer, and I'd store it in my head. I hadn't the foggiest about his style of play, but I'd make it up and claim it as my own. The following day, while hitting the ball between the tractor's wheels, I'd commentate, 'And Beckenbauer shoots' or 'Beckenbauer goes for the header and . . . Goooooooal!' That was difficult because I had to throw the ball up myself. I imagined playing in the biggest, most famous stadiums. Interestingly, however, I never visualised the fans in my head. Maybe that's why I was never scared of the public. I was always able to block that out and I didn't care about my surroundings, whether there were 100,000 people in attendance or there wasn't a soul watching.

I also believe nothing happens by chance, that there is a reason for everything. Since those early days I've had the ability to notice something powerful that you can't see, but does exist. A vital force, an energy field that makes the world go round, an aura that accompanies people, which gives lots of information about them. It's in my skin, I feel it. Karina and I call it 'universal energy'. My wife helped me get to grips with it and gain a more in-depth understanding. Others helped me explore those feelings further. It isn't superstition or black magic. I believe there is science behind it. It helps me break down day-to-day life, comprehend things, even possibly my own past.

I come from a family of Italian immigrants hailing from Piedmont. My great-grandfather ran a bar that doubled as a grocery store. He cut an intimidating figure, commanding respect – especially when holding a knife, with which he was skilled – and laying down the law. He was called 'the Sheriff', without anyone knowing where it had come from, and he acted accordingly; he was the authority in the place.

My grandfather followed in his footsteps, and often got into trouble. I was around 14 and he was in his sixties on a day when there was a scuffle in a game that I was playing in at a local village. My father and grandfather both got involved in the punch-up and swung at anyone who got near them, knocking people down.

I went to my grandfather's house that evening to see how he was and he was laughing.

'What did you do, Grandpa?'

'Well, a guy was pissing me off and I knocked his block off.'

That was my grandfather. I enjoyed listening to him tell stories about Murphy. People there weren't scared of anything or anybody. I was living in Europe when I had to go back to Argentina to see him pass away. He no longer recognised me, but I was able to say goodbye.

*

My grandfather cut my father's dreams short, as was often the case in Murphy. When he was little, Dad was a good footballer and received offers to play for local teams, although not on professional terms. My grandfather strictly forbade him. It couldn't happen. My father was the

63

eldest of many siblings and he had to follow in his dad's path by taking charge of the land.

My old man went to school until he was 12, after which he had to work day and night. There was barely any space for fun, such as going to the cinema or playing, unless he ran off for a bit, of course. On one of those escapades he met my mother, who was from a nearby town, and he married her at 19. She was two years younger.

Just like my grandmother, my mum commanded respect. They both ran their households. When my children have a fight with their mother nowadays, they say, 'Shut your mouth!' Imagine saying something like that to your mother back then! You'd get slapped so hard that your head would fall off. I don't remember the last slap, but I did get a fair few before moving to Rosario when I was 14. My parents showed me exactly where the limits were, but I still took it upon myself to be a bit naughty. I would sometimes get found out and receive what was the universal punishment back then. In any case, my father was my idol and I was always following him around. There were things that really got to him, such as when his children showed one another a lack of respect – he had a way of instilling values that have stayed deeply rooted within me.

My father helped me become a footballer. Without his support, I would never have achieved it. Maybe if my grandfather hadn't banned him from playing, Dad might have reacted differently. He stopped working to take me to training and to matches, and he'd sometimes give me a lift to Rosario. He made sacrifices in order to give me a chance.

If he hadn't let me move to Rosario on my own, I wouldn't have made it as a professional. Back then, it was very common for Argentinian players to move far away from home to try to achieve success. However, letting your offspring take off can create a gap between parents and children, years pass, a decade or more, and we end up becoming different people – still relatives but strangers too. That's the price to pay for being who I am today. As is often the case, my parents found it difficult to keep pace with my developments. After a while it becomes difficult to relate to them.

When I was already settled in Rosario, we would speak on the phone only on Saturdays, just for a bit, meaning there was no way to explain the daily routine, the emotions, the experiences and the ways in which I was becoming a new person. So there comes a time when your parents become strangers. Or, more accurately, we become strangers to them. Distance turns into intolerance. When you're young, the energy which makes you achieve greatness can also trigger pain, haughtiness, an inability to understand your elders.

Time goes by and you can't retrieve the past. Your relationship with your parents is like one of those thick cables made up of thinner ones that make it almost indestructible. If the thin ones start breaking, though, it gets weaker and is difficult to repair. Impossible sometimes. Yes, I'm their son, but I'm also a famous person who has created a life which they aren't part of. I think they find it hard to separate the son from the celebrity.

Nowadays I don't know how to build the bridge that will bring me closer to my father once again. I find it hard to talk about this, it causes me great pain because that distance has almost become a rupture, and I feel responsible.

Nor do I have the close relationship that I'd like to have with my two brothers. In fact, it's the worst relationship imaginable. I have more emotional links to friends and acquaintances than I do with my brothers. Is that my fault? How does one get into that position? They are valid questions because I don't want it to happen to my kids. I tell them that they can fall out with one other when there's a conflict of interests, but they must never lose respect for one another.

Another thing that worries me is that passing on values to our kids often depends on where we are in our own journey through life. Six or seven years ago, when Sebastiano was 15, I was in another world. I was completely different from whom I am today. I understood life in a different light, my levels of patience weren't the same and I communicated in a particular way . . . My relationship with Mauri, his younger brother, is entirely different. We're very close, but, now that I have changed, now that I am different from the person I was six or seven years ago, have I managed to instil in both the same values?

Just like all parents, we demand so much from ourselves. Perhaps too much. And we don't always get it right.

I have to call my folks.

*

One day I almost died in the flat in Rosario where I was living. I remember it as if it were yesterday.

I spent my first year at Newell's in digs near the stadium. My father then bought me a small one-bedroom flat. I trained in the mornings and went to school in the evenings from seven until 11. I then took the number 15 bus back to the flat. There was a bar opposite the stop and, as its kitchen was shut, the owners would make me some sandwiches, I'd grab a bottle of water or a Coca-Cola and walk home.

I would switch on my black and white 14-inch Noblex TV, the same as the battery-powered one that we had in the countryside, although in Rosario there were two channels. It was pretty chilly in the flat in winter. I'd shut the door to the rather minuscule kitchen, the bathroom door and the dining-room door before going to my bedroom. I'd take my TV with me and watch it for a while until I fell asleep. My father had always told me to switch off the mobile gas heater before going to bed in order not to use up all the oxygen and I always did, but it was bloody freezing that night and I thought, 'I'll lie down for a bit and watch some TV, I'll leave the heater on for another half an hour to heat the room up and then I'll switch it off.' I fell asleep.

When I woke up, I was dripping with sweat, I couldn't breathe. I instinctively switched the heater off. There was a window near by which I opened and stuck my head out of. I was out of it. Getting some fresh air kind of woke me up and so I opened all the other windows before going back to my room. I didn't know if it was my head or my body that hurt, nor what I was doing or where I was. I got into bed completely soaked.

I woke up in the morning cold to my marrow. It was freezing! I closed everything and had a shower. I was hurting everywhere, even the nail on my big toe. I went to see a doctor who checked out my temperature, throat, head . . . 'Go home, get into bed and stay there for a week,' he said. I didn't go out for three or four days. I just ate rice and eggs, as that was all I had. I didn't have a phone or anything like that. On the fourth or fifth day I went to the club. My father didn't know anything when he came to visit me the following weekend. The flat was in a real state. I even had pans of old food under the bed! I was

15 and he couldn't believe what had happened. I got a bollocking. He chucked it all away and bought me an oil-filled electric radiator instead.

It's incredible the way things happen. Someone up there was looking after me and gave me a nudge, 'Get up and open the window.' Why else did I wake up?

*

Do you need to experience great suffering to be a footballer?

There are many ways to become a professional. In life suffering does not equal reward. It takes a mix of effort, desire, passion and responsibility to achieve your objectives, and not exclusively in football. If my son wants to be a footballer, he doesn't necessarily have to go through what I went through. That's what I'm fighting for. To be a footballer, you have to feel it. It has to be very deep down. I always had the need to become one, although I don't really know why. My brother also liked playing football and my father gave him the same chance as me, but he didn't grab it because he didn't feel it on the inside. If my son doesn't have that feeling, he won't be a footballer, whether he lives in digs from fourteen or not.

The day after accepting the Tottenham job, we had a meeting with Southampton, whom 12-year-old Mauri played for. The coaches wanted him to stay and offered him a contract. Of course, he was over the moon and didn't want to come to London with us. What should we do? Split the family in half or allow him to stay behind? After analysing it over several weeks, we decided that we'd buy the house where we were living in Southampton and I'd stay in a hotel near the Tottenham training ground, while regularly travelling down south to be with the family. After the first few drives, I realised it wouldn't work, it was all too much effort. I told Mauri that if he was going to be a footballer, he could do so anywhere. We ended up not buying the house and he accompanied us to London.

If 16-year-old Mauri comes up to me now and says he's off to Málaga and that he has the maturity and ability to do it, I'll give my seal of approval. Back then, however, he was too young. But, do you need to leave and distance yourself from the family to fulfil your dreams? I don't think so. In fact, if I were the one to suggest that he suffers as much as I did, he'd certainly resent me for it. You can't ask a teenager from the first world to suffer these days.

It saddens me that my sons haven't had a taste of nature in the way that Karina and I have. Emotions only seem to be aroused now if accompanied by tangible presents, and the more expensive the better, rather than growing a flower in the garden which was a regular happening during our childhood. The simple things, the silliest things that you can imagine, are just what made us happy. Now it is too much about material things.

Our boys though have been good. Sebastiano, who was born in Barcelona, was always well behaved and could be taken everywhere. One day we went to a restaurant which happened to have King Juan Carlos I of Spain as a regular. Children don't go there, but we made Sebas part of our social life and our friends didn't mind us bringing him with us. In the middle of dinner, he began reciting García Lorca and the restaurant manager couldn't believe it. He was only three or four. What a personality Sebastiano was. He grew up with adults. He was always with older people, listening to adult conversations. We basically improvised his education as the three of us were alone in Barcelona, without the influence of any grandparents, aunties or uncles.

We then went to Paris and after that we spent six months in Bordeaux, where we lived just opposite the main theatre in the city centre. The change took some getting used to because Mauri was very little and Sebastiano was still adapting to life in the capital when he had to change schools again, which always creates drama.

I remember buying Sebas a bicycle and one Sunday afternoon I promised myself that we wouldn't leave the park until he learnt how to ride it without stabilisers. We were there for three or four hours. Two elderly ladies watched us the whole time and when Sebastiano finally managed it, they started applauding joyously.

Look at him now: he's a sports scientist who is forging his own path. The other day he was asked what he wanted to achieve: 'More experience and being known as Sebastiano, rather than the manager's son.' A few years ago, he was working with our academy in Belgium and a group of players from London rebelled against him, didn't pay any attention to what he was saying. He had to earn their respect and did not use his family name once. I know he wants to take off, but maybe it's better if he stays with the family for a bit longer.

Mauri might look very shy but he has a great sense of where he is and how to behave. It must be hard to play for the club where your father is the manager. He knows he will be judged differently but he lives calmly with it. We're ascertaining whether it's worth accepting a scholarship which would allow him to study and train at the club. He wants to do it. It is in his hands to take advantage of the opportunity and show his value, and his values.

I can't chat with Mauri about football as much as I can with Sebas, who is in a more mature phase of his life and has a job that forces him to be reflective and seek out more answers. It's hard to speak to a 16-year-old footballer who thinks he knows it all. He has to believe that he's right. I understand that has to be the case – I was probably the same. That arrogance protects you during a period that is normally filled with doubts. If he were overly aware of his own limitations and the potential difficulties involved in becoming a footballer, he would stop trying. On top of that, I'm his father and although I'm a manager, there's still a level of suspicion about what I have to say.

I used to analyse the situation without a father's emotions, when the normal scenario is to always think that your son is the best and if he didn't play well, it was because of the shortcomings of his teammates. When he played well, I told him so, but when he played badly, I also told him so. That can of course hurt his feelings. Now I try to sidestep that conversation. When he doesn't play well, I don't say anything. Well, I say, 'Tough game, wasn't it?'

Family. Home. A place of rest, where I can be myself once again. If I ever forget what that means, I can look at the photo of the boy smiling gleefully with a ball under his arm.

*

Monday 5 September. It was a calm weekend. England were in action. This upcoming week will be quite tough because the boys will be coming back on different days depending on their schedules at international level. The fitness coaches and other members of the coaching staff are preparing tailored drills and recovery plans for them. Some of them landed yesterday, Son arrived today and a few others get back tomorrow.

Espanyol goalkeeper Pau López has joined us on loan in the last few days. He has huge potential and is lucky enough to be training with Toni, who has created his own methodology.

Incidentally, I've received a gift from Dejan Lovren who is now at Liverpool and was previously at Southampton with me. It was a watch with a note saying, 'For my footballing father'. It was unnecessary, but also wonderful.

Above all, this week will be about getting the team settled because the transfer window has shut, the players know there won't be any more changes and their individual situations are being addressed. We've also agreed new contracts for six players. The chairman intelligently called a meeting with Jesús, me and a few others after the transfer window closed and I got back from my trips to Barcelona and Ibiza. He invited me in for a quick word beforehand to remind me that the two of us have the last word over which players come and go. Authority isn't something that you can buy in a shop, it's bestowed upon you by others.

I ate too well when I was abroad. I need to lose some weight, so I've taken up sport again. While on the running machine, I found myself thinking about the extraordinary light of Barcelona.

*

My wife grew up in a house with a large garden, like our current one where we live; she needs to feel space around her. And it's not just the garden – the rooms are also spacious. We chose this area because it's nine miles from both the training ground and school, but we know little more about it. It's mainly residential and is characterised by big houses with patios. Neighbours tend to keep their distance. We only know one and she happens to be a Tottenham fan. We originally moved in opposite her and one day she brought over the entire Spurs-supporting family to introduce themselves. Even the grandchildren came and they were all lovely. We have moved since then, not too far away, and she's still the person who keeps Karina up to date with everything.

While I am particularly fond of nature, when I discovered city life I fell in love with the culture of having a coffee and a chat. It doesn't exist to the same extent in London. That spontaneous aspect of socialising, where you can accidentally bump into someone or ring a friend and be with them in 15 minutes. That's why we fly to Barcelona whenever we have a free day or two. We go there, to our spiritual retreat, to share time with friends, in search of a different light. Even the boys (Sebas still lives with us) press us if a few months pass without us going.

Karina's day revolves around Mauri. She has to pick him up, give him a meal and take him to training. My wife probably spends three hours in the car every day. She's studying cooking and nutrition – one of those eternal students. There's always something new to learn. She goes to the gym and she cooks, spending endless hours in the kitchen. She is a wonderful, adventurous cook.

We know that this is a productive period for me and I'm working round the clock, taking time away from my partner and sons. The day will come when the offers dry up in Europe. They may want me in Japan or the United States, and just the two of us could go for a new experience for a couple of years. So far we've made all the decisions as a family, sometimes more for their sake than mine. Even when the boys were little, we'd sit down as a four to decide. We'd imagine the scene: where would we live? What about schools? And our house? We'd create the trip before embarking upon it.

When I have a decision to make, if a grain of doubt remains after considering the options carefully, I hold back. As a friend used to tell me, if I have a chance to mull it over for one more night, I do so. Something may appear which will help me make up my mind. I don't know how to explain what it is, possibly that intuition I spoke about earlier. It inspires me and reveals the right answer. When I do find it, it's rarely wrong.

But moving is never an easy lifestyle choice. As a player, I turned down many chances to leave Barcelona. Sometimes the timing isn't right. You'd like to leave when your son finishes secondary school, but it isn't always possible. I cried for days and days when I knew I had to leave Barcelona for Southampton. I knew it was a real blow for the family.

*

Saturday. We played Stoke today. We didn't make a good start in the first 20 minutes, we're finding it hard at the beginning of games; we're

71

lacking those automated patterns of play and our performance didn't flow, although they didn't create any chances against us.

I have been thinking about our preparations. Was it a good decision to lighten the workload on a Friday? Everyone was finally back after the international break, so we showed them some videos and did a variety of exercises. We also played an 11-a-side game against the academy team and Son played but should have been more clinical. We had other options for the Stoke match, but I was convinced it was the time to show him that we have faith in him. He had been considering leaving the club and this was our way of saying, 'You're staying, let's start over.'

In the 19th minute, Son, who was having a good game, was fouled in the box, but the referee didn't blow up. He reminds me of Lamela, who arrived at the club a year before I did. Just like Son, he was an expensive signing and young players really feel that pressure. They want to prove themselves at all times and find it hard to accept not being in the starting line-up. The settling-in period is essential. Lamela needed a year or two to start performing. Players nowadays are rather impatient; they want it all straight away. It's like modern-day society. You go on the internet and you have the information you need two seconds later. In life, however, it's a process, involving maturing, working and learning.

We had a chat with Son during the week when he got back from the Olympics. A club in Germany wanted him and promised that he would play. I always say that promises are the death of a footballer. It's better to be reassured that if you're better than your teammate, you'll play. If anything is written in stone beforehand, there is a risk the player will rest on his laurels. We were clear with Son that he has to earn his right to play, as we tell everyone. He wanted to leave after a bad year, but I told him that he was part of my plans and we weren't going to let him go on the cheap. He decided to stay. He'd only played in one international game and he came back to train with us for ten days. He earned his starting berth against Stoke.

He opened the scoring in the 41st minute.

Son has a big entourage around him, including a secretary. The works. His father is his agent and he has many sponsors, too. Managing all that isn't easy. I've been told that he's a huge star in South Korea. In the summer when we were in Australia, a Korean girl asked me for an autograph. I asked her if she knew who Son was and she said she didn't and asked who he was. I ended up having to show her a photo. The Korean didn't even know him!

I really must tell him that one.

We were in the lead at half-time, but we knew something wasn't quite right and we made some adjustments. Eleven minutes into the second half, Son got on the score sheet once again. He also notched an assist and put in a solid defensive display, earning the man of the match award in the process. We won 4–0 and Kane bagged his first goal of the season. We're fifth.

*

It's a Champions League week. Our starting XI is more or less fixed and the players are up for it. We've had several chats with individual players after the international break. We wanted to see how they were mentally. Harry Kane was one of them. We discussed his contract situation and goalscoring drought. Scoring against Stoke was certainly a positive.

In a recent morning chat with Eric Dier I mentioned to him that there are a few aspects of the game that he seems to have dropped from his performances. He asked to speak to me again that afternoon. We trained at Wembley and afterwards I showed him videos from the session and also from our previous match. In the end he admitted, 'I didn't think it was such a big deal.'

We're playing Monaco tomorrow. Jesús told me that he had to give the boys a boost during the warm-up against Stoke by changing the last planned exercise. He thought they had a passive approach. I imagine that tomorrow we'll have to rein them in and calm them down in a new stadium in front of 90,000 on a historic evening. These are the moments we dream about as youngsters.

I played at the old Wembley for the national team. I believe it was in 2000. It looked like I was set to start, but I didn't. Five minutes into the game, Bielsa sent me to warm up alongside Bonini. I looked at my teammate and said, 'Five minutes in? What has he seen that made him get me to warm up?' Nobody was injured, nobody was struggling.

I'd been warming up for five minutes when Bielsa said, 'Get changed.' What do you mean, get changed?! There were barely ten minutes on the clock! 'Sensini off, Pochettino on.' Bielsa saw things that the rest couldn't. I simply loved what Fernando Redondo did next. He grabbed the ball when we next had a free-kick and called me over. 'Poche, Poche, come here, take the free-kick. There we go, now you've had a touch to settle the nerves.' The epitome of Argentinian guile and quick thinking, of a streetwise guy, a *potrero*.

*

Wembley. A place where there is nowhere to hide, where you find out if you know as much as you thought. Where many of the things we stash away from our experiences in hundreds of pitches all over the place come into play.

A coach's education begins long before his first match. We have to make a hundred choices a day and hope we get most of them right. But these decisions aren't made in isolation: they are the offspring of our experience, our emotions and the circumstances. They are often engendered by other people, father figures such as Jorge Griffa, who brought through an extraordinary generation of players at Newell's and taught me a great deal.

First and foremost, I learned from him that you have to be brave in life. Griffa was a fearless person who, from the very first time I met him, impressed me with his energy, his gruff, imposing voice and his aura of invincibility. He didn't spin yarns like a poet; on the contrary, he was very direct, and his words would get straight through to you, resonating deeply. And he acted as he spoke.

Even after establishing myself as a top-flight player, I didn't have an agent. 'Mauricio, you don't need one,' he told me. 'Trust me, the club isn't going to take you for a ride. It doesn't matter that the others have representatives; you're not going to end up out of pocket.' And it proved to be the case. The day I went to sign my first contract, having won the title with Newell's, Griffa said: 'This is your first big payday, isn't it? From now until the end of your career as a footballer, you should be living the good life. But remember: when you hang up your boots, you need to be able to live even more comfortably.' Keep your head, he was telling me. You reap what you sow. He wasn't only talking

74

about money, but also about life: if you look out for people, then they will look out for you.

There's another thing he told me that I repeat to my players. 'Mauricio, football will take you where it wants to, not where you want to go; go with the flow, do your best and believe.' Often lads seem weighed down by problems and I tell them: 'Play football and be happy; football will take you where it wants to.'

Then there's Bielsa. It is no coincidence that so many of us who played under him at Newell's from 1990 to 1993 became coaches and are still working in football: Scoponi, Gamboa, Berizzo, Martino, Zamora, Franco, Berti . . . Bielsa made us understand the game and his passion was contagious. That's not to say that our footballing philosophies are the same, though. The Marcelo I knew, the one I enjoyed and suffered in equal measure, based everything on the opposition having possession and how you win the ball back off them. That used to be the axis of his methods. His philosophy has evolved since but I am not with him daily, so I don't have on opinion on it.

My approach has got some common ground with him but also with many others: we've got the ball, you try to get it off us. I'm not as obsessed with the opposition as Bielsa was – he even asked his assistants to dress up in disguise to sneak in and watch opponents train behind closed doors. We both demand our charges play with intensity and at a high tempo, I want my teams to provoke a controlled disorder, to create so much movement that it distresses the opposition.

I'll never ask my players to dedicate their entire lives to the cause. At Newell's sometimes, around the key stages of the Copa Libertadores competition for instance, we could spend up to three months holed up together – we were only allowed out on Thursday mornings. We'd train on Monday and Tuesday, play in the Copa Libertadores on Wednesday, leave the camp on Thursday after training, and then come back that same night. You had hardly any private life. Bielsa would be with us at times and absent at others. We'd spend all day there and there was only one telephone, which would be disconnected at 10 p.m. If you wanted to talk to your girlfriend, you had to be waiting by the phone when she called, because if someone else picked up, they'd say you weren't around – they, too, would be waiting for a call.

*

Ironically, it was an unanswered phone call that, sometime later, paved the way for me to become Espanyol coach.

The club president, Dani Sánchez Llibre, brought me back from Bordeaux to help the team when they were in trouble. Two years later though, the talk in town was that he wanted me out. I called him but he didn't answer his phone. One day I got wind that he was having lunch at the Hilton and I went to see him. 'Can we talk when you've finished?' I asked him. We ate at separate tables and then spoke afterwards. 'Listen, *presi*, you were wrong not to take my phone call. If you don't want me to stay, say the word and we'll settle things in two minutes.' I duly ended up retiring.

Shortly after I quit playing, there was speculation that I wanted to be the new president. Even surveys were conducted. I phoned Dani: 'I want you to know that all the reports are untrue.' He has since said that he never would have endorsed the sporting directors' idea of appointing me as coach in 2009 if I hadn't straightened things out with him. In fact, those two conversations strengthened our relationship.

I will always be grateful to him for placing his confidence in a person who had played for Espanyol for many years and knew the club inside out, but who had never coached before. I became the third manager of the season, taking over a team languishing towards the bottom of the table, five points from safety. It was a difficult dressing room to be entering, as it was the end of an era and nobody had dared to carry out the necessary overhaul. I knew what I had to do.

What I lacked in experience, I made up for with clear thinking.

From the first day, my backroom staff and I would arrive early at the training ground, which we gradually transformed. We'd drink *mate*, discuss things and have a natter. I listened to what everyone had to say and then made decisions based on a combination of intuition and reflection. I haven't changed all that much – though perhaps my team talks have improved. We used to do a few strange things; we even tried hypnosis!

After drawing with Guardiola's Barcelona in the Copa del Rey, we also shared the spoils with Valladolid in our first league match. Our director of football, Paco Herrera, resigned, and Ramón Planes – who had been the technical secretary – replaced him, provisionally until the end of the season. That's what he was told, that his position would be reviewed at a later stage. Everything was up in the air. We were tipped for relegation to the second division.

People bad-mouthed Ramón to me, and also vice versa. That's typical in football and naturally it led to an almost irreparable rift. I kept my distance from Ramón, but we continued working together. I left the door open. I observed him. We got to know each other. The quality of his work and his perseverance, courage and high principles spoke volumes. Ramón and I had more in common than I had first thought, and we joined forces to get the club to where it belonged during complicated times, of which we would endure many. We knew that we had to overhaul things and we were committed to putting our faith in youth. Soon after, he was the one who brought in Jesús – whom, in my need for a fresh boost, I eventually made one of my right-hand men.

But first, before any big plans, we had to survive that season.

The team bought into our ideas from day one. We felt we had to be proactive, take to the pitch with confidence and play at a high tempo. To be bold. And if someone, anyone, wasn't on board, then that was fine – someone else would play in their place.

'Now we're definitely staying up,' I told Ramón after beating Barcelona in the Camp Nou. We always took the game to them in the derbies and we earned points that cost Barça league titles.

As the season was progressing, we had to cope with tension; the atmosphere was incredibly intense. The stress was tough, but it had its good side too. Winning a game with Espanyol, hard as it was, always brought a huge feeling of happiness: that is how we felt when we got up, when we read the paper, when we went for a walk. It was pure joy, albeit fleeting.

We fell eight points adrift of safety at one stage, but we took 32 points from 19 games to seal survival with two match days to go. Job done: the club was going to begin life in the new stadium in the top flight. With a bunch of naive idealists in charge.

Moving to the new Cornellà-El Prat meant the end of an exile in Montjuïc that had begun with the demolition of the club's iconic Sarrià Stadium in September 1997. I still remember the Saturday when the two main stands were knocked down; a very sad day. We lived five minutes away and that night I went with my wife and my son Sebastiano to look at the ruins. We asked the security guard to let us in. It was impossible to hold back the tears as we walked towards the middle of the pitch. We felt like we were witnessing Sarrià's death throes, the energy of the place slowly fading away.

I literally dreamt of being in charge for the opening game at the Cornellà-El Prat Stadium. And luckily that dream came true. We brought over Rafa Benítez's Liverpool on 2 August 2009. A crowd of 40,000 turned out for the occasion.

And something odd happened. A bird, a chick, flew into the stadium – it was either green or white, I don't remember which. I picked it up, then let it go, and it flew off. I'd also seen that in my dreams.

We won 3–0.

And six days later, at the height of pre-season, Dani Jarque died.

It's very hard to explain. There are situations that you have to deal with, but you can't help but wonder why you have to go through them. And why something like that happens to such a young, healthy kid.

I remember every detail of that Saturday morning. We'd trained at the Italian Football Federation's headquarters in Coverciano, Florence, and he'd seemed perfectly normal. We were preparing for a game the following day in Bologna. After lunch, I told the players to have a nap if they wanted to, and then to go for a wander round Florence. Dani walked by me and said to the doctor, who was sitting opposite me, 'Doctor, can you give me an aspirin or a paracetamol? I've got a bit of a headache.'

I chimed in: 'If you head into Florence, have a coffee and it'll go away.' He replied that he preferred to stay in and rest because he was tired.

Those were the last words I ever heard him say.

Later, I was in a square in Florence with Feliciano Di Blasi, my assistant, when I got a call from Iván De la Peña, our best player. He was crying and asked me to go back to the hotel because something had happened to Dani. When we got there, there were doctors in his bedroom trying to revive him. They tried for three hours, but he never responded. He'd had a heart attack. At the age of 26. It was harrowing

– a trauma, a collective trauma. While the doctors were doing their job, the players were crowded around, sprawled on the floor, crying, clutching their heads, distraught . . . I felt powerless as I looked on and realised that he was leaving us, this kid that I loved, who was part of my life, to whom I had just given the captaincy, who reminded me so much of myself . . . and there was nothing I could do. He had gone. I was devastated.

The silence on the flight back from Florence that same day tore me apart. It was deafening.

We had to keep going, though, and to protect the group and rally around them. We had to channel everyone's energies towards recovering and building up confidence. To use the pain as a driving force. Every glance, every word and every gesture took on new significance.

We suffered a few defeats and struggled to get into our groove. Dani's girlfriend, Jessica, was pregnant when he died and gave birth to their daughter, Martina, on 23 September. That very same day we secured our first competitive win at the new stadium. We dedicated the victory to them.

*

That summer we had begun the required shake-up of the squad. We gave a number of academy lads a chance, like Kiko Casilla, now at Real Madrid, who had been wasting away in the third division with Cadiz, where he was on loan. And Víctor Ruiz, today at Villarreal. He was at centre-back when we lost 4–0 at home to Racing Santander and he had a torrid time. After training the following Monday, I told him: 'Hey, you've got to play without fear, go out there and take no prisoners.' Our next game was against Barcelona and there was no doubt in my mind: Víctor had to play. In the event, we almost claimed a point, but Xavi dived to win a penalty, from which they won it.

The signing of Dani Osvaldo in the January window that second season (2009–10) is perhaps the best example of how we operated. We weren't scoring goals and we had no money, but we were offered the option to sign 'Chupete' Suazo, who came recommended by Bielsa and had been a leading scorer in both Chile and Mexico, where he had amassed incredible stats. Ramón and I spent hours mulling it over. Everyone saw it as a no-brainer – except us. 'What happened to that kid [Osvaldo] we saw two years ago at the Toulon Tournament, the Argentinian who was an Italy Under-20 international?' I asked. Ramón told me that he'd scored three goals in two years and was hardly playing. But he couldn't have forgotten how to play football at the age of twenty-two. We watched him again. I told Ramón, 'I really like this bastard. Shall we sign him and see what happens? If it goes wrong, they'll slaughter us.' We already had Raúl Tamudo, a club legend, in that position, but we showed our balls by signing Osvaldo. During his first training session, Ramón and I looked at each other and said, 'We've screwed up, he's washed-up, he's an ex-footballer.' But we whipped him into shape. In his first five games, he scored just once. But he ended up becoming Espanyol's record sale: we signed him for €4 million and sold him for €17m. Just a year and a half later.

We watched hundreds of academy matches, we handed debuts to more than 20 kids, many of whom are established professionals today: Jordi Amat, Víctor Ruiz, Dídac Vilà, Javi Márquez, Álvaro Vázquez, Javi López, Raúl Rodríguez . . . But perhaps the thing that most helped me grow as a coach, and so quickly, was my showdown with Tamudo: an iconic figure, one of the best players in the club's history and their all-time top scorer, who was nearing the end of his career when I took over.

I had to grapple with a situation from which other, much more experienced coaches had shied away. Nobody had dared to open that can of worms. I knew what I had to do, though, and I cut straight to the chase. When what I'm doing is right and truthful, I don't give a damn about any other considerations. I tackled it head-on.

I didn't want to mistreat a cult hero, but the steps I took were necessary. In any case I couldn't afford for them to backfire because I was a rookie and the club's position was on the line. Although we'd survived the previous season, our limited budget made it hard for us to emerge from the lower reaches of the table.

Raúl was my friend, we'd shared happy moments in the dressing room, including when we won the two Copa del Rey titles, but sometimes players put their personal interests before the collective good. I had several conversations with him to try to make him see that he wasn't behaving appropriately, that something else was expected from a leader, legend and veteran like him, and that he'd probably reproach himself for it in the future. He'd been in the first team for 13 years and he'd almost certainly suffered due to the responsibility and weight on his shoulders, but that didn't entitle him to forget about the group.

When that season began, the memory of Dani Jarque was in the foreground, but attention shifted to Tamudo, who was gradually phased out of the squad. When I was asked about it, I said that he wasn't fit to play. In the end, he only played 376 minutes all season, featuring in six of the 38 league games and starting just four. In the other two, he came on with half an hour to go.

Raúl didn't understand or rather did not *want* to, which of course only complicated matters.

I remember seeing him in tears when I hung up my boots. Just a few years later, we were arguing and saying hurtful things to one another. There were clear-the-air talks, but when something is broken, it's broken. I'm sure that we both could have done more to avoid a lot of what went on – especially as it was painful not just for us, but for those around us too.

I can only imagine that he matured as a result of what happened to us. I'm sure I made mistakes in how I handled it; over time you learn and improve. Now, after ten years as a coach, I wouldn't go rampaging into battle like the bare-chested, lance-wielding Mel Gibson in *Braveheart*. You've got to be able to calm things down.

These days we're not on speaking terms. Many people contributed to that state of affairs; the environment at Espanyol is such that, when something is wrong, it is invariably made worse. But I'm at peace with it, because every decision I made was justifiable: there were very solid grounds for each of them

Nowadays he's part of the club's backroom staff and I'm sure that, from that different vantage point, he'll have realised that you have to take many things into account when you make decisions. And he'll probably disapprove of players who behave the way he did, and if he does encounter something similar, he'll make choices to ensure a good atmosphere among the group. To do so, you need to have real conviction and discipline, and know what values you want to instil.

Anyway, the fact is that, during what were lean times for Espanyol, I kept the club well clear of trouble for three seasons – we even flirted with Europe – and surpassed 150 matches in charge. But the dream ended in November 2012.

Or was it already over before then?

The summer between my penultimate and last seasons had been really challenging; the club had a lot of financial problems, so we couldn't sign anyone and had to sell. There was a moment when I thought to myself, 'What's the point of carrying on when it means sinking further into the mire?' At that time, I got an offer from Sampdoria, who had just been promoted to the Italian top flight. They were willing to trigger my release clause and pay me double what I earned at Espanyol. I was about to embark on my fifth season at the club. All summer, we were in two minds about what to do. I heard myself tell Ramón, 'No, let's stay and, bloody hell, let's fight!' Karina told me she couldn't stand seeing me so exhausted, urging me to quit. We couldn't go on like that, she said.

In the end, I told them, 'I'm leaving.' The Sampdoria owner agreed to come over and finalise everything the following day.

But when I got up that morning, I called the Italians' sporting director and told him that they shouldn't come because I was staying. I'd analysed everything and could see the disaster looming at Espanyol, but my pride continued to make me think that we could turn it around. There was no money, but we would be creative. My romanticism got the better of me; it had taken over my mind and no one could talk me round.

My family are Espanyol fans and that'll never change. But we ended up losing any romantic notions about the club. You get disillusioned when you see that your vision, football as a vehicle for ideas and values, isn't shared by the rest – that your plan to lay down deep roots won't come to fruition. I suddenly realised that it was not possible, that no such thing exists. It's so difficult to keep business and emotions separate! There are genuine people for whom the club is part of their DNA. But then there are others who use football to make money or serve their own interests. That's enough to kill dreams – that, and the sole pursuit of results. Are results really all that matter?

As early as pre-season on the 2012–13 term, I saw things I didn't like. We lost matches and lacked drive. There was also a cumulative sense of tiredness, both on my part and among those around me. When a coach makes decisions, some people benefit, but others lose out. When you're in a position of responsibility, you can never make everyone happy. There were a few unhappy people. People needed a new face.

The club told me I couldn't leave until the assembly of delegate members had been held to elect the new president. Joan Collet, a powerful figure within the existing structure who was running on a continuity platform, was the favourite and any changes in the dugout risked ruining his campaign. But we were all utterly exhausted. I asked Collet to let me leave. 'Please, let me go,' I said. He said no. One day, two or three weeks before the assembly, I reiterated my plea at my home, in front of Karina: 'Joan, please, if you win the elections, let me leave the next day.' He agreed. 'Joan, I've got this year and one more left on my contract,' I went on. 'I'll waive the second year's salary, but you have to pay off my staff, because this has nothing to do with them.' It wasn't too much to ask, even considering the financial difficulties that were hobbling the club. For example, Miki, my close friend and assistant, was on less than €45,000 a year before tax. Collet accepted.

That is how it finished. It would take a lifetime at another club to go through what we experienced at Espanyol. I feel there was a balance between what I got from the club and what I gave. We're even. I feel very grateful to the club and the people around it. It's thanks to them that I was able to move to Barcelona and to experience some great moments as a player and coach.

Ramón Planes says that I was a samurai in another life. I think he's referring to the fact that I have values, I'm a fighter and I forge ahead without fear, especially when the going gets tough. And that I'm loyal to and honest with my people, and willing to kill for them. Just like my great-grandfather and my grandfather, although with no knife.

I don't know what I make of that. But I'm proud that someone I worked so closely with, and alongside whom I went through so much at Espanyol, pictures me that way.

*

14 September 2016. We lost to Monaco in front of 85,011 fans, a record attendance for an English club in the Champions League. Deservedly. 2–1 at home.

Worse still: we let ourselves down badly.

In my first Champions League match. Our first Champions League match.

*

Tonight my family and I left Wembley at 11.20, after having something to eat in the Manager's Room. We listened to music in the car; none of us spoke a word. We'd said everything there was to say. When we got home, we went to bed. I put some Spanish radio on and listened to a bit of everything, switching between stations and shows: Hora 25 to COPE, ONDA CERO, El Larguero . . .

As usual, I have my iPad in bed, so before calling it a night, the day warrants one final reflection.

I'm angry. It was a historic night. How often do you get 90,000 fans cheering you on like that? Then there's the Champions League music . . . If that doesn't spur you on . . .

We lost because of a failure to show passion and excitement at playing in the Champions League. It's not that we're not capable in footballing terms, that we don't have the requisite quality. We weren't up for the game mentally. That's what rankles with me.

As the boss, I have to take responsibility and question a whole load of things. What's difficult is what Messi does: to pick up the ball, dribble past five opponents and score a goal. But it should never be difficult to run and be aggressive, to remain vigilant and positionally disciplined, because all that is motivated by desire. Sometimes things don't pan out the way you've planned, but you should never hide. At no point did we display the attitude that's required in these sorts of matches.

In the days building up to the game, I'd been living a dream. So it was a rude awakening when we went and conceded twice in the first half, and in that manner – due to schoolboy errors.

As a result, at half-time I turned into a blabbermouth. I couldn't stop talking; I didn't want to. What was happening was plain for all to see. 'What is this team doing? How can we let in goals like those? Is there no blood running through your veins?' I told the players all that and more. I punched a television and almost broke it. I think they were a bit scared to see me like that – it's the first time I've ever got that heated with this group.

I asked them to go out and show more respect for the fans. I told them that I didn't care if we won or lost, but that we couldn't forsake what we are: a brave, aggressive, committed, high-intensity team. There was no need to talk about tactics or positioning. We'd worked on all that the day before: which flank to attack down, how to defend against them. The way we'd responded to the throw-in for the second goal . . . it was disgraceful! We were getting rid of the ball too quickly and winning it back too deep; all the signs were bad. It would've been easier if it was down to one player being poor, or the centre-backs being soft for the goals; then I could just haul them off. It was a broader issue at this level, but you have to really think decisions through before you make them, because they can have consequences for the rest of the season.

I saw more aggression after the break, but it was too little, too late after rolling over for half the match. We ran seven kilometres more than the opposition, we had 15 shots, we dominated possession, but we lost to a team who competed better.

When I faced the media, I told them that playing at Wembley – which the journalists themselves were suggesting was to blame – was no excuse. I said that we'd lacked passion.

I'd imagined something else entirely: that I'd have to restrain the lads, put the brakes on them, stop them from being too aggressive. We thought any mistakes would stem from overexcitement. But I have an inkling that the pain I'm feeling is because something that I suspected, but didn't want to see, has been confirmed. Something that goes all the way back to that day in Newcastle. Something that seemed coincidental, but isn't.

There are some things even hard work can't improve. When certain moving parts, certain personalities, are put together, it affects the group. And to progress, it's not enough to train, to have a good philosophy and working methods; sometimes you have to replace parts that don't function.

I even blurted out in front of my family, 'Newcastle was awful, but so is this.'

This defeat has taught me a lot. You mustn't let emotional attachments blind you.

I'm going to start preparing mentally to make whatever decisions are necessary come the end of the season, because we're here to win.

*

In the end I fell fast asleep, albeit only for three or four hours.

I met up with Toni, Miki and Jesús at the training ground at 7.30 a.m., as usual. While we were watching certain incidents from the Monaco match for the third time, the chairman walked into the office. We were talking about the game and we showed him why we'd been left with such a bitter taste in our mouths. Part of our job is to show the chairman stuff that the fans don't see, and which you can't see on television. These are often the most vital things. The conversation with Daniel was a very interesting one. Then he explained why he'd come to see me.

'Do you remember David Bentley, that player I signed all those years ago?' he said. 'I spent big money on him and he scored that goal against Arsenal in one of his first games. Now he's running a restaurant in Marbella. He has a good relationship with Dele Alli's agent, and I was thinking it might be good for him to meet up with you. It occurred to me that he could talk to the youngsters and give them some advice, because these days they listen too much to what agents have to say and make lots of bad decisions, like he did.'

Good idea with the best of intentions. But part of my job is to decide when and how to apply strategies to help our players. I liked that the chairman wanted to give us a hand, but we have to be careful. Society is changing very quickly and it might not be wise to use an example from the past, as it is not certain to have the desired effect on a different generation. Things that we were sensible to say a decade ago hardly ever provoke the same response in a younger group. This is a challenge for the coach. We are friends, psychologists, trainers in search of solutions which are different to the ones that were applied to us when we were the players' ages.

A while later, we also spoke to Georges-Kévin N'Koudou, a new arrival who spent a month at a hotel waiting for his transfer to be completed. Now he's just moved into an expensive house and comes to training in a high-end car. That doesn't strike me as the image of someone who is hungry to conquer the world. He has just landed, but he has to show his value. We told him as much.

Simon Felstein, our Head of Communications, a good lad, hard-working and funny, had a car accident yesterday. It could've been very serious, but he came away unscathed. We all celebrated his lucky escape.

*

Two days after the Monaco match, spirits have started to lift again ahead of tomorrow's game against Sunderland. Today we divided the group into the guys who played and the ones who didn't, and I did some tactics with the latter.

There was no need for a video debrief of what to improve on from the Monaco game: the message had already been conveyed in no uncertain terms. But I did hold a meeting with some of the players to explain what we had to do and how to lead from within.

At my presser ahead of the Premier League fixture, I reiterated what I'd said before: that we'd lacked passion. I also noted that it's a young team and it's our job to help them grow. And suddenly more details of that tough conversation with Bielsa, right after he joined Espanyol, came flooding back to me.

'How would you rate your performances last season?' Marcelo asked me. That year I'd won an award for the best centre-back in the league.

'It wasn't quite nine or ten out of ten. I'd give myself a seven.'

'Listen,' he replied, looking me straight in the eyes. 'I've watched all the games back and if I'd been the coach, you wouldn't have played, because you've stopped doing lots of things that you used to. You're not the player I used to know.'

And, obviously, I reacted. I lost weight and trained harder. I was called up by the national team, signed for PSG and played in the World Cup.

Such is the power of words.

At lunchtime, I discovered that Harry Kane wanted to talk to me. I avoided him; my anger hadn't fully passed yet. And when I'd finished eating, I decided to perform a little test. I got up and went to sit in an armchair by the balcony. Let's see who comes over, I thought.

Out of the corner of my eye, I saw Kane grab a piece of fruit from the buffet. He went back to his table. A short time later, he took his dirty plates over to the trays near the sofas. And then he sat down next to me. We ended up speaking until 3 p.m. I admitted to him that Bielsa had made me cry that day when he told me those home truths.

Tomorrow against Sunderland, in our first game since the Monaco debacle, we'll only be making two changes to the starting line-up, one of them because Dembélé is available again after serving his six-game suspension. In other words, it'll pretty much be the same team that played against Monaco.

I've got a slight earache. The doctor says it's a minor infection.

*

It's Saturday which means it was matchday. I had a bit of a temperature this morning, so I showered at the training ground to cool down. I put my tracksuit on and we headed to White Hart Lane. There isn't even time to complain. Or stop. Today is the 18th and we don't get another day off until the 28th once we're back from Moscow.

It was goalless at the break, but there wasn't much to change. We thought the goals would come. We decided to wait a while before switching it up and it ended up being a good idea. Kane scored the winner in the 59th minute, but he also sustained an injury. In fact, injuries forced us into all three substitutions, which hardly ever happens. Dembélé and Dier aren't real causes for concern, but Kane will be out for a few months.

*

Ahead of the League Cup tie against Gillingham, I dared to say that Marcus Edwards, a talented 17-year-old from Camden, reminds me of Messi. He moves in the same way, touches the ball many times while on a run and comes out of congested areas with similar ease. I also said that we have to be patient with him and the way he builds his own future. The way he perceives the profession and his relationship to it, will determine the type of player he becomes.

Maybe that's why the stadium was packed out. Marcus is one of those rare players who can get people off their seats whenever he's on the ball. There aren't many of them out there. When he came on for what was his debut, he showed glimpses of quality. On one occasion, he picked up the ball out wide, cut inside, played a one-two and ended up hitting a shot that would've been shown on all the sports channels if it had gone in.

Janssen converted a penalty to score his first goal for the club. Eriksen captained the team which boosted his confidence. N'Koudou showed sparks of brilliance, but overall it was a day to celebrate for the academy. We won 5–0 and young Josh Onomah grabbed his first goal. Fittingly, everyone who celebrated that moment with him was also an academy product.

*

We picked the squad for today's away game against Middlesbrough with an eye on the away Champions League fixture against CSKA Moscow and the following one against Manchester City. We didn't take any risks and left out Rose, Dembélé and Dier. Son Heung-min scored both our goals which took us up to second in the league. We lacked that killer instinct to notch a third after going 2–0 up. There are no easy games in the Premier League – we ran out 2–1 winners.

After the game, we had a chat with Aitor Karanka, who got all his coaching badges with Toni and me at the Spanish Football Federation complex in Las Rozas. His job is far from simple: he has to manage a newly promoted squad containing many new faces.

Marcus Edwards travelled with us which was a new experi- ence for him, although he didn't make it on to the pitch. I'll speak to him again tomorrow. A photo was taken of us during his debut against Gillingham in which I'm grabbing him around the neck and hugging him. It reminds me of one I have with Maradona in which I'm also grabbing him around the neck. I'm going to show it to Marcus.

*

Today, the day after the Middlesbrough game, we had training and a talk. I'd wanted to mention something to them for a long time about a fashionable energy drink which they consume so regularly. First of all, it does your body no good. Second, it's unnecessary. I know what they're after: confidence and security. Sometimes footballers cling on to things out of fear and they look for strange solutions (or shortcuts) to block their weaknesses from their minds.

When I was at PSG, we had tests to check our stress levels. As games got closer, the technically gifted players like Ronaldinho and Arteta became less tense, while stress increased for the less technical ones. You have to know how to manage anxiety. We must give them the tools to increase their confidence.

We discussed weight with a couple of players. We have so many games at the moment and we can't train that much or do much extra work. When that is the case, players must control themselves, watch what they eat and relax in order not to put weight on.

As for our match preparations, Sissoko took a knock to the head and the doctor wasn't sure that he would be fit to play, so, as always, we took the medical advice seriously and he won't be travelling to Moscow tomorrow.

*

We are staying at the Four Seasons near the entrance to Red Square. We spent some time at the hotel before heading to the stadium for a light training session in which we split into two groups: those who'd played on Saturday and those who hadn't. During my press conference, I felt that the Russian journalists were full of confidence. They said how foreign teams often find it hard in Moscow. I reminded them how Espanyol beat Lokomotiv in 2005 and later looked for a photo in which you can see a group of Espanyol players celebrating that victory in Red Square.

After that, we headed back to the hotel for dinner.

Earlier in the week, Toni had received a call from a former teammate of ours, Dmitry Kuznetsov, who is now assistant coach at Rubin Kazan. We met up at the hotel bar and I reminded him his arrival, as he wasn't European, got me into trouble when we played together at Espanyol. Back in our day, you could have five foreigners in the squad, but only three on the pitch. José Antonio Camacho was the coach and I was usually a starter. If we were losing, however, he'd take me off to bring on a different foreign player, often Kuznetsov. He did it many times and one day I got the hump. Camacho asked me what was wrong and I told him I didn't think it was fair that I was always the one who had to come off. He told me that only three foreigners could play, but after that discussion, he didn't sub me again. What are players like, eh?

Before going to bed, which was already later than usual, the coaching staff and I wanted to see Red Square, but it was shut, so we had to look at it from the hotel entrance.

After breakfast, I went back to the square with Jesús, Toni, Miki and Xavier, our chiropractor. We had to go with a security guard because it was the first time that an English side had faced a Russian team since the trouble at Euro 2016. Our fans were asked not to draw attention to the fact that they were English. How exactly could they do that, I wonder?

We took a few photos, went to a shopping centre and then went back to the hotel to get ready for the game. Lunch was followed by resting until teatime, and then the team talk.

Lamela came into the starting line-up, as did full-back Kieran Trippier, who'd only played one game so far, but had performed very well. We showed videos of our opponents and their set-pieces. It was then time for kick-off.

And we won. CSKA 0–1 Tottenham. It all went to plan. We were in control and got into their final third on many occasions, but didn't have that finishing touch. In the second half they created more chances and we decided to make a change. We brought Janssen on and added pace down the wing through N'Koudou. Lamela moved into the middle and given that he isn't a pure number 9, he added energy to the attack and created space by moving their centre-backs out of position. That's how the goal came about. Lamela dropped deep to play in Son, who scored again. We were happy, but felt that we must be more lethal in front of goal.

Although it was a charter flight, the journey home was horrible. First of all because of the time difference. Moscow is two hours ahead. You get a short day when you fly out there and a long one coming back. The first team travel in first class, a privilege not shared by the youngsters competing in the Youth League.

The seats don't convert completely into beds, but they are comfortable. The table is big enough for a good flight menu and to put the iPad on it after dinner. We have just discussed the game with the coaches, but not in great depth. It's still so fresh and the emotions from the match remain present. At this stage of the season everyone in the squad has played except the third goalkeeper. We have stayed in tune with our style but can improve. The players have been more focused since the transfer window shut. We're second in the league. Our record in all competitions reads six wins, two draws. This season there has been just the one (painful) defeat.

I am going to have some wine and will try to get some kip. We are going to land in London at 5 a.m., more or less, so I have given them the day off.

4.

OCTOBER

S *everal challenges lay in store in October. First of all there are four league games, the first of which was against Pep Guardiola's Manchester City at White Hart Lane, as well as the chance to get back on track in the Champions League away in Germany. The League Cup fourth-round tie is against Liverpool. Along the way, chairman Daniel Levy took the coaching staff on a business and pleasure trip to the Alps.*

Thursday 29 September. We gave the players the day off on Wednesday, having arrived back, not at 5 a.m. but an hour later from Moscow, and we returned to training today. The majority of the players were exhausted, so we lightened the workload. We staged a 45-minute 11 v 11 match: the substitutes who didn't feature in the CSKA game, the guys who didn't travel and some who were coming back from injury like Rose and Dier, against an Under-21s academy side.

Later I took the opportunity to have a tough chat with Wanyama, because he needs to change some of the things he's doing on the pitch.

It's interesting, for instance, that he thought that he'd put in a good performance against Boro and CSKA, until we showed him some video clips. Victor is a very special, emotional lad who really takes things to heart, and of whom I'm very fond because there's a real nobility of spirit in him. When I signed him for Southampton from Celtic, he was just a big, strong baby of 21 years old; giving him a talking-to made me feel bad, but it has to be done. These days, I know which buttons to press and how far I can push him.

We're going to carry on doing recovery work with the rest of the squad on Friday, so that they're in the right physical and mental condition to take on board more details on Saturday – including practising set-pieces, which we think will be important in Sunday's game. Late fitness tests will determine who's available: we know that Harry Kane is still out, while Dembélé has a knock on his foot and I don't think he'll make it. Hugo Lloris has resumed training with the group.

*

Friday 30th. I had my press conference today and the narrative was clear: first against second, with table-topping Manchester City – who have a 100 per cent record and the division's best attack – up against the league's meanest defence. Simon Felstein warned me it would be billed as Guardiola v Pochettino, Barcelona v Espanyol, and he was right. English football is in thrall to the cult of personality, which explains why this collective sport is transformed into stories about individuals, why goalscorers are lauded, why anyone who makes a mistake is lampooned, and often deeper analysis is avoided. Every week there's a different story of ready-made heroes and villains.

I do have fond memories of those Catalan derbies though. Mindful of Barça's superiority, we always set out to rattle them and make them play in a way to which they were unaccustomed. If you let them develop their game, it's not a question of whether you'll lose, just by how many. It was really funny when, earlier this week, Sky Sports screened the Barcelona v Espanyol match that we won in my first season in charge, when we were bottom going into it and inflicted a first home defeat on Guardiola's team. A lot of players gaped at me because they see Espanyol as tantamount to a neighbourhood team – so I beat Messi's

Barça with a neighbourhood team! It's good for them to see that such things are possible. And it's a reminder for me that I'm finally in a position to go toe to toe with a Guardiola side.

Pep and I always had a relationship of respect. I think our teams contested something like eight to ten derbies and there's a tradition in Spain according to which, ahead of the game, the coaches get together on the pitch where it's going to be played. There came a point at which we stopped doing it because we were coming face-to-face so often, but our encounters were always entirely cordial. Plus, we lived near one another in Barcelona, so we sometimes bumped into each other in the neighbourhood.

We overheard Pep talking about me on the TV in my office. I didn't hear the whole interview, but from what I could pick up he had some interesting, well-argued things to say. 'If I were a young, aspiring coach and I saw Tottenham, I would say, "I'd like to play like them." I don't think he's one of the best managers in England; he's one of the best managers in the world.' He seemed pretty sincere to me. Everyone knows that footballing battles aren't just won on the pitch, that it all starts at the press conference. Since I find it strange when people talk about me in such terms, and because praise can cause complacency, as we were listening we thought to ourselves, 'What's he up to?' But honestly, I think it was a genuine show of respect.

I made my opinion clear at my press conference: Pep is one of the best coaches in the world, not only because of his results but also because of his philosophy and the style of football he favours, which are very similar to my own.

It'll be a great pleasure to greet him, as well as City's fitness coach Lorenzo Buenaventura, who is a good friend of mine, and particularly Mikel Arteta, who has embarked on a new adventure. I'm very fond of him and he'll make an exceptional coach.

*

Saturday 1 October. We strive constantly to improve and develop our system, method, or whatever people want to call it. We insist on our ideas and we tweak training slightly depending on our next rivals. This game has a series of connotations different to any other we had played before. The team feels it too. There is no need to motivate the troops, maybe just insist on our principles.

Several conversations with Harry Kane come to mind because that is what we did with him from day one. I know it was really tough for him at the start. We had to win over hearts, minds and bodies so that they would keep pressing and running up and down the pitch. But I refused to entertain any doubts about this being the way forward. 'If you do it, and continue doing it, and you're tired at the end, don't worry,' I told Harry and the rest of the team. 'I'll introduce someone else to do your job, but you can't leave anything in the tank.'

Before I arrived, his game was a bit more back to goal, holding it up, waiting for chances to come, getting in the box. Whereas now, he is always on the front foot, always trying to press. And if we have the ball, he has freedom to move around, not just wait for the ball to get to him. He has to be alive every minute.

This is how we've turned the team with the worst defensive record in the top ten into the best defence in the division. And without playing defensive football – far from it, in fact – or making many personnel changes.

It is all about being brave. I love that word in English. We must display bravery at all times and, since mental preparation is crucial nowadays, we send daily messages to this effect in different formats and packaging.

Today, before the session got underway on the pitch, we showed them a five-minute video of some aspects of City's game, and especially how they bring the ball out. They've won every match so far, but we've found some good examples of how pressing can disrupt their build-up play. I like to spark debate with the players, whether in the team briefings or during the tactics sessions: their ideas can generate new solutions. It also helps them to feel invested in the process. We record absolutely everything, even what goes on in the gym; we flag up mistakes to the players and correct them using videos.

We analysed their Champions League clash against Celtic on Wednesday and I'm convinced they're going to line up tomorrow with

Fernando and Fernandinho in central midfield. We know what they look for, so we think the keys are: outnumbering them in the middle of the park; harrying them so they don't have time to build from the back, getting in their faces and not letting them pass it about, which is what they enjoy; and, finally, using the ball well when we get it, being bold and pushing forward without fear.

I told the squad all that and then restated it differently by reminding them about when England played Spain in Alicante. It was 0–0 at half-time, but 2–0 to Spain at the final whistle. The England internationals returned home happy, reckoning they'd given a good account of themselves in the first half before conceding twice in the second. I told them, 'Excuse me, but I disagree, because at no point did you seek to take the initiative or be brave. Truth be told, it was clear right from the warm-up that Spain were going to win. The only question was whether they'd score in the first minute or the 90th, but the match was a foregone conclusion. Football is all about attitude.'

The message was clear: let's go out there, take the game to them and dictate.

I've decided on the starting line-up. Sometimes I keep the players guessing until the last minute; I can really channel the emotional and psychological state that suspense creates. But on this occasion, I told them earlier today, and the team in question had a dress rehearsal against an academy XI who replicated City's approach. We've opted to go for the most attacking team we can, with a lot of pace up front and plenty of movement in the side to cause them difficulties in the transition game.

Son will operate as a false nine, a role he's played before at Bayer Leverkusen and at Hamburg, as well as a couple of times for us last year, such as against Borussia Dortmund. He offers us the ability to press their centre-backs and take City by surprise, because he can exploit the space created by the movement of Alli, Sissoko, Lamela and Eriksen. We'll carry a threat from deep.

That's the plan. We have a good feeling; we played well in Moscow and are confident. After training, we gave the squad the afternoon off.

*

Sunday 2 October. The day of the game has arrived.We met up at the training ground: the players not in the matchday squad came in the morning, while the rest arrived in time for lunch and the subsequent briefing. I once again repeated the previous day's message: that we had to capitalise on the opposition's weak links and try to hurt them.

We got to the stadium around an hour and a half before kick-off and showed a couple of clips from yesterday's training session to Sissoko, Wanyama, Alli and Eriksen, to remind them of the idea behind our game plan and point out a few positional tweaks. We're always open to making late changes. Even though we'd settled on our line-up, following some video analysis we adjusted one player's position to try to make the most of his qualities and avoid putting him in compromising situations.

In the pre-match interview, a journalist asked me how we were going to play, since we didn't have an out-and-out number 9. I kept my answer vague.

Ossie Ardiles came down to the dressing room to greet us, as he does whenever we play at home. He told me that Pep's praise of me had made headlines in Argentina and that it'd help raise my profile there. Afterwards, I changed out of my tracksuit, had a shower and put on my club suit for the game. My two kids arrived and spent a little while with me in the Manager's Room.

*

This is what I said in my post-match presser: 'It was a great, great victory for us against this opposition. It is always so difficult to play against them. Sometimes when you have a plan, it works, sometimes it doesn't, but to make it happen against Manchester City, against such a great team, makes me very happy.

'If you play like we did today, with passion and aggression, then you will always have a chance. It is always about mentality. That is what helps us run and play as we want to. We need to follow this after the international break.'

It's been a great day. I feel very satisfied.

*

Despite the sense of calm, there had been a palpable vibe in the air before the match: we all knew it was an important match. We knew too that we could win it if we got things right.

We had put the team on the starting grid. Whether we won the race depended on the players and their decisions.

This was the line-up: Lloris; Walker, Alderweireld, Vertonghen, Rose; Wanyama; Sissoko, Eriksen, Dele Alli, Lamela; Son Heung Min.

We set out our stall really well; we had a clear vision of how to play against them. I think we caught them off guard. For long stretches they weren't able to build from the back; they had to resort to a lot of speculative long balls, which limited their ability to attack. We pressed high up the pitch, with intensity, and so we won the ball back quickly. That opened up lots of options for us in transitions, dragging the opposition out of shape and causing them to make mistakes.

It helped that we got the opener so early, after just nine minutes. We were dominant even at that early stage, but we got a slice of luck when Kolarov turned a Danny Rose cross into his own net. We continued to mark our territory by maintaining our dizzying tempo in the first 25 minutes. This forced them into rejigging things and we took a few minutes to adjust. In the 37th minute, after a turnover, Son picked out Dele Alli, who fired home a low, first-time finish to Claudio Bravo's right from around the penalty spot. So we can still score even without Kane . . .

I got up off the bench more than Pep, but no more than usual. It was one of the matches in which I've felt calmest, so confident was I in our preparations and in the players' concentration, which is usually relentless in these types of games. I'm often more nervous when we're up against a team near the bottom of the table, because you have to be wary of players getting overconfident.

We were 2–0 up at the break, when we just ironed out a couple of small details. We went out in the second half with the same attitude, hitting the ground running again. City kept trying to take us by surprise by having their players interchange positions and switching formation, including sticking Sterling at centre-forward alongside Agüero and moving to a diamond in midfield, but we stayed alert.

We were awarded a penalty. If Kane had been on the pitch, he'd have taken it. In his absence, it was between Son and Lamela. They are free to decide. Lamela ended up taking it and missing. Then Agüero tested Lloris a couple of times, hitting the post once.

Something funny happened in the 84th minute, when I wanted to bring on N'Koudou, and we both wound up cracking up with laughter. The problem is that he doesn't speak any English: he only speaks French, although he understands Spanish. I usually get Miki to translate everything into French for him. Anyway, when he came over to receive his final instructions, I started talking to him in English and he looked at me with an utterly bewildered expression. I could've been telling him how to cook paella, for all it was worth. So then I said to him, 'What language do you want me to talk to you in? Spanish?'

'OK, sure,' he said, laughing. So I started explaining a couple of things to him, with no idea whether he was understanding – it was total confusion. Only then, when I'd finished, did he reveal that 'Miguel had already gone over everything'!

I don't force them to speak English, I wasn't forced to when I arrived in England, but they learn fast.

We didn't celebrate too effusively, but inside we felt a huge sense of satisfaction. Everything went to plan. We were happy not just about getting the win, but about how it was achieved. When my backroom staff crossed paths with City's near the dressing rooms, they said we'd deserved it, that we'd played really well and hadn't let them get a foothold in the game.

I was already at my press conference by then. The journalists sang our praises. Since the main story told itself, one of the talking points was the penalty incident between Lamela and Son. The press do love to stir up controversy! I spent an hour with the media, almost the length of a game. I understand that the broadcast rights holders want exclusive content, given how much they pay. But it can be exhausting to talk to the radio, the daily newspapers, the Sunday papers, do a press conference and then round off by speaking to the club's in-house television channel. It's crazy but we know these are obligations that we have to fulfil.

When I was coming back from my last interview, Jesús and I ran into Ferran Soriano, Txiki Begiristain and Guardiola in a corridor. We had a chat for three or four minutes about what we're going to do in the coming days, with the players set to head off on international duty, and about our Champions League opponents. General chit-chat.

The traditional ritual of managers having a glass of wine together after matches doesn't exist in Spain. I'm not really into it myself – I think I've given it a miss following every away game. My coaching staff are more partial to it, though, and my opposite number will usually come into our Manager's Room. It's an odd moment because normally one of us is angry and the other is happy. Still, it's like an interlude in which colleagues recognise that they are all in the same boat, whatever level they are working at. So you discuss your respective problems superficially, your counterparts ask you about your team selection for the next match and you comment on the latest transfers . . . It's largely small talk for the sake of keeping up the tradition.

The chairman came down to the dressing room after the game. Simon told me that was a first. He brought wine – a much better bottle than the one we'd already opened in the Manager's Room. We toasted the victory. He looked chuffed.

Son was named the man of the match after a livewire performance, but in my book the standout performer was Victor Wanyama, even though he got himself booked too early, after half an hour. He broke up play and was aggressive, as well as enterprising, having a hand in the second goal.

I didn't see him after the match, so I asked Jesús to go and fetch him. When he walked into the Manager's Room, I laid into him: 'Sit down, I'm really angry with you! How can you pick up a booking so early? That's unacceptable!' A serious expression came over him, he sat down and I thought he was going to burst into tears, so I got up and gave him a big hug. It briefly got awkward as he didn't understand what was going on. 'Victor, now you really are the king. I told you – you've got to be the boss on the pitch. You're in charge, you're the king.' Only then did the penny drop and he hugged me back with all his might. Then he started laughing, his boyish face lighting up with that somewhat shy smile of his. He showed everyone what a great player he is today.

There were no further celebrations. It was a great win, but we had to keep things in perspective. Plus, we were all tired because it was our seventh game in three weeks.

So everyone hauled themselves off home. Since things were dragging on, I asked Sebas, who had driven in, to take his brother home. Jesús, Miki, Toni and I later went back to the training ground in a minivan taxi. Jesús then gave me a lift home. When I got there, I had a glass of wine and something to eat, and watched some football – Espanyol were playing Villarreal. Or rather, I watched a match: there wasn't much actual football on display.

My wife had stayed in to watch our game on TV and had tuned in for the full coverage, so she recapped everything the pundits had said. I relived the build-up, the action and the post-match reaction. And everything in between.

*

We're second after seven games, one point behind City, who remain top. We ran 5.7 miles more than City. We completed more sprints than any other side this season. We're the only Premier League team that are unbeaten domestically. We've only conceded two goals. It's the club's best start in fifty years. We've won seven matches this season, drawing two.

We've lost just once: that bloody defeat to Monaco.

We had yesterday off. I spent most of the day at home. In the afternoon I took Mauri to training after picking him up from school.

It's going to be a relaxed week. Today we'll work with the five first-team players who are still around. Wanyama is one: he would've been called up for international duty, but since Kenya weren't in competitive action, he asked to be excused for fitness reasons. There's also Trippier, Carroll and Winks, plus N'Koudou, for whom the week is vital: an opportunity to gain muscle mass and improve physically. We'll also catch up with the injured Dembélé and Harry Kane.

Given our position in the table, we've got to make the most of it and enjoy this moment; if not, when else will we? We'll ease up in training, while drawing up a work plan for the packed schedule ahead: another block of seven games in three weeks. That includes three different competitions – the Premier League, the Champions League and the League Cup tie against Liverpool at Anfield – and four away trips.

Before then, though, Jesús, a few board members and I will be joining the chairman on a trip for a couple of days.

*

Daniel has invited us to his house in the French Alps, near Mont Blanc, for a few days. It is a small gathering of people from his inner circle – eight of us in total – in a spectacular setting. But there's often a a quid pro quo with the chairman: with Daniel, you hardly ever get anything for free. I sometimes joke about it with him.

As a host, he is warm and attentive, making you feel at home. Would he have been that way even if we'd lost our last match? Like anyone, he doesn't like losing, but he's always even-tempered. At least with me. He's never shown sadness, frustration or the slightest sign of aggression. He's been nothing but supportive, open to dialogue and eager to find solutions.

In the mornings we enjoyed going for walks, but at lunchtime and dinnertime, while devouring the sensational meals prepared by his chef, we had what, however they were dressed up, ultimately boiled down to business meetings. We spoke about current goings-on and our respective visions for the future.

Even after two and a half years, we're still laying the foundations. In all professional relationships – which always have a personal element to them – it takes time to forge that close connection. That applies even more strongly in our world. A climate of mistrust surrounds football clubs, because this is a business in which everyone thinks they know best.

But at the end of the day, it's those of us on the inside that have to make the decisions, and it's not always easy. For example, a manager can't just click his fingers and expect the club to sign a player that he wants. It's not that straightforward: we don't always have all the information to hand and factors that we're not aware of come into play.

Equally, it's a mistake for a club chairman or owner to think it's easy to handle 25 players and the staff, to suppose that coaching and selecting a team is simple. Sometimes we're guilty of not respecting each other's roles. It's difficult for a chairman to trust a manager and vice versa. You each have your own people and ideas. But Daniel and I have embarked on this road to mutual understanding, which is essential for any long-term relationship.

We're getting there.

Paul Mitchell – the former head of recruitment at Tottenham, and at Southampton before that – had a take on the situation that gave me food for thought. Because of our work here, we can attract players who would earn more elsewhere. But soon Daniel will have a problem, he argued: less prestigious clubs, for example Crystal Palace, can pay better wages than us. My influence, working methods and style of play will therefore start to become less relevant. And then what?

Paul told me that Daniel has been lucky with us. It seems that our arrival was part of a process to recover the club's identity. We have implemented a style which is popular with the fans, we have promoted academy kids and restructured the squad based on our own philosophy. More than a process, this has therefore been a meeting of minds and identities, the one from a club in search of its essence and the one we brought in.

In my playing days I always tried to steer clear of the 'back office', because the president would try to get you onside and distance you from the coach, to have you on his side or to get information out of you. Ultimately that's foolish because that information is not necessarily put to good use; they subsequently have to make decisions without knowing the full story.

I can put my hand on my heart and say that no club president's attempts to exert his influence ever stopped me from being loyal to any coach I worked under, even when I didn't get along with him. Whenever I had something to say, I said it to his face. I like addressing conflicts and resolving them on the spot. I'm not the sort of person to file things away, let them eat away at me and then bring them up the next time I see someone, a year later. I don't hold grudges.

One of the disputes in which I was involved was highly public. While at Espanyol, after a loss to Cádiz at Montjuïc, our coach at the time, Miguel Ángel Lotina, decided to lecture the team in the middle of the pitch. A television camera captured the events. I learnt a lot from that experience.

After a home defeat, I'd never dream of holding a meeting in full view. The coach came over and told us that we were a bunch of mercenaries. I spoke out. I asked him whether his intentions were to make a negative statement about the players. 'Yes,' he responded, 'I've got to say something; I have to deal with the media.' That struck me as pure demagoguery, because we'd never have come out after failing to get a win and said that our game plan was a disaster, putting the blame all on him; you win and lose together.

So I replied that, with all due respect, his words only served to drive a wedge between him and us, rather than help find answers. 'Boss,' I told him in front of everyone, 'if I was one of the parents in the stands that took his son to the game and you, the coach, go and publicly claim that we players don't give a damn whether we win or lose, I'd want to run over and smash in everyone's faces. What is the point of making such a prominent statement?'

Catalan TV channel TV3 even aired the footage with subtitles to make sure that the audience wouldn't miss a thing. As a consequence, the coach saw me as an enemy within, fabrications were concocted and people started saying that Tamudo, De la Peña, Luis García and I were some axis of evil, that we were running the show and so on.

It's true that we ended up winning the Copa del Rey, but the toxic atmosphere also led to bad results and we were on the brink of getting relegated. A last-gasp goal from Corominas against Real Sociedad on the final day kept us up – thank goodness.

*

Today is Friday. We're now back in London and looking back over the trip, I think it was his way of making us feel more part of the club. Not just on the footballing side, but in terms of everything Tottenham represent. The chairman's office is next to mine and we communicate via WhatsApp every day, but that getaway in the Alps has taken our sense of mutual understanding to new heights. I plan to spend most of the day at the training ground shooting scenes for the advert for *Championship Manager 17*, having agreed to be the face of the game. I get a lot of offers to do publicity, but I reject most of them. I don't want to get distracted.

*

The team had the weekend off, so on Sunday I went to greet Gareth Southgate, who has just been given the England job following Sam Allardyce's departure. The England national team regularly use our facilities and I spent a while chatting to Southgate and Steve Holland, who strangely is part of the international set-up while also remaining the Chelsea assistant manager. I went back on Monday for their open training session, but left afterwards because I didn't want to be a bother.

Our players have been filtering back after the international break. The last returnees were Lamela and Son; no sooner had they come back yesterday than they started their recovery work.

It's Thursday and only today will the group train together again for the first time. We've got to tread carefully and see what shape the players are in before picking our line-up for the visit to Tony Pulis's West Bromwich Albion. His teams are always rugged and difficult to play against. We've got three more away games to come this month, in Leverkusen, Bournemouth and Liverpool. We have to manage the workload, run tests and rotate if necessary, fielding the guys who are freshest.

Often during the international break, players not only suffer from jet lag and lose hours of sleep, but their routines are also disrupted. A sort of decompression effect sets in, so we've got to get them back in the zone. The faster they get back into the swing, the better their chances of making the starting XI, because we're going to need to fight and cover a lot of ground against West Brom.

The BBC requested an interview with me. It turned out nicely. I don't give many interviews because I hold press conferences every three days, but this one has gone down very well. I spoke about passion, about the need to play football with the same enthusiasm as during childhood.

When we're kids, we kick a ball around for the pure pleasure of doing so. Who's to say that we can't recreate that in our young professionals? Why do they fall out of love with football so early?

*

After our England internationals reported back to the club, I had the opportunity to talk to them about Sam Allardyce's departure following a single game in charge. He may not have committed any crimes when he was secretly filmed talking about money, but when you occupy a high-profile post, you don't just have to be squeaky clean – you've got to appear so too. Unfortunately, it gave the impression that those in power invariably exercise it to further their personal interests. As a fellow member of the managerial guild, the whole affair saddened me, because it cast doubt on us all.

In any case, this isn't just an issue of one individual's decision-making – it's about the workings of this business, which also make footballers seem like commodities. Since coaches hold most of the keys to the door that decide players' futures, this only reinforces that feeling among the footballers themselves that they are goods to sell and buy.

I've received all kinds of approaches during my managerial career, but I'm not an easy target for agents or the business world. For starters, I haven't had an agent since I became a coach. I'm not against agents per se, but I prefer to be the master of my own destiny, mistakes and all. My decisions stem from my gut feelings and I avoid the danger of being led astray by an agent's hidden agenda. I've been told that Real Madrid and AC Milan wanted to sign me as a player, but that my agent had asked for too much money or didn't get along with their sporting director. I don't know whether or not that's true, but such things inevitably sow seeds of doubt.

Ever since I began my coaching career at Espanyol, I have negotiated my own contracts, as well as Jesús's, Toni's and Miki's. And I feel extremely comfortable with that situation, because that way I don't owe anyone anything. If someone wants to find out what I want or think, they have to talk to me or my people.

*

15 October. The West Brom match went as we'd feared. We dominated but, not for the first time, we lacked ruthlessness in the opposition box. Ben Foster, their keeper, was the man of the match. Dele Alli equalised with a minute left, after we'd conceded in the 82nd minute. They gave us a scare, but we reacted in time.

We had to leave Son on the bench and only introduce him for the last 20 minutes. He hurt his ankle in his country's first match of the international break and still they played him again in the second one. He arrived back with the joint swollen and we didn't want to run any undue risks. National teams often don't protect players and we pay the price. If his condition improves, he'll start against Bayer Leverkusen in midweek.

I've been pleased with Son's maturity since the summer, when there were question marks hanging over him. We told him, 'Son, we're not stupid, we know what you're capable of, you've got our support and what it takes to reach the next level. If that's what you want, focus on playing football, enjoying yourself and getting better every day.' I monitored him closely after his two wonder goals against Stoke, because such things can easily go to a player's head, but he's shown the humility required to keep kicking on.

*

They say you should start the day as you mean to continue and I don't like to get up in a hurry. The first alarm is set for 6.30 a.m., but I stay in bed for another ten minutes. It's one of those simple pleasures: not quite ready, I enjoy just lying there for a little while longer. At 6.40, the alarm goes off again and I get up. Some days I have a flashback to my playing career because I have a sore back, neck or knee. As a player, pain is your faithful companion.

My wife gets up at the same time as me, and Mauri follows suit. Sebas doesn't always sleep at home. While I prepare the *mate*, Karina makes the green smoothie that we drink together with Mauri. Then she takes him to the bus stop at around 7.15, which is when I usually set off for the training ground.

That's the perfect sequence of events. It's not always like that, of course: sometimes my son oversleeps, my wife yells at him, or they can't find his tie, his backpack or a book he needs at school that day. If something goes awry, I may leave a little earlier.

On my way to the car, I enjoy walking over cobblestones, a sound that I relate to the start of the day. Which car I choose depends on my mood. I'll take the Smart car when I'm feeling playful, the 4 × 4 when I just want to get there as soon as possible, or sometimes the Bentley that the chairman gave me. Whichever it is, I leave it running for ten minutes beforehand to warm it up. It's all about being prepared.

Toni, Miki, Jesús and I get to the training ground at around 7.30, when the car park is all but empty. It is soothingly silent as we make our way to my office, which is on the second floor and overlooks the training pitches. Toni steeps the *mate* masterfully while we catch up on the latest in our respective families since we last saw each other – i.e. since the previous night. We share information and talk about the latest news with the television on in the background. Then one of us will make some comment about the day ahead and we seamlessly transition to preparing for the session. We discuss individual cases, and watch and edit videos. We fill up folders. We analyse everything while the surrounding offices gradually come alive with the hustle and bustle of the morning.

It's a bit of everything rolled into one: a gathering of friends, a business meeting and a routine. And you miss it when it's gone during the summer break.

By 9.00, all the planning is done, so I head to the canteen, which is on the same floor. I like to wait for the players sitting on my sofa, and for them to come over and say hello. This is our first conversation, our first contact. I need to see what state of mind they are in.

Sometimes I show my face even earlier. The day after the Monaco game, I was in position just after 8.00, observing if anybody was earlier than usual and keeping an eye on their expressions. I sip coffee or *mate* while they have breakfast, and then I head back to the office to finish off bits and pieces. My door is always open if anyone wants to talk – no appointment is necessary. My wife makes one, though, so she can be sure I'll be able to receive her. I think she got fed up stopping by and having to wait for interminable meetings to end before she could see me.

Jesús, who always stays on top of everything, returns from the medical briefing bearing the latest updates: such-and-such a player has slept poorly or has felt a twinge ... We finalise the details of the session, deciding whether we need to talk to anyone in particular and whether our plans need to be changed or finessed. Then we head off for the session.

109

After training, we have lunch and then more meetings, chats, phone calls, maybe a visit to the gym. Time flies by at the training ground. I'm gazing at the trees behind the pitches. Their leaves are changing colour. I've just realised that autumn is here.

And that it's already almost 3 p.m. on what has been a typical day.

*

After arriving back in London at around 2 a.m., I have so much going through my head. A lot happened in the Bayer Leverkusen game.

Once again, we weren't clinical enough; we had clear-cut chances and didn't convert, hitting the woodwork once. Hugo Lloris, who is in the form of his life, saved us. He's one of the world's best keepers. The first half belonged to us and the second to them; 0–0 was a fair result. If the Champions League campaign started afresh now, we'd have a better chance: our game and attitude have progressed, and we've taken something from both of our away matches. It's very tight after three matchdays. There are only three points between the teams at the top and bottom of the group, and we lie second on four points.

But we drew a blank and struggled for pace up front, in part because the West Brom game was gruelling and some of our players were tired, and partly because our back-ups aren't ready to be starters. We weighed things up before the game and considered starting N'Koudou on the wing to give us speed and fresh legs, but sometimes players knock themselves out of contention.

During one of the training sessions ahead of the trip to Germany, one group continued recovery work while the rest contested a seven-a-side game. I played for one of the teams. Sometimes I forget that I'm no longer 20 years old: I get stuck in, throwing myself into slide tackles. My body can't hold up any more, but I'm as hungry as ever. N'Koudou's mind seemed elsewhere, however. We wanted to know the reason for his lethargy and spoke to him about it. We felt we couldn't rely on him for a Champions League clash and we told him as much. He was out of the running to start against Leverkusen.

I was eager to see how he'd react.

N'Koudou turned up at the stadium wearing a backpack and head-phones, which he didn't take off until just before kick-off. I took him

This is my favourite photo because it seems to express something essential about me. You can see a plough, a ball and a broken shoe. I was wearing some sort of nappy and had not yet turned three. That is what summer is like over there.

I played outdoors all the time during my childhood and always loved animals.

Here we were playing in the Third Division for Newell's second team and had just beaten our rivals Central 4–0 away. Marcelo Bielsa is on the left in a suit. He looked old even when he was young. I was with them for seven or eight months. Batistuta was also there – we broke into the first team together.

This is the day when Karina set her sights on me.

With my father and my brothers Martín and Javier.

With Jorge Griffa, the coach who handed me my debut and was in charge of Newell's youth academy. He came with me to Barcelona when Espanyol signed me in 1994. Here we are visiting the *Mundo Deportivo* editorial department. He was like a second father to me.

José Manuel Lara, as majority shareholder, played a key role in that period of Espanyol's history. His family's company, a publisher called Planeta, purchased my playing rights and loaned me to the club. They always looked after me.

With Toni, Spurs' current goalkeeping coach. We have been through so much together.

We could see them blowing up Sarrià from our flat in September 1997. It was a sad day. Karina wanted to leave flowers by the wreckage, but they did not let her.

With Marcelo Bielsa, who was at Espanyol for a few months at the start of the 1998–99 season before the Argentina national team poached him.

Enjoying success with Espanyol was particularly special. We won the Copa del Rey in 2000, after 60 trophyless years, meaning two generations had not seen the club win anything.

Karina, Sebastiano and Yolanda on the day of the Copa del Rey final at Mestalla. Later, when the ground was empty, we spent some time on the pitch. I was unable to celebrate because I had to join Argentina for a World Cup qualifier against Bolivia a few days after.

I'm actually crying in this picture. We were going to Paris. It was tough to leave Espanyol behind, although I later went back. Karina was pregnant with Mauri.

I scored against Marseille in the Coupe de France at the Parc des Princes by heading in a Hugo Leal corner. It was a different PSG and a different league back then, filled with good teams: Lyon, Lille, Bordeaux, Marseille, PSG . . .

Diego Maradona invited me to his Boca testimonial versus Argentina. It was a star-studded Boca side, featuring René Higuita, Carlos Valderrama, Hristo Stoichkov . . . It was one of the most wonderful experiences I had on the pitch. Diego's speech had us all in tears. He exudes charisma and energy wherever he is!

Ronnie had just come over to PSG from Brazil. His technique was extraordinary, but, above all, he oozed charisma. My son Mauri, who was still little, almost learnt how to say 'Inho, inho' before 'Papá' from an ad Ronnie used to do. When I brought him to meet Ronnie, he was gob-smacked. He did not know if he was with the real Ronnie or the one from the advertisement.

I am extremely fond of Mikel Arteta, who will go on to be a wonderful coach. He is alongside Guardiola at present. He was like my younger brother. He was 17 when he joined PSG and you could see that he was heading for greatness.

With my mother Amalia and my brother Martín on my farm.

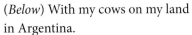

(*Below*) With my cows on my land in Argentina.

This photo of me with Simeone and Batistuta is from the 2002 World Cup in Japan.

After the 2002 World Cup, we went to Disneyland with my children and my in-laws, Ana Castro and Antonio Manuel Grippaldi.

With Zinedine Zidane. I had the photo taken because he was a Bordeaux legend. It was pre-season, so I was very thin.

In Bordeaux, I discovered the magic of wine. I bought books and started taking a real interest in it. In fact, I signed for Bordeaux (I turned Villarreal CF down) partly to live close to and enjoy the best wine region in the world. There were châteaux everywhere. We lived just behind the main theatre.

to task: it's a matter of respect for his teammates, who were preparing for battle. But he was on a completely different wavelength to the rest of the group that day.

We'll see how it goes in training tomorrow. It won't be easy because we'll be tired after travelling today.

We've lost two more players. Danny Rose hurt himself during the match – we don't yet know what the injury is – and Marcus Edwards rolled his ankle in training yesterday. Though he'd travelled and trained with us, he was due to play for the Under-19s in their Youth League fixture today.

Sometimes I wonder whether it was wise of me to liken him to Messi. He's only 17. At that age, Messi was making his debut for a Barcelona side featuring Ronaldinho. They're from different families, backgrounds and cultures. One of them thinks like an Argentinian and the other like an Englishman. Marcus is still in the process of adapting to the rigours of being a professional, which require that you act and think differently, be disciplined and make sacrifices. He has authority and behavioural problems, and we have to look at the bigger picture and find out the root cause. There was a time when it would have been seen as impossible for him to play professionally, let alone make it in the Premier League. Our challenge is to get him to accept the pathway we've laid out for him, and it's our responsibility to make sure he behaves himself when he trains with the first team (with all the rules and obligations this involves). He has no shortage of talent, but there are gaps to be filled: he has to learn to score ugly, run more and be committed.

The reason why I said that he was 'our Messi' is because Leo is the target. Marcus needs to have the conviction that he can become a top professional and believe in the journey separating him from that destination.

It's a shame that injury has now halted that process.

*

N'Koudou trained well today. He's got the message that the only way to push for a place in the starting XI is to work hard. And put the team first.

*

22 October. Another goalless draw, this time against Bournemouth. It leaves us fifth, with 19 points after nine games. It's the sort of game we need to be winning if we want to challenge for the title, but we came up short in front of goal again. We've been missing that little bit of quality.

Since we were contesting the early lunchtime match, we knew we'd move top if we won, if only for a couple of hours. But we made a really sluggish start. We lacked focus and intensity, and in the opening minutes they created what would be their clearest chance of the encounter. Lately, we've been struggling to put our game plans into practice. It was a match in which we wanted to attack more down the flanks, rather than centrally, but we only managed to make inroads down one wing in the first half and down the other in the second. We were sloppy and weren't sharp enough, and that showed in both our build-up play and our finishing.

The three games over the last week have been tough and we're going to have to totally reshuffle our line-up for the League Cup clash in three days' time. Last year, we were able to rotate nine or ten players in different competitions, particularly in the Europa League. That number has dropped to one or two this campaign, three at most, because of the demands of the Champions League. What's more, we haven't had a full-strength squad all season.

Moussa Sissoko, who is usually quite a level-headed lad, elbowed Bournemouth's Harry Arter and I've been told that the FA could take retrospective action because the referee didn't see the incident. We've no grounds to appeal because you can clearly see him raising his elbow in the footage. He'll get a three-match ban, but it could work in his favour because he was the last to arrive for pre-season and still isn't in peak condition.

*

Today I invited Toni and Jesús – who lives next to us – back to the house. We'd had dinner out, so I brought out some wine and chocolates. Sebas joined us. We watched the end of the Real Madrid match, Marseille v PSG and then the Rosario derby, Central v Newell's. The game was level with a minute to go and Newell's, who hadn't won in ten or 11 matches, got one last corner.

Someone, I don't remember who, said, 'It must be incredible to win a derby in the final minute, and all the more so from a corner.' And lo and behold: boom! Newell's scored from a corner, and Sebas and I celebrated as if Argentina had just won the World Cup.

*

Today's League Cup tie against Liverpool was useful for seeing how far some of our young players have come in terms of their development. Given our injury problems, playing at a packed-out Anfield was a wonderful opportunity for them to announce their arrival on the scene. We travelled on the same day because, as it's our fourth away game in a row, I wanted them to have an extra night at home. We arrived, had a siesta and headed to the stadium which has a redeveloped stand and new dressing rooms to boot.

Our promising centre-back Cameron Carter-Vickers made his debut. Harry Winks played the full 90 minutes. We found ourselves 2–0 down thanks to a Sturridge brace, but Janssen scored a penalty and Shayon Harrison had a fantastic chance to equalise near the end. We ended up losing 2–1 and were missing a bit in every department. It was a game of men (Liverpool who, like Chelsea, aren't in Europe and went with a fairly strong line-up) against boys. We have the youngest squad in the Premier League and the fans should be proud of that, but we must also demand more. Nowadays football is physical, technical and increasingly psychological. We have to be stronger mentally. We'll see what happens next time Harrison is presented with a similar opening. N'Koudou came on towards the end of the game. Onomah didn't do badly, but they all have to take a step forward. Making up the numbers doesn't cut it, you have to show something different.

There was another incident during the game.

Liverpool debutant Trent Alexander-Arnold went in for a challenge early on in the first half. It was worthy of a red card, but, perhaps being his debut, the referee decided against giving him his marching orders. We didn't complain about it, but there were a few routine tackles on Liverpool players towards the end of the tie and one of Klopp's assistants and their fitness coach jumped up out of the dugout. They overreacted and made disrespectful gestures towards me telling me to zip it. When the game ended, Jesús went over to their fitness coach and on the walk towards the tunnel, said to him, 'Listen, don't do that ever again. We're assistants and we should never tell managers what to do.' The guy started raging, insulting him and speaking in German; it seemed as though he wanted to knock Jesús out!

The final question in the press conference was, 'Do you think Liverpool were lucky to finish with all 11 players on the pitch?' I didn't want to drop the kid in it because you can get carried away and make mistakes on your debut, but I answered, 'In the first half I think their full-back maybe should've been sent off. That's why it was strange at the end of the game when they started to complain about us.'

I didn't tell the boys all that, but it was a lesson for them in 'the other football' that you can't learn in training.

*

It's Thursday, two days after the Liverpool game and two days before the league clash with Leicester. Miki, Jesús, Toni and I are mulling over what's been happening to us since the win over Manchester City. We just haven't got off the ground. We've had some niggling injuries affecting three mainstays in the team: Alderweireld, Kane and now Lamela. It's been an intense period with so many away games back-to-back and it's affected the players. The first consequence is that we'll be having recovery-based training sessions today and tomorrow ahead of the Leicester match. We need to tone down the pace to see if the nine players with injuries improve. I'll wait until the last minute to pick the team.

Despite all that, we feel we've only had one bad half of football all season, which was against Monaco. We struggled in the second half against Leverkusen because they put us under pressure, rather than because we didn't perform.

The Lamela situation is worrying. He was a key player for us last season. I started him on the bench against Liverpool partly because he'd had a hip problem since the Sunday before. Nothing serious it seemed. He came on in the second half at Anfield and finished the game unscathed. The day after, we wanted to switch up his training routine, but he said we didn't need to and he was ready to join up with the group. At the end of the session, however, he told us that he was in a bad way and couldn't see himself being fit for Leicester. He needs a detailed examination because it isn't clear what the problem is.

There's an atmosphere brewing, which is why I arranged for a video clip to be cut from training this week. I set up a meeting with the players, staff and coaches in which I started talking about how important the people who work around the team are. I asked Danny Rose and captain Hugo Lloris to say something about the topic. Miki handed me a trophy that was around and I unexpectedly awarded it to the winner of Performance of the Week: Stan, the kitman. 'You did something remarkable, you put your own safety at risk to save the team,' I told him, very seriously. Everyone looked at me flabbergasted. 'Play the video.'

On the big screen we saw how Stan was putting the mannequins that we use in training on the buggy that he drives around. He put one in the driver's seat. The base of it must have been near the accelerator, because the buggy suddenly started to move off by itself. Stan ended up having to run after it and managed to get it back under control, preventing anyone else from finding themselves in danger. We burst into laughter. He proudly took the trophy away with him.

As you might expect, that lifted spirits and we left the room chuckling, with more energy than when we'd come in.

Canadian former NBA player Steve Nash visited us. He's a Tottenham fan and we'd already seen each other in Toronto. He came to the training ground and even got involved in a few *rondos* with us. I also took part, but my back was not best pleased. Eriksen and Wanyama started showing off their basketball skills, but I have to say they're better footballers than they are basketball players.

*

29 October. Matchday. We were back at White Hart Lane. We met at the training ground to decide the starting line-up to face Leicester City, the reigning champions, who are struggling from second-season syndrome and the challenge of trying to prolong unexpected success. Winning the Premier League is one thing, but backing it up isn't easy. The injured players stayed at the training ground to work on their fitness away from the rest of the squad. During the briefing, I focused on tactics and set-pieces. It became a long one. I wanted to go into detail

about the opposition attack, especially their use of those long balls that can be so hard to stop. We ended up arriving at the ground slightly later than expected. We already knew that Islam Slimani wouldn't be playing, having been informed by sources close to the player. Information can come from the most unexpected places. It was a pleasure to see Ros Wheeler, the Southampton secretary, and her husband once again who were our guests on the day. Ros may well be the person who's been at a top-tier club for the longest and she really looked after us when we first arrived in England.

As for the game, we dropped two points, or, at least, that's what it felt like. We had a few clear-cut chances which Kasper Schmeichel saved and another one that clattered the woodwork. We need to be scoring goals from more sources when they dry up for Alli, Eriksen and Son, and while Kane is out. It ended 1–1 and Leicester picked up their first point on the road this season.

The press asked me about the team because we've picked up four draws and one loss since unleashing positive vibes with the win over Man City. Next up is Bayer Leverkusen at Wembley and then a trip to the Emirates for the derby against Arsenal. I told them I was calm, the team have been dominating games, the schedule has been tough and we've been rotating much less this year because we can't afford to do otherwise.

I left it there. It's a key period and we've come into it with fatigue. The risk of illness or small injuries increases with tiredness. The immune system suffers, but the stats suggest we are fine. We're unbeaten in the league, we're fifth and only three points behind City, Arsenal and Liverpool at the top. The competition is tougher than ever ten games in and we're one of the five teams bunched up at the top.

We're also discovering what we're made of. We've gone from playing in the hope of giving our best to being a position where we feel we have to win, which is reflected in the management of information coming through from fitness coaches and doctors. Those small details that we may have previously let slide now need to be tracked because they could prove decisive. The pressure is on the up. There's less time to rest and more trips to embark on.

Beating Bayer would almost see us through to the next round of the

Champions League. Putting in a good showing against Arsenal would strengthen our position as title challengers and provide us with a real platform to build on. Are we ready?

5.

NOVEMBER

T*he season had reached a crucial juncture. The business end of the Champions League group stage had been reached, with Tottenham needing to beat Monaco and Bayer Leverkusen to qualify for the knock-out stages. In addition, they faced three straight London derbies in the league, against Arsenal, West Ham United and Chelsea, the rivalry against the last of which had grown on and off the pitch.*

Simon Felstein just brought in his son Sebastian to say hello. I still remember when he was born and how many months went by before we got to meet him. I kept sending Simon messages saying, 'Come on, bring him in! You can leave him with me, and you and your wife can go out for dinner.' He must've thought I was joking. He is a delightful kid.

*

We lost 1–0 to Bayer Leverkusen at Wembley to a second-half goal. The result has absolutely nothing to do with the stadium. It's totally irrelevant. Where could be better to play football than Wembley? It's true that the pitch is bigger than the one at White Hart Lane, but when teams park the bus against us in the league we'd love to have the space there is at Wembley. There is no perfect scenario – just a set of solutions that you have to be able to apply.

We were poor today. It was embarrassing. We mustn't hide behind cheap excuses. The reasons lie within us. We've lost three times this season. One was against Liverpool in the League Cup, which was understandable, unlike the other two, which came in Europe. We've gone winless six games in a row right when the time was ripe for us to push on. Now we need to win both of our remaining Champions League games, or we're out. Even then, it's not in our hands. We're three points behind Bayer and five adrift of Monaco.

Granted, the build-up to the game wasn't exactly smooth.

*

After the Leicester game, which marked our third consecutive draw in the Premier League, we had a day off and it did us all the world of good. But on Tuesday, the day before our Champions League game, something incredible happened. I'd decided on my starting XI and the training session was all but over. I went to see Kane, who is working on his own with an eye on being fit again for the Arsenal match, and asked Jesús to do some set-piece practice with the starters. Then, in the last attack in a short six-a-side game, when Jesús was about to blow the final whistle, one player went flying into a tackle on another. The latter fell and smashed his nose on the former's knee, as well as colliding with a teammate. The ball stayed in play and a couple of seconds later, there was another hefty challenge that left two more players in a heap. There were four players on the ground! And one of them was supposed to start.

Jesús and I decided we should give it four or five hours to see how the players progressed before definitively settling on a line-up. We knew that Kane wasn't ready yet, while Lamela still hasn't returned to training. Sissoko is suspended in the league but can play in the Champions League. You have to make do with what's available, so in the end we opted for the guys who were freshest.

The match at Wembley made for a frustrating watch. We couldn't impose ourselves or control the game in the first half, and several players made mistakes. We lacked dynamism on the ball and our movement wasn't good enough. They pressed us when we brought the ball out. The most important thing when that happens is to outmanoeuvre them to get the upper hand. We've worked on that a thousand times in training, but we weren't able to execute.

Meanwhile, all of our attacking forays came to nothing. But at least we were still on level terms at half-time. At the break, I showed the players a couple of clips of how we should've been building from the back and reminded the defenders that it was paramount that they be bolder and hold a higher line. We often play one clip of something being done well and another showing the same thing being done badly. We have a member of staff who is responsible for editing the videos during every match. Miguel passes on a message detailing what we need – based on what we've been discussing in the dugout – and the clips are ready when I get to the dressing room. I wait a few minutes for people to relax a bit and then I play the footage and explain the changes we've got to make.

On this occasion, we didn't have a single example of good build-up play from the first 45 minutes.

In the second half, we conceded a goal that was easily avoidable. Bayer are no superclub, they're actually a younger team than us, but they've got more experience than we have in this competition and some top-class players. Maybe we need to ask ourselves if we're good enough to play two games a week at the highest level. To do that, you need all your players to be on form. Last year, the team was more than the sum of its parts for long periods thanks to the players performing above their level. That's not been the case so far this season.

All we can do is stick to our principles, stay consistent in what we do, analyse things as objectively as possible, hope that this rough patch passes and circumstances change, and in the meantime try to reduce our mistakes to a minimum.

Jesús, Miki, Toni, Simon and I all had input into the message we wanted to get across at my post-match press conference. After my media commitments, I headed back to the Manager's Room, where we stayed until shortly after 11 o'clock, ruing what had happened and talking things over. We're only three points off the top of the league, so still in contention, but we're all at a low ebb.

However, when you've been working for two and a half years

– through video and tactics sessions, plus all manner of speeches – to stamp out certain individual errors and they are still repeated, that likely means they have no solution. What's the use in getting angry, then? What you have to do is make decisions at the end of the season and hope everyone at the club is brave enough to act on them.

After getting home, I received a couple of messages from Jesús. He told me I'd done well post-match, both with the squad and with the press. That I'd avoided any further damage. That I'd not sought to make excuses and had exuded calmness.

That calmness wasn't just for show. But I know that we've got to try to turn everything around in time for the derby against Arsenal. We've got four days.

*

Tiredness. The tyrant that takes over everything when it arrives. It's not only the cut and thrust of competing that is tiring; the same goes for being the driving force of a set-up that constantly requires you to make decisions. Hundreds of them, every day. And this fatigue may also flow from another source: expectations, the inner battle between what we'd like to be and what the reality is.

When it comes upon us, it can cause bad moods, negativity, inattentiveness and a lack of clarity. We no longer see what a player is or isn't capable of. Our problem-solving capacity goes to the dogs – and we become erratic, whereas consistency is key when you're leading a group of fifty-plus people.

And, worst of all, we stop seeing the extraordinary in the seemingly ordinary – which is one of the things that sets us apart as humans.

Although I consider myself a good delegator, and Karina and Jesús are there to help keep my life in order and screen out many things, the demands are relentless. I have to liaise with the chairman, agents and the academy. Recently I've concluded that individual meetings with players are very productive. I've also got to ensure Miki, Jesús, Toni and I are all on the same page.

Arsène Wenger once said that 'a coach's face is a mirror of his team's well-being'. Sir Alex Ferguson has stated that he spent more time looking after his people than taking care of himself, and that he sometimes regrets it. A manager's first responsibility, he asserted, is to himself. If you don't eat well and stay fresh, it's impossible to keep your emotions on an even keel.

But it's easier said than done when you love what you do and a modus operandi has been established – one which I endorse – under which all decisions are elaborated collectively, even though the final decision is mine.

Of course, there are times when I feel like my mind is bogged down and, as a consequence, I get the impression that I'm no longer being creative on the pitch. Amid so many meetings, my ability to devise new ways to work with the group, new exercises, is impaired. The other day, John McDermott told me something that stuck with me, which he had heard Graham Taylor say: 'Make sure you're not too tired to think.' Graham used to give his staff a week off during the season in which they weren't allowed anywhere near the training ground. He deemed it essential so that they would have sufficient energy come April and May. It takes strength to lead by example like that. Perhaps I'll have to give up this profession in six or seven years. I enjoy my job with an almost child-like enthusiasm, but the frenetic pace can be hellish.

It's when you feel exhausted that mental fortitude kicks in: are you capable of continuing to make decisions until you're on the mend? It's not so much about taking days off; the group comes first and I'd practically have to be on my deathbed to stay at home. Rather, to combat tiredness, you have to do things like find a place where you can recuperate.

The training ground is our HQ and it's very comfortable but, inevitably, it's awash with emotional, physical and psychological noise. That's why sometimes I need to go somewhere quiet to recharge my batteries.

When I turn up at the academy manager's office out of the blue and plonk myself down on the sofa by the window, which is slightly hidden from view, he knows what I'm doing there, that I need to unwind. We either chit-chat or don't talk at all.

There are other ways of getting away from it all and taking your mind off things. I found spare hours that I didn't think I had to watch a fascinating television series, *House of Cards*. I recommended it to everyone. My wife and I binged on it; it's TV at its finest. It contains examples of leadership, both good and bad, plus lessons in strategy and politics. And then there's Claire Underwood. Every man's dream. All the staff are big fans of Claire.

The chairman has arranged a trip to Argentina after the game at the Emirates. The change of scenery will do us all good. It remains to be seen whether or not we head there on a high.

I'm going to leave this diary behind – like a thief in the night, it too is robbing me of rest.

*

While we're struggling to perform at the level to which we aspire, Arsenal are on form: they've won 11 of their last 12 games in all competitions. They're three points ahead of us at the top of the table. I've just been told that this is the best start Tottenham have ever made to a league season and that we're the only unbeaten side in all four divisions. I haven't lost any of my four meetings with Arsenal so far and no manager in Spurs' history has gone five without defeat. How necessary perspective is – and what sweet reading statistics can sometimes make.

The build-up has been bumpy, just for a change. Ben Davies has an ankle niggle. Érik Lamela, formerly a nailed-on starter, is going through all sorts of difficulties and won't be back for a while. And it doesn't stop there. After the Leverkusen game, I decided that we needed reinvigoration. When the players are flagging, you've got to switch things up tactically. We're having trouble going forward, we keep attacking down the same side and the full-backs aren't delivering everything they're expected to, so I thought it would be a good idea to change formation.

We watched some footage of Arsenal, picked the line-up and then did a tactical session to prepare the players for certain things that could happen in the match and explain how the new system should work. But then, in the last few minutes, Dele Alli got injured. It was important to react well and I asked the remaining ten players to continue with the tactical drills. It was my way of telling them that they were doing well and nothing had changed.

The good news is that Harry Kane is back. I'm going to throw him into the starting XI: we need a breath of fresh air.

At my pre-match press conference, I highlighted the fact that Arsenal, despite all the criticism of Wenger, deserve praise. They are one of the most consistent clubs in world football, because they've been at more or less the same level for the last two decades. We, on the other hand, are still progressing as a club and team – we're at totally different stages.

One more thing. Miki, Jesús, Toni and I tip our hat to Arsène and all his staff. Arsenal are perhaps our biggest enemy in footballing terms but we've never had any problems with them. They behave excellently on the touchline. Having been doing this for 20 years, Wenger could conduct himself arrogantly or believe that he's above the rest, but he's shown us nothing but respect.

*

6 November. We've just played against Arsenal.

Although Dele Alli said he was fit, we didn't want to run any risks with him. One of the other players hadn't slept well, another had a stomach ache and another's foot was bothering him. And we didn't know whether Harry Kane would be able to manage more than an hour. Kick-off was at 1 p.m. and in the morning we were still plagued by doubts. Some of them were eradicated in the warm-up. In the meantime, we had to keep calm – both outwardly and inside. We knew we could deliver a good performance.

In the end, things went almost entirely as we'd hoped. We came out strongly, didn't back down and created chances, whereas they didn't have many and the ones they did have were largely the product of us giving the ball away and making mistakes.

We went for a three-man defence against Arsenal. Without Lamela, we're short on attacking wide men. The injuries to Alli and Alderweireld have weakened us through the middle. Rose and Walker can operate perfectly well as wing-backs. A 3-5-2 also meant that Kane wouldn't be isolated, as he'd have Son Heung-min up top alongside him. The risk of getting exposed at the back was minimised by our pressing effectively when we lost possession.

The new-look formation left a good taste in our mouths. Now there is talk of us having a plan B, or even a plan C. Before people used to criticise us on that front, saying that the team always played the same way, but that's not true. We may have continually lined up in a 4-2-3-1 to begin with, but through non-stop movement and positional interchange, how we attacked would vary depending on the opposition and the state of play.

We went behind just before the break, but we didn't feel we were being outplayed – far from it. Harry Kane, who ended up playing 73 minutes, equalised from the penalty spot early in the second half. And we had clear chances to win the game. In any case, the most important thing was to give a better account of ourselves after the disappointing display against Leverkusen.

At my press conference, I was asked to describe Mousa Dembélé – who had to come off in the first half of the Champions League match, but was magnificent today – in one word. When he's on his game, he gives us something different, so I went for 'genius'. Now we'll have to make sure he keeps his feet on the ground. I'll give him a little clip round the ear when I see him.

*

One last entry before I take a break from this diary for a few days. I love having my people around me. Seeing Toni, Miki and Jesús nodding off on the plane brought to mind one night back in Southampton, at the hotel where we lived for the first six months. It was an intense period, an enjoyable apprenticeship. Our workdays began at seven in the morning at the buffet and ended at nine or ten at night. The hotel didn't have satellite TV, so we had to make use of obscure websites in order to watch football matches. Since the Wi-Fi signal wasn't great everywhere, sometimes we'd set up shop with the computer in the middle of the restaurant, the four of us hunching over the screen trying to decipher what was going on in a game. We watched as much football as we could. One Thursday, the Europa League was being shown on terrestrial television and I suggested we go and watch it in my bedroom. Jesús sat on the couch, Miguel was in a chair and Toni lay next to me on the bed. Five minutes later, we had all fallen asleep. When I woke up, the other three had left. That story epitomises those days.

Jesús was the last addition to the gang. Every coach needs someone who they can trust implicitly – an extension of themselves in the dressing room, on the training pitch, in the gym and in everyday life to boot, because ultimately a rapport like that can't just be built through work. Ramón Planes brought him to Espanyol and from day one I felt comfortable sharing my knowledge with him, and my vision for the future. He has gone on to become one of the key figures in my career.

He initially joined the club to provide methodological assistance to the youth set-up and the Under-21s, but it wasn't long before he started working with first-team players who were coming back from injury or needed extra conditioning. At the beginning of the following season, the person responsible for editing videos of the opposition left for Barcelona. I'd paid for an analysis programme, which featured cameras and whatnot, out of my own pocket and I asked him to help me with it. Little by little, my way of thinking rubbed off on him. This was a time when he was arguably lacking a bit of love for football – he saw it as just a job. Right away, I realised that he had a great work ethic and was hugely adept at understanding new things. It just so happens that I parted company with the fitness coach I'd been working with – Feliciano Di Blasi, who was from the old school – and so I brought Jesús into the fold.

'What do you want to earn?' I asked him early on.

'Whatever you give me. I know you will always value me well. I will never give you a figure.' And that is how we have worked since then.

Jesús humbly says that when he came on board, we were already on course, but I've grown a great deal since I met him, and especially since we put together our current group. Together, the four of us have risen to a whole different level. Their commitment and intelligence continually push me to better myself and challenge me. We're a humble group which is free of egos, which is essential in order to constantly be improving. In football, you never get the ideal scenario – there's always something amiss. That's why we've got to adapt to what we've got, which is something they help me do.

Certainly, the leader of a group is usually the person who embarks on a path, before being joined by others along the way. But the beauty is that it's not the 'Mauricio Pochettino method': it's a group effort. We are a coaching team who believe in a way of working, a way of playing and a way of living; that's what matters most. The goal isn't to feel safe or protected, but rather to enjoy what we do, and to share emotions and ideas, and when it comes down to it, I have the final word. It's fundamental that we safeguard all these things from day to day.

On occasion, people have asked me whether I would be better served by shaking up my coaching staff in search of new stimuli and to avoid becoming so enamoured with our philosophy that I refrain from constantly putting it to the test. But I'm surrounded by three guys who are hungry to improve and learn, so I don't need to make changes.

Miki has been a great friend of mine since our teenage years. We met in Newell's youth ranks when we were 17 or 18; we shared many a moment when we were both dreamers. Our girlfriends later met one another and we'd spend long days together eating and watching football and basketball together; it was the Chicago Bulls' heyday. I had a car and I'd go and pick him up on the way to training. Miki says that those journeys to Bellavista from the centre of Rosario, where we lived, were always a lot of fun – in spite of the music we listened to, which I'd always choose. One day he broke the door of my Fiat Uno. As we were about to get out of the car, I said to him, 'Careful, Miki, it's windy.' He opened the door and the wind ripped it clean off! Truth be told, it was about as sturdy as a toy car, but for years I jokingly went on at him about how he'd broken the door of my Fiat and never reimbursed me for the damage.

He, too, experienced those interminable training camps organised by Marcelo Bielsa at the Funes Military College, on the outskirts of Rosario, which we only left in order to play matches. We used to talk to the fitness coaches a lot; physical preparation is something that's always interested us, and to which I always pay careful attention with my teams. Our favourite pastimes were ping-pong and a couple of other games; we also had restricted use of a television and VCR, meaning we were able to watch films once in a while. It wasn't easy to be away from our families for such long periods. Nowadays I try to ensure my players can be at home as much as possible – there's nothing like the comfort of sleeping in your own bed.

Those fitness coaches were the old-school sort, the type that 'punished' you. The sessions were really tough. When I got promoted to

Newell's reserve team, who were coached by Marcelo at the time, I was placed in the hands of a fitness coach by the name of Trusendi, who told me I was a little chubby and made me train wearing a sweater on top of my shirt. Pre-season was in January, so it was extremely hot and muggy in Rosario.

Still, Miki and I laughed a lot together in that prison.

Karina and I served as witnesses at his civil wedding ceremony. Then followed a period when we went our separate ways and he spent time in Ecuador, Mexico and France, but the idea of working together one day was always in the back of our minds. When opportunity knocked, I offered him a job at Espanyol, asking him to film our training sessions. At the training ground we built a tower made from scaffolding pipes so Miki could start filming. It is still there. Gusts of wind would always be blowing and there was Miguel clinging on for dear life while recording. His reward for putting himself through this major health and safety hazard was coming with us to Southampton.

Jesús is tasked with channelling all the information we get from the sports science and medical departments, and handling a whole host of things so that they reach me in a digestible format. I also have him by my side at press conferences in case there's something I don't understand. He's present for most of my conversations with club staff. Miki, meanwhile, runs the analysis and scouting operation, and Toni is in charge of everything related to goalkeeper training.

My relationship with Toni is a whole other story – an up-and-down journey that I'll return to later.

Toni lives with his wife, Eva, near the training ground. He has a 32-year-old son, Enric, who lives in Granollers; another son, 22-year-old Toni Junior, who has been based in Southampton for a while; and a daughter, Cristina, 16, who lives with her parents in London. Miki's wife, Carina, and their seven-year-old son, Thiago, are both with him in England. And Jesús also moved over with his wife, Olga, and their two daughters: Paula and Marta, aged nine and 14.

Life has brought us all to England.

Naturally, Toni is coming with us to Argentina. We're off to Lago Escondido.

*

It's Monday and we're about to land in London after one of the most extraordinary trips I've ever been on. We had gone away bruised following a tough month and a half, albeit happy with the draw against Arsenal. But, while in Argentina, we were able to reconnect with dormant energies and with the people around us. I think whatever we achieve this season and in the years to come will be the upshot of what we said to one another, saw and shared in Lago Escondido.

As if that wasn't enough, Miki almost died.

It was Daniel who suggested that we should go to Lago Escondido one day. It's owned by Joe Lewis. Daniel and Joe own ENIC, which owns 85 per cent of the club. Joe has an estate there and told Daniel that we should come over and take advantage of it. That was a while back. I said that it sounded great to me. A couple of months ago, before our bad run, Daniel brought it up again. I told him that November would be a good time, because it's the beginning of spring in Argentina and the weather would be good. And so it was the four *amigos* plus the chairman and Allan Dixon, who assists the first team players, who set off at 10 p.m. on Sunday, the day of the draw with Arsenal, on a British Airways flight from London to Buenos Aires. Beforehand, I had one fear: if we got a bad result that afternoon, who knows what the flight would be like? But in the end we even deserved to win and suddenly the trip seemed like a good opportunity to stop and take stock of what was going on, as well as to spend seven full days with the chairman.

We whiled away the time on board watching films and drinking *mate*. People gave us some weird, quizzical looks: *mate* on a plane?

We touched down on Monday morning. They were expecting us, so we were fast-tracked through security and then went to a private terminal where a jet was waiting to take us to Bariloche, from where we travelled on to Lago Escondido in two minivans. Nicolás, the caretaker of the estate, was in one of them. I told him all about the land I own in Arelauquen, by Lago Gutiérrez, one of a number of lakes we passed on the way to Lago Escondido ('Hidden Lake') from Bariloche. I also mentioned my ranch in Murphy which stretches across 500 hectares, and is home to some 3,000 cattle. It is a haven of peace, a place for family barbecues. It's been five years since I last set foot there.

We stayed at the owner's mansion and when we got there we were welcomed by his assistant, Silvana, who is a local. She and Nicolás accompanied us for most of the activities we did during the week. We were in good hands.

I'd wake up at 7 a.m. to a beautiful view and we'd go out walking for a couple of hours. Then we'd come back and chat over leisurely breakfasts, with croissants and *dulce de leche* providing a sweet touch. Next we'd go off fishing, rafting, horse riding or quad-biking, or play paintball or padel ... At lunchtime, we'd have a picnic wherever we happened to be, in the mountains or by a lake. We'd have dinner at the house, but always in a different spot. And we spent hour upon hour talking – mostly about football, of course. And about wine, which Daniel and I both love. We spoke about things for which we don't find time at the training ground, even though the chairman's wife says I'm the third member of their marriage!

Football remained the main topic, though. Sometimes club presidents and chairmen appoint a coach because of his CV, but until they make a real connection, they don't truly understand what they've brought to the club. Spending so many hours together helped Daniel get closer to how we think. We spoke about being more effective, about strategies, about how we can improve and become more competitive. About why I prefer to give home-grown kids chances rather than signing players, and the problems that can be caused by buying players you don't need. Leaving a signing on the bench is not the same as having an academy graduate as a bench-warmer.

We reprised a really interesting game we'd first played a while back. We had to split the Premier League squads into good players, very good players and stars. In doing so, the different opinions we each had about these categories became apparent, and some very constructive discussions ensued.

A chairman and a manager can only really talk football at a superficial level. But I was able to explain to him in detail how, the more defined your playing style is, the more difficult transfers become, because either a player gives you something specific that you're lacking, or you're better off not signing anyone. We also came away with a better understanding of the club. Tottenham are building a players' lodge and a stadium. We must be one of the few clubs that turns a profit every year, and that's where the money for those projects comes from. An interesting change of role among the coaching staff took place during this conversation. Toni, Miki, Jesús and I always debate everything, with everyone saying their piece, no prisoners taken, whereas when we talk to the club, to the chairman, we become one voice.

On the second day, we crossed the lake by boat and went hiking in the woods for around three hours. We walked across brooks, drank water from streams, stopped to hug 3,000-year-old trees. We duly got back on the boat and rode to an island, where we wolfed down barbecue fare: the whole hog, from grilled Provoleta cheese to *empanadas* (pasties) and roast baby goat.

I did my best captain act and made as if to sail the boat 'home', but we were still in the mood for more. 'How about we take the quads for a spin?' By the time we were careering down a steep slope, with no brakes, the idea no longer seemed such a good one.

Being so far from the city sharpens your thoughts and senses. The ideas that come to you may not be ingenious, but they seem so at the time. I massively enjoyed the moments we spent together as a group, as well as the odd solo outing to the wharf, a quiet, enchanting spot. One day when I was cycling, I bumped into Jesús, who had gone for a run. We decided to press on together; he jogged and I pedalled alongside him. There was this incredible energy – we didn't need to talk, we just kept going, our surroundings making us feel part of something much bigger than ourselves.

On the Friday, we gave a talk at the estate's on-site community centre. We brought together people from the local football scene and showed them how we work. We didn't have all that long because, as usual, we had other activities lined up. After lunch, we went rafting around the lower River Manso, the eight of us plus the guide. We covered 18 kilometres, the first few of which were relatively calm.

'You'll fall off at some point,' they warned us, 'but don't worry, we won't leave you behind.' The first to take a tumble was Jesús, at the very first rapid, and the guide grabbed his leg and pulled him back in.

No sooner was the next rapid upon us than Jesús once more plunged head-first into the water. We were all laughing at him, but then we started going through rougher patches. Still, everything was going more or less fine until the last rapid.

Suddenly, the boat flipped. Instead of punching through the wave, the raft swerved and several members of the group were flung out. Jesús once more went flying, on this occasion joined by Daniel – who was in the middle – Nicolás, Toni and Miki.

They were scattered in different directions. Jesús fell right in front of us and the safety boat accompanying us went to fetch him. Toni, who ended up behind us, was spotted by the guide; to the right were Nicolás, who was hauled up by everyone in unison, and Daniel. I'd promised the chairman that I'd fish him out if he fell in, and I was true to my word.

I saw Daniel in the water, looking at me, a picture of seriousness. I grabbed his hands and heaved him in. Then we joked about how I should've demanded a new contract, telling him, 'Daniel, either you double our salary or you're not getting into the boat.'

And Miki? We didn't even realise that he was missing.

Some 15 to 20 seconds had gone by. We were all focused on the water, on rescuing everyone we'd seen. And we hadn't thought about Miki, who'd wound up under the raft, underwater for several interminable seconds, unable to come up for air. Finally he emerged to the left. 'I'm drowning!' he kept yelling. We pulled him into the boat. We were extremely shaken!

I don't think I will be recommending it to the players . . .

We went out walking early the next day. At one point, it suddenly hit us that our week away was coming to an end, and we concurred that we'd all felt it had been special. After returning from the walk, we had breakfast and packed our bags.

Something really strange happened to me. When we were saying goodbye to the 15 to 20 people who had welcomed us and shown us such warmth and patience over the previous days, I burst into tears. If someone had asked me why at the time, I wouldn't have had an answer. We'd created a group chat for everyone on the trip and in one message I wrote that you can't hide in Lago Escondido. You can't conceal who you are. In the middle of nature, all the masks slip.

My wife made the most beautiful remark on the subject, which I drew inspiration from: 'Do you want to know why you felt so good and it made you cry? Because nature didn't judge you; because you felt free to be yourself for seven days.' She hit the nail on the head. We live in a world where everyone does that very thing: pass judgement. From your neighbour to the guy over there on a motorbike; when you go to the airport and people look at you, they're judging you in their minds. Ultimately, all of us in this world are nothing but actors on a stage. And what we felt in Lago Escondido was liberation.

We flew to Buenos Aires, to San Fernando Airport, and a van came to pick us up which jarred completely with everything that had come before. It was cramped, barely seeming big enough for the suitcases, there was stuff on the floor, including paint cans, and it was dirty and completely dilapidated. We laughed about it, picturing ourselves arriving at the hotel and the concierge asking us, 'Who are you lot? Are you from the orchestra?' We chatted for a while at the hotel and had a great grill platter washed down with some excellent wine.

We went for another walk after dinner. Toni and Allan were walking, talking and hugging each other ahead of us, and someone drove by and yelled out, '*putos*'! Allan turned to the car, not having understood what was said to him, and greeted the excitable young men. Toni, still with his arm around his shoulder, proceeded to explain to him what they had just shouted. 'It means "prostitutes", Allan'. His reaction – pushing away Toni's arm with all the masculine force he could muster – was hysterical.

We had a good chuckle before heading off to bed.

*

We got to London at 5 a.m. on Monday and after a brief stint at home, we met up at the club once again. Janssen, Kane and Eriksen were not playing in their countries' second international fixtures and were already back. The rest of the players have been gradually arriving throughout the week. I've been keeping a close eye on everything in training. I've led defensive, attacking and positional drills and

I've worked on set-pieces with the goalkeepers. I even got everyone involved in the Mannequin Challenge which did the rounds online. It was absolutely hilarious. Today, 18 November, we've all managed to train ahead of the home game against West Ham. The starting line-up has been decided.

There was no alternative but to get straight back to normality. To the relentless rain and traffic.

*

We came away from the Arsenal game happy, although we hadn't won. We needed to get back to winning ways against West Ham, but we found ourselves behind with 89 minutes on the clock.

I handed a first league start to Harry Winks, a Tottenham fan through and through who's been with us for eight years. We tried out a slightly different formation which was a diamond with two forwards. It didn't come off, although it'd gone well in training the day before. At no stage were we able to play as we wanted, we conceded a goal from a corner and I decided to switch to a classic 4-4-2. The team performed better, but we still went in at the break 1–0 down. We didn't show the players any footage from the first half; we just repositioned the attacking line and explained how we were going to go forward. We made a good start to the second period and young Winks equalised on his full debut and in a derby!

We were looking good, but we conceded again. We made a few tweaks to the formation which didn't come off. Son came on and lost the ball with his first five touches before providing the cross for Harry Kane to equalise in the 89th minute. Two minutes later we were awarded a penalty for a foul on Kane which he converted himself.

The referee blew for full-time: 3–2. We really needed that win.

Winks, who was grateful for the faith that I'd shown in him, came to our dressing room and we gave each other a big hug before greeting the rest of the coaching staff. The chairman also came down, just when we were with West Ham's cohort. We exchanged formal greetings and when they left Daniel gave me such a big hug that he almost lifted me off the ground. It was an emotion-filled game where we really had to dig in.

My shoulder was hurting the day after. To be honest, I could feel pain pretty much all over my body. Tension levels were high. Maybe we didn't perform that well, but we didn't think West Ham were the better side. It was our perseverance that helped us turn it around. Harry Kane was our saviour with two goals and three points to keep us within three points of the top. How could we not miss a striker like Kane for ten games!

It's Monday today and we're off to Monaco for a key Champions League fixture. Some of the boys are now coming back from injury. We'll get to see Kane play the whole 90 minutes. We have to check on Dembélé, Alli and Vertonghen's fitness after such an intense derby. Last year we were seemingly immune to injuries, not so much this year. Harry and Toby have already missed three Champions League games, for example. But any other team can tell a similar story.

Only a win tomorrow will do.

*

22 November. We were beaten by Monaco.

We kept them at bay in the first half. Son missed a golden chance for us, just as he and Kane did at Wembley against the Monégasques. It was Dele Alli's turn against Bayer. You pay for that at this level.

Despite making some tactical adjustments, we conceded straight after the break. We responded by equalising through a penalty during our next attack. Monaco were still in a strong position, given that they only needed a point to get through. What followed summed up our European campaign rather fittingly.

After we had equalised, they kicked off and four passes later, in the 53rd minute, Thomas Lemar scored what would prove to be the winner. We conceded with 11 players behind the ball! It's very difficult to fathom. Do we lose concentration at key moments? Is it an accumulation of individual mistakes or a collective one? Is it down to quality or mentality?

We did create more chances, but didn't look like winning the game. We were lacking that attacking aggression that Monaco displayed in abundance. They caused us problems whenever they went forward. We seemed to end up going backwards whenever we had the chance to push on.

It was hard to watch from the dugout. I stood in my technical area for the last 20 minutes, trying to project an image of calmness. When things are going wrong, it's important they don't get any worse.

The challenge in the Champions League is more mental than physical or tactical. It's a matter of knowing what it takes to win when the pressure is high. We don't lack quality, just that psychological strength that enables you to play at the top level with only a few days' rest. We've only scored one goal in Europe from open play, which was Son's winner against CSKA. The other two were from a free-kick and a penalty. We've now lost three out of five games. There's plenty of in-house debate over how we can change the way we play and the best way that the players can combine in order to maximise our resources and compensate for our frailties.

We had plenty of discussions about it with the chairman in Argentina. As well as helping this young squad mature, it is absolutely crucial we have to be both imaginative and brave to improve and continue being competitive at the highest level.

I prepared for the press conference with Simon and Jesús. I had to say, as serenely as possible, that we haven't been able to show who we are, although every loss has only been by the odd goal. Add to that the fact that we're taking steps forward, but we still have to improve the squad. Everyone has to learn from this, starting with me.

Maybe our heads are moving faster than the evolution of the team. We have to be critical of ourselves. Tonight I asked Jesús if he thought that maybe we were putting the players under too much pressure, knowing that many of them are already giving their absolute all. 'Maybe they have no more to give, but without pressure, they'd give less,' he answered.

*

Getting knocked out of the Champions League by Monaco was a tough blow that I didn't expect, just like most blows in life. When you want something and it escapes your grasp, it takes something away from you. It didn't lessen my strength, but I was disappointed, above all with myself, for not finding the way to overcome that obstacle. I'm responsible for our premature exit. Maybe we didn't do enough. I didn't find the right way to get the significance of the competition through to them. I've watched the games back, dissected them and gone over them in my head. I've asked myself where I got it wrong.

I've noticed that I've been isolating myself while on this path of self-reflection in order to think and create something new.

I've even distanced myself from my family. When I get home, I put music on or watch a match.

I'm seeking out energy and excitement, that light at the end of the tunnel.

But if I switch off, it'll all come crashing down.

*

After the setback against Monaco, we had to turn our attentions to the game against Chelsea, the best side in the league alongside Liverpool, in my opinion, with both freed from the shackles of a European campaign. We knew that we were one rung lower down on the ladder than them, but we still wanted to win. We only had a day to prepare for the fixture, which was on Friday, and we had our doubts, but we still thought we knew how to hurt them.

'Keep your heads up, boys,' I said to them. 'It's 11 v 11.'

We managed to make life hard for them. That was five days ago. It's now the Thursday after the game at Stamford Bridge. It's been a week of contrasting emotions.

It isn't easy to gauge what happened.

We put in a marvellous first-half display against Chelsea. We didn't let them dominate, we were on the front foot and kept up a higher level of pressure and aggression than we'd shown for some time. We were convincing going forward, were flying at times and Christian Eriksen scored after 11 minutes. Chelsea had only two chances, one of which came from a weak Hugo Lloris goal-kick and, the other, two minutes later in the 45th minute, led to their first goal. We went in all-square at the break, as unfair as that felt.

Something that Jesús showed me some days before sprang to mind during the second half when we made a defensive error that almost cost us a goal. He had passed on a television clip in which someone explained how a defensive player should react in a certain situation.

I was taken aback by the explanations, which stuck in my mind. One of the things I am working hard to control are my emotions during a game – instead of being controlled by them. After our mistake, those words came to mind. Jesús was totally focused on the game and I shouted, 'See how that guy was completely right?' Neither Jesús, Miki or Toni could believe their ears – me talking about some video in the middle of the game. Realising Jesús had not understood at all what I was talking about, I sat next to him and started explaining in detail, jokingly, what I was referring too. 'Look, Jesús, what I mean is . . .' We couldn't stop laughing. It was a small moment to lift the tension for a bit.

Victor Moses scored early in the second half and we lost 2–1, but something had happened. Something good. We've only won one game in ten, but I'm convinced we're on the verge of turning things round and not purely because we went toe-to-toe with a team that could well win the league. I realised something. Continually going over things, looking for something that doesn't exist and trying to square the circle are unnecessary endeavours. The solution lies in having sustained belief in the process. And in finding in oneself the passion and answers to overcome any obstacle. That's what the trip to Lago Escondido taught us.

The entire squad was in training and we didn't have a midweek fixture for the first time in a while. We shared out the workload based on minutes played. On Monday I started speaking to some of the players, using videos of their performances. It was more of the same on Tuesday ahead of a double training session.

We prepared two different videos for Wednesday, one for defensive players and the other for the more attack-minded members of the squad. I always go over my talks with Miki, Jesús and Toni, but sometimes something happens that throws me off track. I showed the footage to the first group and was prepared to do the same with the second, but I saw a few expressions on some of the players' faces that I didn't like.

Enough was enough.

I didn't say much about football, it was more about life and what it means to be professional and to respect your profession.

In reality, it's not so much a profession as a sport that we all started out in not to earn money but because we love it.

I went down that path and was very firm. I don't think Miki, Jesús or Toni had ever seen me like that. Unbelievably the more mad I get the better my English is.

We always try to protect the players. The coaching staff spends twenty-four hours thinking about how to look after them, improve them and help them, but not only on the pitch. Maybe more off it than on it. When a footballer doesn't respect football, he doesn't respect himself or the people working hard for him. And I feel I have to act.

If as a player you lose your passion for the game or your love for being in contact with the ball or the smell of the pitch, if you use football as a way of achieving other things (money, being in the press, enjoying perks, millions of Twitter followers . . .), if you like all that more than training or sharing moments with your teammates, if running or going to the gym bores you, if you don't fancy taking care about what you eat or the amount you rest or if you don't keep yourself in good shape, you should revisit your targets.

You give some players an inch and they take a mile. That hurts me and it hurts them even more. I try to iron out the problems and warn them, and warn them again. I can't go in hard too early. It has to be the right time. To avoid confrontation isn't a sign of weakness, it's simply foresight.

But sometimes you have to go a bit further. I gave clear examples of players who weren't doing what was needed. Mistakes in games are the consequence of the way you live your life and what you demand from yourself. There is no separation between tactics and emotions; it's all linked. I hadn't previously singled players out in front of the others, but some of them didn't react after what transpired at Newcastle or after discussing that painful defeat as a group. Nothing. I had to grab their attention once again to remind them of our principles as a group.

'We get everything ready for you from seven in the morning when you arrive until you go home. In exchange for that, we don't ask you to win, but we want you to keep up the standards that are demanded of you individually and collectively. For example, if we take the risk of building from the back and get the ball into midfield, our attacking players can't hide. I don't want you to dribble past three players and score, I want you to stay within the team's positional intentions. It's the same for the defenders: take risks, push up without fear when asked to do so. Be more aggressive. You're in your comfort zone at the moment. I prefer you to make mistakes than not try anything. That's the difference between winning and losing, between being a normal player and a great player. It's about the amount you demand and the risk.'

It wasn't one of those talks that you can have every week, or even more than two or three times per year, but it was needed. I'd planned for 15 minutes with each group, but ended up speaking for an hour. I'm sure everyone, including the players, felt good about it. I did.

After that, on the pitch, we worked on the position of the defensive line as well as three attacking phases. We also did some drills with our forwards. It was intense. We tried to boost stress levels to a high to take the players to their limit and show them the different responses required in each situation. The boys were wonderful.

After such talks, the reaction is instantaneous. It can have miraculous effects because, after reminding them that this is not a job but something they used to love, it takes players deep into their consciences and they each go back to a certain point in their past. You don't know exactly where – they may remember playing with their father, friends, or starting out in Denmark or Argentina – but it takes you to a reunion with a younger version of yourself; the kid who loved football and the person you are now become one again. When that happens and they go back out to train, they're enjoying themselves again, laughing, running around and making a momentous effort. They're more aware, receptive and open to what they're told. It's remarkable. Our objective is to maintain that feeling and to keep it going for as long as possible.

This week I have to play them the video for 'Love My Life' by Robbie Williams, a song that sums it all up. It's a hymn to feeling empowered, loving life and being at peace with oneself. It is where it all starts.

*

It's Thursday. After yesterday's physical and emotional rollercoaster, it's a day for recovery. I also have a press conference. You have to be coherent, tell the truth and protect your players in front of the press. All at the same time.

I know they'll quiz me on Sissoko – whom we decided to leave out of the squad for Chelsea for tactical reasons – and on an incident with Antonio Conte's assistant. On top of that, we've only won one of our last ten games and the media, who usually treat us well, have to be a bit harsher on us than before. Let's see. I'm heading down to the press room.

*

Do I regret the line-up against Monaco? Not at all. What did I say to Conte? One of his fitness coaches told me to shut it in the second half. Before the game ended, I summoned Antonio, with whom I had a very interesting chat when he came to the training ground while still in charge of Italy. I put my hands on his shoulders and told him to tell his coaching staff that they mustn't approach me and that my assistants are banned from speaking to the opposition dugout. Conte told his guys to shut up.

And Sissoko? Why wasn't he in the squad for Chelsea? My message when interviewed on television after being knocked out in the competition was that we hadn't played well and couldn't compete at a high level twice a week in two demanding competitions – that was my take and how I felt. I added that the team's progress over two and a half years showed that we were going the right way. Sissoko said in the mixed zone, 'Maybe we should go back to White Hart Lane, rather than play at Wembley . . .' How could he speak about White Hart Lane? He's just arrived, and with injuries and suspensions he's barely set foot inside our ground! All that combined with mistakes in his game, a lack of concentration and struggling to adapt to the demands at Tottenham meant we decided to give him a second straight football-free Sunday.

I did tell the press that he wasn't in the squad for football reasons and he had to do much more.

There was very little talk about our upcoming opponents, Swansea City.

*

I remain confident about what lies ahead. First of all, we're doing much better than our results suggest. Second, Argentina did not give me rest, but got me back on track.

6.

DECEMBER

Tottenham were fifth in the league, with the team's record reading eight wins, seven draws and five losses from twenty games played. The club's Europa League berth was at stake in December against CSKA, with a third-place finish in their Champions League group needed. There were also five league games to get through, including a visit to Old Trafford to take on José Mourinho's Manchester United and a return to Southampton that resulted in mixed feelings for Pochettino.

An Argentinian friend told me that lemons absorb negative energy and cleanse the air, which is why I have a tray of them in my office. We all have the potential to see the energy that surrounds objects and people, although not everyone has honed that sense. For whatever reason, I've been able to develop an ability which allows me to see others' auras. Do I believe in God? Yes, because my parents baptised me and I made my First Holy Communion. I do believe, however, that there is an external force that differs from the God of Catholic teaching.

I often say to my sons: 'Dream, develop the idea before you go to sleep and throw it into the universe. Believe in the stars. Go to sleep and relax.' Ever since I was a boy, I've been convinced that the universe conspires to help you fulfil your dreams. That's the energy source that I feel is with me. Decisions, personal relationships and absolutely everything else are a matter of energy. Good or bad, small or large.

I also noticed it as a player. When I was the PSG captain, I spent countless hours speaking to fitness coach Feliciano Di Blasi, whom I later made my assistant coach at Espanyol. Feliciano brought his energy skills to the forefront and would analyse individuals through their auras. He'd share his experiences with me and I was fascinated. That's how I gradually learnt how to develop that sixth sense.

I need data and tests, but what most influences my decisions is my ability to see if the right energy is flowing. I can foresee things that are going to happen and the associated consequences, or which path each player is going to take. I can see it in their auras.

I am convinced humans have many mental abilities that are yet to be developed. Being aware of them, however, doesn't make you special or allow you to get it right every time. Or to win games.

Football is filled with unexpected moments that you can't control. Our preparation for, say, the away Monaco game was good, yet we lost. During my short time as a manager, there have been matches that we were well prepared for and went as expected, that are as you imagined them, and others that went badly. Each player's mental state is always crucial and his performance may hinge on how he's slept, if his child is ill or if he's had an argument with his wife. It's not at all easy to manage.

The attempt to understand and control the uncontrollable is where some of the magic of this profession lies.

*

There is a type of player I admire. One that is always ready, who hardly ever doubts himself and knows how to give, and how to take. That's what Harry Kane exudes. He's signed a new contract and the photo from the signing has been doing the rounds, as have those with Jan

Vertonghen and Hugo Lloris. I'm wearing the same suit as when Danny Rose, Dele Alli, Harry Winks, Eric Dier and Christian Eriksen penned new deals this season. I was wearing a tracksuit for Tom Carroll and Kyle Walker's extensions. I look so serious in that last one.

The team's future is in good hands.

*

In 1991 I played in a friendly for Newell's in Figueres against a second-tier outfit whose goalkeeper sustained a serious injury. A youngster took his place and ended up replacing him for the rest of the season before earning a place in Spain's Olympic squad where he got the nod over Santiago Cañizares and won gold in Barcelona. When I signed for Espanyol, the first thing that our goalkeeper Toni Jiménez said to me was, 'I won an Olympic medal thanks to you and your team.' That guy is now a great friend of mine and the Tottenham goalkeeping coach. The chemistry between us was obvious immediately and is the type that will last for ever, although at times he was a difficult teammate.

Toni was very demanding, especially with defenders. He would really give them a mouthful. Not everyone took to that approach, but I knew where he was coming from and a quick glance was all that was usually required for us to understand one another, which is essential for a centre-back and goalkeeper. If anyone ever laid a hand on him, I was there to protect him.

The moment that confirmed our strong connection possibly occurred during the 2000 Copa del Rey final when on opposing sides. He'd signed for Atlético Madrid and was having a tough year. The team weren't performing well and ended up getting relegated. As for family life, his father became very ill. He'd come back to Barcelona every two weeks, call me and I'd drop whatever I was doing to go to play dominoes with him and his old man at the hospital. That's how Toni's dad spent his last months on earth.

In that final, Toni experienced something that changed not only his life, but also football. Tamudo stole in to nick the ball with his head when Toni bounced it and ended up scoring a crucial goal that helped Espanyol win the cup. It was the last time that such an incident took place because the rules were subsequently changed as part of the increasing protection of goalkeepers, and such play has been considered an infringement ever since.

Toni was in tears at the end of the contest. He was crying while he picked up his medal from King Juan Carlos, who even felt compelled to give him a hug. He cried en route to the dressing room. He was inconsolable.

I was thrilled with the club's first trophy in 60 years, but I couldn't feel completely ecstatic. I went to see him in the Atlético dressing room. The atmosphere was awful. I sat next to him and didn't say much. There was no need.

During my second spell at Espanyol, Toni was also back at the club but wasn't the same guy that I knew and I told him as much. He'd gone off track. He thought he had everything right and everyone else was wrong. Not only was he no longer a starter, but he'd lost his passion for the game. I think he understands that much better today than he did back then.

We hung up our boots at the same time and got our coaching badges together. He started working at Girona, but we kept meeting up once a month to continue the gradual process of defining our footballing philosophy. Given that the goalkeeper is the player who, at the start of moves, defines your attacking and defensive intentions, because, for instance, the build-up is dictated by whether the ball is played out from the back or kicked long, we brainstormed about how to include him in the group. As soon as I had the chance I brought him to Espanyol as an assistant, as we already had a goalkeeping coach. After working together for a year and a half, we headed to Southampton together.

I like taking shots against goalkeepers and getting involved in their training sessions. When I do so with Toni, we still understand each other with just a glance. He sometimes makes remarks to provoke me, warm up the atmosphere or change direction and has an unwavering ability to make us laugh, which is always refreshing.

On top of that, he can be a pushy so-and-so. I remember that after three days at Southampton, he already wanted to change something that he didn't like about the goalkeeper. 'Coach, I have to sort this out,' he said to me. He went to speak to the player and didn't stop saying 'because, because . . ', one of the three English words that he knew. I think he made himself understood. He ended up becoming Nicola Cortese's favourite to the point where the chairman wanted to name a training pitch for goalkeepers after him.

His English has been improving, but at no great pace. On a day when we had to record an interview for Spurs TV, I had an idea. Jesús would hide behind Toni and answer in English, while the latter moved his lips. But it was impossible. As soon as Toni opened his mouth and Jesús started to answer, we all burst into laughter. In the end, he did it in English himself. Someone commented about his language skills online; it must have been an Arsenal fan.

*

A week after the defeat by Chelsea and a series of intense briefings, dispatching Swansea with ease did us the world of good. We completely dominated, scoring five goals (two apiece for Kane and Eriksen, and one for Son), but it could've been a lot more. The statistics showed that only once in Premier League history had there been such a disparity in terms of efforts on goal. We racked up 28 shots, 15 of which were on target, while the visitors didn't force Hugo Lloris into a save.

I enjoyed our centre-backs' performances. Vertonghen and Dier, whose focus has been on the up, displayed intensity and impressive anticipation, held a good line and communicated well. The response to the two team talks has been satisfactory overall.

We're still fifth, but we have two more points than at the same stage last season, despite the poor recent run which I hope we've managed to turn around. We're being touted as title contenders, but the players still need to perform even better, while Chelsea (who have 19 more points than last season) and Liverpool (seven more) need to be slowed down. We've benefited from the fact that Leicester City and Manchester United have underperformed, while Arsenal, City and Everton are at the same level as last year. Given the context, we haven't done badly; it's just we are who we are. Expectations have grown more than we have.

After the match, the journalists asked me about Dele Alli's fall for the penalty which Kane converted. I cracked a small joke comparing it with Michael Owen's dive against Argentina. Now I can see online that the newspapers are really focusing on that. The final stages of press conferences are dangerous. You relax, maybe you're fed up with the questions, and you can end up saying any old thing.

I'm still tired. Last month we changed our routine with the trip to Argentina, but rest time was limited. I eat more than I should when I'm exhausted and I haven't set foot in the gym in a long time.

*

No English team is currently running the show in Europe. We were debating the reasons why ahead of the CSKA game.

The Premier League has some distinguishing features that demand a greater level of physical and mental energy than in any other European competition. The two-week holiday period, or even more in some cases, that breaks up the season in Germany, Italy, Portugal and Spain has a regenerative effect both physically and psychologically, which is key for the players come February and March when so much is at stake. You also expect Barcelona, Real Madrid, Atlético Madrid and Juventus to suffer less because they can rotate domestically. You can't do that here because the league is considered a priority. In addition, teams competing in Europe receive no preferential treatment when it comes to fixture scheduling, so we often head into European games less rested than our opponents.

The CSKA match was our chance to redeem ourselves and produce a top performance. A win would secure our Europa League berth and we also wanted to taste victory at Wembley. We repeated many of the positives, creating several chances, but they scored from their first attack. We managed to turn it around through Dele Alli, Harry Kane and an own goal, but we could've put the game to bed much earlier. It's another step forward after our good displays against Chelsea and Swansea. It's not by chance that it's coincided with Toby Alderweireld coming back from injury and the fact that – besides Lamela, who's yet to return – we don't have any injuries at present.

A statistic has emerged today showing that Tottenham are second only to Juventus when it comes to how many minutes of international football our players have played in 2016, a sign of success, but also a handicap in terms of keeping the team fresh.

*

I was speaking to Simon Felstein in my office back in my first few months in charge and one of the club captains knocked on the door. 'Do you want me to leave?' Simon asked.

'When we're done,' I responded. It was important for him to know that he was part of this, and that nobody was more important than anyone else. I needed him to understand the way we work because he looks after the club's relationship with the media and they provide information to the fans.

When I arrived, Simon asked me if I could speak English in press conferences, which I hadn't done at Southampton. I said that I could and had already discussed it with Daniel. I was very nervous for my first televised interview. I'd already done one with *Revista de la Liga* on Sky Sports when I was at Espanyol, but they spoonfed me the words and they practically recorded me sentence by sentence. It was hilarious.

I speak to Simon before facing the press. I need him to identify likely questions and what they're thinking about, as well as giving me his insight on how I should explain certain matters. He rarely reins me in, but has done so occasionally. He didn't want us to do the Mannequin Challenge in the press room, for example. When we went in, I opened the door for a journalist and reached out to shake his hand. I looked over to Simon. 'Should we do it now?' 'You'd better not,' was the message from his panicked face.

Jesús also takes care of plenty of press matters and acts as a filter. He even keeps an eye on seemingly trivial affairs. The other day he had a go at Simon because Harry Kane went to the press conference . . . in flip-flops!

We like to grant time to the journalists who travel with us the most. When we went to Azerbaijan last season, we had a 45-minute-long off-the-record coffee with them, the type that they adore so much. The same thing occurred in Australia in the summer. I invited them to the players' area while they were away. I explained to them, with the help of a computer and a screen, how we press without the ball. It would allow them to understand our style of play. We spent an hour and a half together chatting.

Sometimes I get tired of the sound of my own voice, but the manager is the club's spokesperson here. That said, I'm not the type to create havoc in press conferences. What I say hardly ever surprises the players or the journalists, who struggle to find compelling headlines. I suggest things to the players during the week so they prepare good arguments and answers for the media. I do know, however, that everything carries more weight if the manager says it.

I do demand that journalists don't overstep the mark. They once asked me about Nabil Bentaleb, who was a regular starter during my first season here. Nabil decided that he wasn't going to stay with us, so he trained with the Under-21s until he found a new club. I explained it by saying, 'The rules are clear. If you aren't part of our plans, whatever the reason may be, why should you train with us?' The following day they wrote that I was ruthless and had no pity, which I feel is actually a positive attribute in Anglo-Saxon culture. But it isn't strictly accurate with regard to me. I know what I want and I know when decisions need to be made. But I was not ruthless with him.

I spoke to Nabil a lot, particularly in my second campaign, although his performances were on the decline. 'He's a young boy who can make mistakes,' I said. 'Let's give him a chance.' It reached a point where both parties thought it was better for him to move on. When I make a decision is because I am convinced about it and have plenty of reasons.

Our next game is against the very best at controlling the public message: José Mourinho.

*

I'll always speak well of Mourinho because I admire him as a coach. That's not just because he opened his door to me when he was at the Bernabéu or because he was kind to me when I was at Espanyol and when I moved to England. None of that influences my opinion that he's a really good coach, one of the best, just like Guardiola and Simeone.

I had several conversations with José last summer about certain players. Whenever I phoned him or sent him a message, he replied, but we haven't stayed in contact as much during the season besides the odd call. I'm not one to ask for favours.

I've always been loyal and expect it to be mutual.

*

We arrived at Old Trafford six points ahead of United and with the team back on track. The press were reporting that the Manchester club wanted me ahead of Mourinho, which is a story that I could've done without. It just serves to fire up the beast that rages inside José. We didn't have many attacking options on the bench (Lamela and Janssen were injured) and I left Eric Dier out of the starting line-up, a decision that not everyone could fathom.

We didn't lose because we performed badly or didn't create chances, but because we lacked that competitive edge, particularly in the first half, which is deeply frustrating. In their first three or four moves, we seemed to be saying to Mkhitaryan, 'Play between the lines and we won't do anything to you.' Half an hour in, we suffered a loss of concentration, we reacted poorly and it led to their goal. It could've come earlier or later in the game. We had some clear-cut chances to equalise, but you could see from the opening minutes that we weren't aggressive enough when it came to winning the ball back. It ended 1–0.

The press asked me why we'd picked up only one point from visits to Arsenal, Chelsea and United. I tried to respond ambiguously but we have analysed the situation internally. This year we've been more tactically versatile than ever. We've played in three different formations that have involved varying types of movement in opposition territory. The demands set by international fixtures and injuries to key players have restricted our ability to rotate. Most of our signings, with the exception of Wanyama, are still settling in. Managing this period of transition for our younger players, some of whom are being courted by bigger clubs, isn't proving easy. These are just some of the factors that are holding us back.

The texts that I exchanged with the chairman tonight have been pretty heated, given the combination of frustration and disappointment. We came up short in another big game.

In fact, from this game onwards, I need things to happen.

*

We signed the 20-year-old Eric Dier during our first summer and he was used mostly as a full-back in my inaugural season. He suffered a dip in form, as do all young players, and he ended up losing his place in the line-up, but he's an intelligent lad and kept working hard. He understood our methodology, which was similar to what he'd experienced in Portugal, and started in the League Cup final against Chelsea. We tried to sign Wanyama that summer, but Southampton wouldn't sell. I spoke to Jesús and we decided to use Dier as a holding midfielder in a friendly, playing half the game at the back and the other half in midfield. We were pleased.

While on tour of the United States, Daniel was concerned. 'We need a holding midfielder.'

'Don't worry, Daniel,' I told him. 'I'm going to turn Dier into just that.' I think he thought, 'This guy is either a genius or completely nuts,' while veering towards the latter. I had to battle with the chairman, the head of recruitment and everyone else because they wanted to bring in a holding midfielder, while I was convinced that Dier would do the trick.

He has played well in midfield, although it's not the position for which he is best suited. I've told Eric he has what it takes to be the best English centre-back, but he has to be convinced of that himself. We've put the conditions in place for him to stand out and to improve. But he broke into the national team thanks to his displays in the holding role and ended up scoring a couple of big goals.

After we signed Wanyama, Eric, who now sees himself as a midfielder, felt that we'd treated him badly because Wanyama's arrival would halt his development. His performances have started to suffer this season. We've spoken a lot in recent months, but I've felt that he hasn't been telling me everything. Two weeks ago, I once again tried to understand why he couldn't shake off the shackles and I offered to help him with whatever it was. Nothing. Then I found out that Manchester United have made an approach and the player is being destabilised. His people have been putting pressure on him in recent weeks, although United aren't promising anything.

Mourinho and I had just finished our interviews at Old Trafford and the players were doing their warm-down on the pitch. When José was done with the press, he stood by the entrance to the tunnel and regarded the returning players. He greeted Sissoko and hugged

Dier. They passed by me en route to the dressing rooms, laughing and speaking in Portuguese. Maybe it's a common Mourinho tactic, but he put Eric in a compromising position. You can't do that after a defeat.

'Are you friends with Mourinho?' I asked him.

'No, but I've known him for a long time, from my time in Portugal . . . One of his godsons coached me. He always says hello to me.'

The number of individual meetings with players goes through the roof at this stage of the season. I've recently heard myself repeat too many times that I'd like them not to let me down. Me, the team, their teammates, the fans. We've kept faith in them when they haven't done well. I've never publicly singled out any mistakes. Now is the time to get more in return. In those conversations, the player has often gone from listening, protecting himself and being afraid to show weakness to opening up and letting out plenty of what he has inside.

I sat down with Eric after lunch on Monday and we chatted for four hours about the whole shebang: his agent, family, confusion.

As for the Mourinho incident, 'What could I have done?' Eric asked me.

He told me about United's interest since last summer and I explained the situation to him clearly.

'Look, you aren't leaving because you signed a five-year deal with us in August. You're among the highest-paid players at Tottenham at the age of 22. You're important to us and you could become the best centre-back in the Premier League.'

Ever since that conversation, Eric admits that he could've waited for Mourinho to be out of sight before heading to the dressing room.

*

I've just competed in a darts competition with my sons at home. I won, naturally. I started watching the World Darts Championship when we moved to Southampton. We all love it and think everything about it is interesting, from the setting to the game itself. It takes real talent.

I've surprised Karina by organising something all by myself. We're going to see Rod Stewart at the O2 tomorrow. We haven't done much together this year. The climate has been our enemy. On the few free

Sundays that we've had, it's been cold or raining. Or, in truth, we've simply been too lazy to go out. Also I don't know what other coaches are like, but my mood hinges on results.

*

Today in training ahead of the Hull game, we didn't watch videos of our opponents or correct mistakes from the United match. Instead, we let the players do their recovery work. In the press conference, a journalist suggested that we could consider new attacking options in order to improve. I thought, 'We have a point more than last year and we're in the Europa League as we were last season. This once again confirms that the level of demand has gone up.'

One of Hugo Lloris's friends, the coach of a Slovenian team, came to visit and we spent the afternoon together. Walter Zenga and Pako Ayestarán have also recently paid us visits. A coach of a Japanese side who played with Ossie Ardiles is coming next week.

Karina regularly asks me when I'm going to take her to Japan. I could see myself living there one day. I've visited three times, one of which was for the World Cup when that infamous Michael Owen penalty incident took place.

I stupidly fell into a trap that day. I always say to my players, 'It wasn't a penalty, but you can see why it was given because as a defender you can't be so naïve when facing a player like Owen, who I knew was fast, intelligent and lively. As soon as you gave him a chance, he'd kill you. I shouldn't have gone in for the tackle, I should've held off, I should've read his intentions better.' During my four years in England, the topic has come up several times. Of course the players have seen the video. I've shown it to all the centre-backs. 'Obviously I've made mistakes, too,' I tell them.

We were all dead after that tournament, but none of my teammates or anyone in the coaching staff accused me of anything. These things happen in football. After getting knocked out, the press banged on about it for a week and then it wasn't discussed again. Until I moved to England, that is.

*

14 December. We headed into the Hull game planning to play three at the back, with Eriksen in midfield and Sissoko given another

154

opportunity. We played a back-three on occasion last year as well as against Arsenal this season. We usually leave three in defence when we go forward: the two centre-backs and the holding midfielder, while the full-backs push up, which they certainly had to do against a deep-lying Hull. We need our full-backs to give us more because we haven't been getting in behind enough recently.

Our distribution wasn't great and our wide players were only fleetingly involved in the first half, although we were in control and created plenty of chances. At 1–0, we were denied a penalty for a foul on Eriksen and Hull then spurned their best opportunity. There's such a fine line between the 3–0 win that we picked up and what could've turned into a very tricky contest! Eriksen, who scored twice, rediscovered that attacking flair that had been missing.

It felt rather strange to see Ryan Mason on the Hull bench. It was a mixture of affection and sadness.

After the game I was asked about Eric Dier, who once again played the whole game: 'I know there are a lot of rumours, but he's 100 per cent our player. He's very important for us. He signed a contract after the Euros and showed his commitment to the club. There's no doubt his future is at White Hart Lane.' I should have added, 'And at Wembley, where we'll play our games next season while our new stadium is completed, and at the new White Hart Lane.'

These seemingly small things that escalate into larger issues are tiring. They make me question whether the job we are doing is really understood. We keep winning, which lessens the pressure, but it takes up so much time with meetings between games and demanding a level of effort from some people who, frankly, shouldn't need to be pushed.

Is it a good idea to establish deep emotional connections with the players? Is there another way to get the best out of them? The exhaustion is exacerbated when you don't get what you expect from them or when that emotional interchange is uneven. Is it fair to expect the same emotional response from them?

I have to switch off now. I need sleep.

*

During the difficult start to our tenure at Spurs, my staff and I began a ritual that we continue to this day. When I get out of the shower after training, I always say, 'Why did we leave Southampton to come to Tottenham?' Then I hang my towel on the wall and lean my head against it. I did it again today and we laughed. Sometimes I'm joking, but on occasions I'm being serious.

As it happens, though, my relationship with Daniel continues to blossom. He is becoming ever more approachable and forthcoming, and our assessments have grown more aligned. The doubts that arose in the first few months after our arrival have vanished: Latin Americans and the English can have more in common than might first appear possible. Daniel's seriousness shouldn't be mistaken for aloofness. He now comprehends what type of manager I am and why things are being done differently to the past. He knows that you have to let time be the judge of things.

The chairman's wife, Tracey, and my loyal and efficient PA, Susan, put on a dinner for all the coaching staff's wives tonight. They'd hired a magician and a great time was had by all. It was Tracey's way of showing appreciation for the sacrifices they make as our partners. It's true that we spend all day at the training ground, but however much we complain at times, we enjoy what we do. But when we get home at night, we don't feel up to much, so it's our other halves who have it hardest.

*

18 December. We played Burnley today. We decided on the line-up yesterday and devised a detailed defensive and attacking game plan, only for Toby to get injured again. We had a choice to make: simply go for a like-for-like replacement or change our approach too? In the end, we opted to switch the system. The message didn't change, though: that the players had to be switched-on for the full 90 minutes, that they'd be able to enjoy themselves, but they'd also have to dig deep, since a lot would be demanded of them physically and mentally. Burnley play a standard 4-4-2, they battle all game long, they're very strong and they're really dangerous from set-pieces. The brief was to avoid conceding cheap free-kicks or corners, and to defend as far away from Hugo as possible.

We went behind following an unfortunate piece of play, in which we gave away possession two or three times and fell victim to a ricochet.

156

But we stayed patient and were rewarded when we equalised before the break, Dele Alli getting on the end of a Kyle Walker assist from out wide. At half-time, we reminded them that we had to move the opposition from side to side in order to find space, and create overloads so that our full-backs could get forward on the overlap – just like we'd worked on.

Earlier this week, I spoke privately with left-back Danny Rose. I wanted to set some things straight and ask him to play a bigger part. So, while we lacked an attacking threat from full-back in the first half against Hull, Rose was magnificent today: he made himself available for the midfielders throughout and marauded forward boldly, putting in several fine crosses. He then scored the winner in the second half. It was no less than we deserved after we racked up 27 shots, of which nine were on target. We're fifth, three points adrift of second place and one off fourth, ahead of the clash with Liverpool, one of our rivals for Champions League qualification. There's no respite.

The 'other game', the action on the touchline, provided entertainment aplenty. I feel for the fourth official, having to listen to what Miguel was saying and also to our opposite numbers with their 'f*****g this' and 'f*****g that'. Burnley felt that Sissoko should've been sent off. And obviously when a coach talks about a possible sending-off at his press conference, everyone else picks up on it. On the other hand, no one mentioned that Barnes's foul on Dembélé in the first half could also have warranted a red card. Neither did I. I dream of a world in which analysis doesn't always focus on the latest flashpoint, in which controversy – fuelled by a coach's words – doesn't block out everything else. Very unlikely to happen.

We have given everyone two days off afterwards. I'm going to spend them in Barcelona with my family.

*

It's funny; we don't rest in Barcelona, what with all the get-togethers with friends, meals and walking, but I come back feeling rested because my mind unwinds, because we break out of our everyday bubble. The strongest memory from this trip will be the meal we had in one of those traditional Catalan restaurants that use vegetables from their own garden.

On the flight back to London, I mulled over the matter of the emotional ties that we've established with the players. There are other ways of engaging with them, but however much experience I accrue, I don't see myself changing on that front. I like to forge emotional bonds with the people that I work with.

Truth be told, this isn't proving my toughest year. My most difficult period came at Espanyol, when every decision, every loss, seemed like the end of the world for me and my family. Nevertheless, English football is five times more challenging. Handling the team is more complex when you're a manager rather than a coach. On top of that, you have less time between matches, which are so intense that they leave you exhausted, and afterwards you have to spend an hour with the press, trying to think up different answers to the same questions.

Paradoxically, I'm usually calmer in defeat than in victory, as I aim to keep a cool head to analyse the reasons for the loss and start searching for solutions. It's always that much more of a stretch to make improvements when you're winning and everything seems to be going well.

Having said that, after losing a match, the most you feel like doing when you get home is having a glass of wine before hitting the hay. Sometimes I take it out on my children or, in particular, my wife. Something she says, any innocuous comment, can light the fuse and I end up exploding.

The 23rd of the month is our wedding anniversary. We've been married 24 years. My dear, patient Karina.

*

We resumed training yesterday, Wednesday the 21st. We were on double duty today. In the morning, we trained out on the pitch, splitting the players into groups, with those of them who are feeling the strain after too many matches continuing with recovery exercises. In the afternoon, we did gym work. At around four o'clock, the families of the squad and coaching staff arrived for some festivities.

Today it was announced – alongside the now-classic picture of me posing next to him, wearing a suit – that Hugo Lloris has signed a new contract keeping him here until at least the age of 35. It makes me proud that so many players have shown their commitment by renewing their deals. In the last year and a half, no one else has tied down as many players who would be of interest to other clubs. That says more than I ever could.

It was all plain sailing with Hugo. We told him we wanted to offer him a long contract. He sat down with the chairman one afternoon and it was all sealed there and then. He then expressed himself clearly in the interview accompanying the announcement, saying that he believes we can do big things and are going in the right direction. I decided to piggyback on the good news by making a declaration of intent on Sky Sports, telling them that, 'Our dream is to win the Premier League.'

More good news: as the meeting with Southampton has been moved from the 26th to the 28th and though we'll have fewer days to recover for the subsequent clash with Watford, it means a lot of the foreign players will be able to fly back to their countries for Christmas. So we'll eat together at the training ground on Saturday 24th and then go our separate ways.

This is the first time in four years that my staff and I are going to have a relaxed Christmas.

*

Our next opponents are Southampton. I sometimes ask myself why we left. If you had to pick one team that played consistently good football over the four years in which we've been in England, it was our Southampton side in 2013–14. It was our first full season and our notable results included running out victorious at Anfield against a Liverpool team who almost won the league. Their fans clapped us off. That's what we left behind.

I don't think we grasped just how good we were. We had a group of 13 or 14 players who changed the way they thought about foot-ball, passionately dedicating themselves to the cause. We finished that campaign eighth, but we deserved better given how we played. It was an extraordinary achievement, the product of enthusiasm and a steep learning curve, and the triumph of a team ethos. And synergy.

It all started with chairman Nicola Cortese's visit to Cornellà-El Prat. We were playing Sevilla that day and Southampton had their eye on Philippe Coutinho. Nicola liked the way I, the coach, handled myself in the technical area and was bowled over by my young Espanyol side that showed passion and aggression on and off the ball. When we left the club in November, Jesús and I decided to set up an office at home and we planned to meet several times a week over the following six months to look back over the job we'd done, organise our training material, improve our footballing philosophy and so on. We agreed to start in the new year, so in the meantime we'd get together to go running, chat or grab a bite. A few offers came in and we even met officials from Dynamo Kyiv and Olympiacos. I went to Argentina in mid-December to spend Christmas there.

While in Argentina, an agent called me. 'The Southampton chairman wants to overhaul the club,' he said, 'and he's been really impressed by what you've done at Espanyol.'

I phoned Jesús: 'Whoa! I just got a call from England.' Then I had Nicola himself on the line and when the conversation was over, I called Jesús again: 'Listen, I've just spoken to the chairman. He wants to meet me. Get ready, we're going to London on 6 January.'

We watched and analysed as many Southampton games as we could, including a 5–1 loss in the FA Cup, and Jesús drew up a short report. We were prepared. We got to the hotel early and saw Nicola's Mercedes parked outside, but he didn't get out until 4 p.m., the scheduled time for the meeting. He was accompanied by Les Reed, the club's executive director.

Nicola spoke in English and I responded in Spanish, with Jesús translating both ways. Three hours went by as we talked about Southampton, football and playing identities. They were looking for an ambitious coach who would fit in with the club's vision with respect to their academy and the desire to instil a high-energy, bold style of play. I asked Jesús to explain that the brand of football we like would work well in the English league: a combination of bringing the ball out from the back, dominating possession and pressing, along with a few other things that suit the English mentality and personality, such as endeavour, physicality, mental strength and teamwork. We would help the players, who I presumed were hungry for success, to be lionhearts – I think I was the one that came up with the cliché. Referees in England let the game flow more, so our team would have to compete intensely and be extremely fit, because the ball is in play for longer here than elsewhere and matches constantly swing from end to end.

As the meeting was drawing to a close, Cortese said, 'I like what I've heard. I want you to be our coach.' In perfect Spanish – the bastard!

We went back to Barcelona and met Nicola for the second time there. We started thrashing out the package for my assistants, but we couldn't reach an agreement, so I said forget it, that we were calling the whole thing off. Two or three days went by and it looked like that was that, that the deal had fallen through because of an inability to agree about the wording of a few clauses – contracts are different in England and Spain.

And that was when Jesús and my wife intervened to help me with the decision.

A private jet was sent to Barcelona to pick us up. There was a bottle of Moët & Chandon on board, plus fruit and other stuff. 'We'd better not touch anything,' I said. Miki, Toni and Jesús agreed. 'We don't want to give them the impression we're here for a lark.' When we touched down that 17 January 2013, the country was covered in three feet of snow. We went straight from the airport to the hotel to seal the deal and put pen to paper, and we later had dinner there with various employees from different departments of the club.

We took training for the first time the next day. Everything remained blanketed in white, so it took the groundstaff quite a while to clear the snow off the pitches – there was no undersoil heating. Then about 200 players turned up! Or it seemed so. There was no induction, introductory talk or anything like that. I led the activities as we broke the ice with a warm-up, some *rondos* and some simple exercises practising game scenarios. All quite light. The chairman and Paul Mitchell, Head of Recruitment, came to watch. On the second day, we added more tactical work and demonstrations, with the help of José Fonte, who doubled as a translator.

We were warned that our first game, at home to Everton just four days after we arrived, could be marred by protests. The fans were unhappy about the sacking of Nigel Adkins, the manager who had guided the club to back-to-back promotions. They were also none too amused by the appointment of someone who didn't speak English and had no experience in the Premier League (but how can you gain experience if no one will hire you because you lack experience?). Many people thought Cortese was crazy.

I didn't give any of that a second thought when taking my place pitchside. The grass was bright green; its aroma enveloped me. The floodlights were on, creating the feel of a stage, a big occasion. The stadium was full; the sound of the crowd was different from Cornellà, bringing to mind a calm, yet powerful wave. I felt a metre taller. That's when it sank in that we had entered a whole new, terrifically exciting world.

The Everton we were up against were a fine side, with David Moyes in the dugout. And we were fantastic. We were aggressive, never letting them breathe, and we got the ball forward quickly. All that was missing was a goal, so it finished 0–0. On the way to the dressing room, I gushed to Jesús: 'If they've responded like this after three days of training . . .' Afterwards, Rickie Lambert came up to me and said, 'I'm sorry, gaffer. We're sorry for letting you down; we should've won.' I'd never heard a player speak that way after a draw. I got the sense that it was the squad's way of welcoming us, of reaching out to us right from the outset, and the gesture felt genuine.

But the moment when we fell in love, the side with us, us with the side, took place in Barcelona. After the Everton match, coinciding with the international break, I took the team to Spain. We trained in the FC Barcelona training centre and I feel that impressed the guys. That and the fact so many people stopped me to greet me or take a picture. 'This guy is somebody', they must have thought. At the first session, our real work started. It was intense, they had to step up to the mark if they wanted to do what we needed of them. Les, Nicola, Paul, they were all watching.

I think, on all sides, it was love at first sight – or fourth sight if you count the previous superficial training sessions and our first game. The players gave us their fullest attention, which is something I'd worried about since I couldn't communicate in English. They gazed back at us intently. They trained at full tilt even though there were things they didn't understand. I glanced at Jesús and Miki and we exchanged smiles. The seeds had been planted.

We acted as if the whole thing were normal, as if we'd been doing this thing of working abroad for years. As soon as we were awake enough, having breakfast before 7 a.m., we'd start talking about training, the players, tactical ideas and exercises. We were like four cables that, when put together, jump-started an engine and turned on the headlights.

We wanted to make the most of every minute of the experience of being in England, so by 7.30 we were already on the way to the training ground. It was still dark outside. The snow lasted for several more days. It was bitterly cold . . . When we arrived, we'd huddle together and drink *mate*. If *mate* gourds could talk . . . For the first month, we were based in an old farm building that would flood when it rained. Three weeks in, the club sorted out an office for us in a dressing room, but it was completely open-plan. We managed to get a folding screen to create separate spaces. Sometimes Miki and Toni had to nip out so that Jesús and I could talk with a bit more privacy.

We'd work through to eight or nine in the evening. Then we'd have dinner together, watch football if there was a match on, and fall asleep.

It wasn't always easy being cooped up together for so long – as was the case from January until our first summer in Southampton, when we finally moved into our own houses – but we'd go to bed looking forward to getting up at six the next morning.

I was the last one to leave the hotel, which felt very big and very empty without the other three.

We were surprised to discover how wide-ranging the role of a manager is in England and we ourselves added to it with new things that suddenly occurred to us. For example, we replaced the laundry detergent that was being used because it didn't have the right smell. I like the club's kit to have a signature scent, to create the sensation that you're putting on something familiar. We tested several options before finding one we liked.

It was at training that we felt most in our element. The squad continued to listen to us, understanding that it was a matter of our way or no way, although we didn't let them lose sight of the need to enjoy themselves. 'If we work hard during the week, everything will seem much easier during games,' I told them repeatedly. We'd play an hour-long 11-a-side game on Wednesdays, with no stoppages – there were no corners or goal-kicks. If the ball went out of play, the game would restart immediately with another ball. It was relentless. Those players have told me since that, even today, they still hear Jesús yelling out 'press, press, press' in their dreams.

That attitude spread throughout the squad. The players did everything at full pelt, whether latching on to the ball, pressing, getting into position or sprinting back to start moves. Then it was on to the next exercise at the same pace, or time to hit the gym. And rinse and repeat: another day, another double session.

They hated the Gacon test, a gruelling intermittent shuttle run. It became a notorious example of the physical demands we make, even though we actually do tougher drills. To start with, the players have 45 seconds to cover 150 metres, with 15 seconds to rest afterwards. In each subsequent 45-second rep, they have to run 6.25 metres further, with the intensity steadily increasing.

We came up with different ways of building play from the back. Our central midfielders would drop in to cover for the full-backs, who bombed forward a lot, especially Luke Shaw. Our main striker, Rickie Lambert, ceased to be a fixed target man; we told him to roam about freely. And so on and so forth. We had a blast.

'We'd need two hearts to play the way you want, gaffer,' some of the players quipped. Kelvin Davis, one of the goalkeepers and also the club captain, once brought the clock from the dressing-room wall out on to the training pitch to remind us how long a session had been. The cheek of him! We laughed.

We worked around the language barrier. I spoke through hugs, contact, with my facial expressions and my gestures. My poor English forced me to find other ways to read people, which suited me just fine. But it also led to some peculiar situations. My third match at the helm was away to Wigan Athletic. After falling behind in the first half, we played really well in the second period and turned the scoreline around, only to concede a last-minute equaliser. I was seething when I went into the dressing room. I started swearing and even kicked a box, before looking at Fran Alonso – who was helping me with interpreting duties at the time, and is now at Everton – as if to say, 'How are you going to translate that, then?' At the end of the day, though, I was just marking my territory; the choice of words in English was neither here nor there.

Roy Hodgson, the England boss back then, paid me a visit because he wanted to call up several of our players. I told him – in the Manager's Room, in front of Nicola – that I'd have to start speaking English soon. 'No, no, no. Carry on as you are,' Roy replied, 'because people are getting more interested in you with each passing day. They're intrigued.'

Nicola expressed similar sentiments: 'Don't worry, you don't need to speak English. You've got an interpreter and it's better that way. Otherwise you could get caught out because it's not easy. You're best off keeping your head down for a bit.'

Having taken charge when the club was in the thick of the relegation battle, we ended that first season 14th, well clear of the drop zone. That summer, we held a pre-season training camp in Catalonia to continue pressing home our ideas. The players tell me that they still remember how we made them hold arrows against the soft tissue area of each other's throats; they then had to move forward until the arrow snapped. Or when they – and I – walked barefoot across hot coals. These were bonding exercises, meetings of minds. And they did everything that was asked of them. They couldn't get enough.

We started the 2013–14 campaign with a victory away against West Brom, with a penalty right at the end, and by the fifth week we went to Anfield with five points. Liverpool were the unbeaten leaders. We began well but Gerrard had the best chance in the first half. I was happy with our pressure, the running, the movement, and felt we were in with a chance in the second half. Less than ten minutes into it, Dejan Lovren scored his first goal for the club after heading Lallana's corner. We left Anfield with the three points and, in fact, we managed to lose only once in the first 11 games of the season. We were flying.

I recently read something written by Jody Rivers, a youth coach and Southampton fan, in which he recalled a moment that perfectly encapsulated what that team were about. We went a goal down to Manchester City and Jody wrote that most Premier League managers would've asked their side to sit back and stay organised so as to stem the opposition's momentum. But within a minute of the goal, 'Luke Shaw was played in behind the City backline and from the byline crossed to the back post. Arriving? Calum Chambers. The right-back. Full-back to full-back. Chambers headed wide but Pochettino jumped and applauded the move. The bravery of young players.' We ended up drawing that game.

Les Reed often told me that we took the Premier League by surprise. That we taught the small boys not to be scared of the big ones, Leicester City being the ultimate consequence of that attitude. Managers and coaches kept asking Les how we trained for the high–pressure game, wanting details of our work. We started getting visitors from all over the place. Les, and others, felt that the Premier League had moved too far from its usual fast and aggressive style, there being too much emphasis on passing, on keeping the ball. And that we brought back the necessary aggression, pressing high and all over the park, a tactic that had not been seen before, or at least not for a long time.

A number of our players began to believe that the sky was the limit. Rickie Lambert, Jay Rodriguez, Calum Chambers, Luke Shaw, James Ward-Prowse and Adam Lallana (the last of whom played in central midfield, a position usually reserved for more physical players in England) have all since won international caps. All except James subsequently signed for other clubs for big transfer fees. José Fonte, Morgan Schneiderlin and Steven Davis, meanwhile, became established Premier League regulars.

Whereas at Espanyol I felt like a father figure to the lads, at Southampton I was more like a big brother. What's more, it was our best year as a family. In the summer of 2013, Karina and the kids moved to Southampton. Sebas had finished secondary school and began university there, while Mauri joined the club's academy and went to a local school. We lived in a beautiful house, one of those modern, prefab-type German houses. It was in the middle of a forest, so we had deer – 'Bambis', in my wife's words – frolicking in our garden all day. It was the stuff of dreams. As Karina told me recently, 'It was the first time in almost twenty years that I enjoyed a whole year, including all the football.'

People were lovely and treated us wonderfully. As for Nicola . . . he was a character. He has a strong personality and knows his mind. But the same goes for me, and we didn't agree on everything. We clashed on a few occasions – including once when he promised a player a particular shirt number when it'd already been given to someone else.

One day he told me I wasn't as bold a thinker as I fancied myself to be. He wanted us to make the players wear head cameras in order to find out what they were thinking and seeing while they played, because he felt that some (and Lallana especially) were making very poor decisions. Since you should always treat your chairman with respect, I side-stepped the issue and said that what Lallana really needed was for us to make sure he had more passing options. 'You're not very brave,' Nicola kept insisting. So I clammed up. In fact, I kept quiet for the rest of the hour-and-a-half car journey to a hotel, where we were meeting a player to persuade him to sign for us. I spoke to the footballer completely normally, but then spent the hour and a half on the way back in silence again, gripping the window handle. We never introduced those cameras.

In May 2013, four months after my appointment, Nicola had a dispute with the club. I made my stance clear: if he went, so would I. In the event, he left midway through my second and last season there, in January 2014, and I'm convinced he wanted me to follow suit. But at that point I couldn't leave the players in the lurch, not when we were building something.

Just before Nicola quit, Tottenham – who knew all about the issues at Southampton – contacted me. I didn't return their call. My staff and I had negotiated a five-year contract at Southampton, but it was never signed. February and March brought a lot of upheaval and uncertainty reigned over who was running the club, what direction they wanted to take it in, what the financial situation and many of the players' futures were. We waited until the end of the season before talking to Tottenham. There was a buy-out clause in my running contract that Daniel was willing to trigger; my first contract at Spurs also contained one, but it was removed when I inked a new deal.

Should we stay or should we go? Our departure from Southampton was a saga. A lot of tears were shed ... After the last match of the season, we spent two weeks going back and forth on what to do. But the instability at the club swayed us and we decided to leave. We also knew that several of our top players had moves lined up; painful as it may have been for them, they couldn't let their bond with us hold them back. It'd only lasted a year and a half, but it was the end of an era: we'd been recruited by Nicola, who was no longer there, and things had changed irredeemably.

Although we'd all seen the writing on the wall, everything happened while the players were away on holiday, so there were no long good-byes. I still remember my conversation with Victor Wanyama, though. I called him; in fact, I called practically the whole squad. Victor, who had only been at the club for a year, sounded upset because he felt we were on to a good thing. 'But that's football,' he said, and I had to bite my lip. 'You've shown me what I have to do to be a top footballer. I'll keep at it.'

'Work hard, Victor. You never know: maybe our paths will cross again,' I replied.

Over and above a fine eighth-place finish, our biggest achievement was having put the club's vision into practice.

Maybe we'll get a warmer reception at St Mary's as time moves on.

*

We've had a good last couple of days in training, including doing an exercise involving coordinated pressing against a 4-3-3. We hadn't worked on that for quite a while and it was new to the likes of Sissoko. We travelled to Southampton on the new team coach the club has recently bought. We watched Liverpool's victory on the way. Arsenal, Chelsea and the other teams near the top all won too, so the onus was on us to get three points.

As ever, the city greeted us with traffic jams, meaning it took us an hour and a half to get to the hotel. Ros stopped by to see us and we spoke about the past and present. We laughed a lot. We were having a drink in a private lounge when a woman walked in with her two-year-old Southampton-supporting son. While the mother asked me why I'd left the club, the kid shouted 'traitor, traitor' at me.

It's true that I never explained the reasons behind my decision, but it hurts to be called that. I understand we had created a bond with the fans, despite my limited English. We'd brought back excitement, belief. And they were let down by my departure, especially because it took place during the summer, without a proper goodbye. They should know it broke my heart to leave. That we thought about it one hundred times before we took the decision. And that, sometimes, we wonder why we really left.

Tomorrow's game is our third against our former club. We got some abuse during the first two. And there wasn't a single word about us in the matchday programme. Ros told me that they would be putting something about us in it this time.

*

Neither their manager nor their captain mentioned Wanyama, nor Alderweireld – another former Saints player – at all in their pro-gramme notes. They weren't referenced anywhere, in fact. Nor was I, for that matter.

Having said that, behind the scenes, the people at the club have nothing but kind, appreciative words when we see one another, and today we encountered a great many friendly faces en route to the stadium.

The team came out half-asleep, we barely touched the ball in the first minute and a half, and then we conceded. You can't legislate for going a goal down so early on. It's galling; your best-laid plans . . . We strug-gled to settle, but after a quarter of an hour, we started dominating and things fell into place. We ended up winning 4–1 courtesy of an Alli brace and a goal each from Son and Kane, the latter of whom missed a penalty. We're still fifth and we've now racked up 13 wins, seven draws and six defeats in all competitions this season.

Around the 87th minute, the Tottenham fans started chanting, 'He's magic, you know, Mauricio Pochettino'. I was standing on the touchline with my hands in my pockets, as I had been all match. I don't normally interact with supporters during games, but today I decided to clap that section of the crowd.

We caught up with many of our former charges after the final whistle. Miki and I then travelled back to London with the team on the coach. Jesús went back by car with his family, while Toni and Eva stayed behind to enjoy a day in Southampton.

We've got the day off tomorrow. We return to business the following day, and then it's New Year's Eve the day after that.

7.

JANUARY

The Premier League teams got up and running in the FA Cup during a demanding January that also featured five league fixtures, including table-topping Chelsea's visit to White Hart Lane and a trip to the Etihad to renew acquaintances with Guardiola's Manchester City. Tottenham began the year in fifth place.

We started January with an away game, although it was only a short trip, to Watford. Since Walker and Vertonghen were suspended, I decided to draft in Kieran Trippier and Kevin Wimmer, reverting to three centre-backs to give us added security.

We met up at the training ground on the first morning of the year. We played the lads a video overview of the opposition and the different systems they use (this information proved crucial), explained how to counteract them and did some set-piece prep. After we wished each other a happy new year, of course. Then we headed to Watford, where two ex-Tottenham players, Étienne Capoue and Younès Kaboul, awaited us.

I made Kaboul captain when my staff and I joined the club, and I was surprised by some comments he made ahead of the match, in which he claimed that he'd been disrespected and I'd frozen him out without any explanation. He was given plenty of reasons in the many conversations I had with him during a period when we were first stamping our authority and were trying to take the team in a different direction.

We thought Watford would go with two up front, because their strike partnership was one of their biggest strengths, but they only named one in their line-up. Then, at the end of the warm-up, a minute before kick-off, we were informed that the wing-back Juan Camilo Zúñiga wasn't going to play and the forward Odion Ighalo was going to take his place. We weren't thrown off, however, because we had prepared for that eventuality.

Everything went as we expected and we managed to storm into a 3–0 first-half lead, allowing us to rest a few players later on. Alli, Rose and Kane were brought off, as we want them to be in fine shape to face a Chelsea side that'll have had an extra day's rest. The 4–1 win with braces apiece by Kane and Alli sealed the full 12 points from our last four matches and our goal difference stands at +20. We remain fifth and have picked up more points over the last twelve months than in any other calendar year in the club's history.

Nothing happens by chance. The last ten days have allowed us to recover physically and focus on our tailored training regimes. It's clear that we've got over the bad run, by sticking to our principles and ensuring that the players have got back to their best. It's working.

As we were leaving Vicarage Road, I bumped into Kaboul and we greeted each other. He didn't comment on a lack of respect, so all that can go down as anecdotal.

*

The restructuring of the club and the parallel work involved in finalising the renewal of players' contracts are still taking up too much of our time. After today's game, the management team headed back to the training ground and stayed there until eight o'clock. I had a glass of wine on the coach. It was my last for a while, as I have to look after myself. Since I retired as a player, I've been on a cycle of getting fat, losing weight and putting it back on. I set myself targets, but I forget and start the cycle again. Now I'm putting my health first by changing my lifestyle and creating good habits. In the past I did one of those brutal fasts that consist of drinking only boiled fruit juice and water. The first four or five days are very tough because your body is used to ingesting many calories and suddenly everything starts hurting. The most important aspect isn't the twelve days of fasting, but the way you get back into your food and the fact that it creates a social problem. You can't just go out for dinner, coffee or anything else. The last time that I did it was in the summer of 2012 when I was getting ready to go to Ibiza. Once we were there, of course, we completely stuffed our faces. I still maintain that a lifestyle change is better – you suffer less and benefit more in the long term.

I'm also going to force myself to do an hour of exercise per day. With 24 hours in the day, saving one hour for my health doesn't seem much. It also helps me think and boosts my energy flow while releasing endorphins and stimulating my creativity.

My best ideas come to me when I'm in the bath, which must be because it's one of the few moments when I'm isolated from everyone else.

*

I've developed a huge amount since the days at Espanyol with Feliciano Di Blasi when we'd say to the boys, 'Look, if you're tired, put your hand on your chest and keep running.' Now I look back and laugh at some of our ideas. But do you know what? They taught me something. Over time you improve your understanding of the game and the way you react to all sorts of situations. Your engagement with the players is dictated by their personalities and needs, and your own experiences.

I tend not to work with psychologists. I don't feel we need one on a regular basis, as looking after the player's mental well-being, and understanding the context and applying solutions beyond the tactical, is one of the manager's roles. Barely anything that we learn about foot-ballers' mentality is written in a book; you learn it along the way. It is only in very concrete moments of trauma or deep confusion that we might look to bring in professional help for some of the players.

Falling in love with your players is a dangerous business. I don't partake in such activities because it's a concept that I save for my other half, not to mention that sooner or later you fall out of love. It happens faster in football than it does in life. The ideal scenario is to strike a balance between what the footballer needs and what I demand. I like to show respect to people who earn it and I believe it's fair to treat the group according to the hierarchy established by graft and hard work.

I like to sign players after analysing them and imagining what they can bring to the team. Given that we want good people as well as good footballers, I also rely on my feelings. I need contact with them, whether it means a quick five-minute chat or an hour-long meeting. On occasion, I've met up with a player, said 'hello' and quickly followed it up with 'I have to go' in order not to see him for a second longer. There have been other cases where five minutes have been enough to sign them or we've been together for three hours because it's been such a pleasure. I've made mistakes, of course, but I always tell them what I want from them up front. That's the only way to kick off a good relationship.

I met Sir Alex Ferguson for a meal in London last year. There were lots of nuggets of information I took from it, as well as memories that will live with me for ever. He advised me that I must never lose control of the dressing room and that caving into the 25 millionaire footballers with whom I work every day would be a monumental error. He preferred to confront a player at the first indication of a challenge to his authority, without hesitating for even a second. If the player overstepped the mark, he would boot him out, as he famously did on occasion. He managed to establish complete power back then, but I think things have changed now. The balance of power has shifted irreversibly towards the player.

I don't dish out fines. I prefer to give a player a number of chances until we reach the point of no return. Sir Alex and I are in agreement on this: you can't have doubts relating to a decision circling around your head when you go to bed. You decide and move on to the next one.

From quite early on in his managerial career, Ferguson decided not to work on the training pitch during the week. He felt it was necessary to come out of that bubble because he could see changes in players' performance levels more clearly from a distance. It gave him perspective and allowed him to focus on their lives off the pitch. Do you have family issues? How are the finances? Are you tired? Observing and seeing things that you don't expect is crucial. Maybe the Ferguson method is the step you need to take for an extended managerial career. I need to be out there, correcting things and demanding more, but often work with the players takes place in my office.

*

Luke Shaw, the youngest member of the Southampton squad at the time, used to come to my office every day, even when I barely spoke English. I'd give him a hug and a smile, which we both needed for different reasons. I'd make him a drink as part of his new nutritional regimen and we'd just chat, even when we didn't understand each other all that well: 'Do you have a girlfriend? Do you still have the same friends? What do you do for fun?' I'd sometimes get angry with him. Luke would often go to London, but I didn't like him doing that; it was an unnecessary and too regular distraction. I told him as much. Was he focusing enough on his profession? Did he enjoy it enough? 'OK, I won't go any more,' he told me. He was living at a club residence, but one day his mother brought him to training. I asked her to come to my office. 'Where've you come from?'

'London, Luke came up to London yesterday,' she replied and I made a joke that cracked us both up. But I felt his head was not in the right place to make the sacrifices and decisions that are necessary at that age. It was a Monday. I didn't utter a word to Luke until the Friday. I don't think he went back to London much after that.

*

I called Victor Wanyama before he signed for Southampton. 'I've seen you play several times and we're going to make you even better, one of the best.' It was the first time that a coach had phoned him and spoken to him in that way. I lit the touch paper. We arranged to meet at a hotel and I noted how uptight he was while sitting on the sofa. I gave him a hug and saw how the tension that he'd given off on arrival disappeared. Both of us quickly felt that we'd known each other for a long time.

From day one, we spoke about life more than about football. I felt like a father to him. He was very shy when he started training with us and he barely spoke. I don't think he was happy. I had to remind him that he was doing what he'd dreamt of and he should enjoy every minute of it. He gradually started to view life in a different light. Football stopped being his profession in favour of his passion.

He gradually opened up.

Sometimes when he looks very serious, I go up to him and say, 'Come on, man. A little smile and it'll all look different.' And he'll laugh. He now says that he trains better with a smile on his face.

*

In our second season, Hugo Lloris fractured his wrist while on holiday in Ibiza in an innocuous incident. I knew nothing about it until much later. Apparently he got it X-rayed and the fracture wasn't visible, so he didn't mention it. The problem was discovered when he went back to France. He felt so ashamed for a week that he didn't dare admit what had happened. I eventually received a WhatsApp from him containing details of what had transpired, but I didn't reply. I know he knew I'd read it. He spoke to Toni who got angry with him. At the start of pre-season I told him to come to my office. It wasn't the injury that bothered me, more the fact that he hadn't trusted me. He told me it wasn't down to a lack of trust, but that he felt embarrassed to tell his manager the injury was caused by something so stupid. It has taken us time to heal the rift that had developed between us. Hugo, who didn't want to mix private and professional matters, now understands what I am asking of him: he can speak to me about anything and everything without my passing judgement. If he's with me, it has to be 100 per cent; 99 per cent doesn't cut it. I share things with him and he does so with me.

*

Alex Ferguson used to tell his players that working hard is a talent and he expected more from his stars than from the rest. I've said as much to mine on occasion. It's also important to get them on your side from the beginning.

When we first played Dier as a holding midfielder, I asked him in the canteen if he'd previously played in that position. 'Yes, for Sporting Lisbon.'

'Ah, OK.' I later read that he said that was the extent of the conversation that we had about his change of position. It's true. I had faith in him and his ability to learn. We'd then correct things along the way.

He's had a tricky six months. 'You aren't the same Eric as last year, the one from the Euros,' I told him in training earlier in the season. Recently, I spent the whole week discussing and speaking about what was happening to him. Every day we looked at different things. For instance, I made a table for him with the headings Good, Very Good, Excellent and Unique. I wrote Maradona, Messi and Cristiano Ronaldo in the fourth one, before asking him where he saw himself. 'Very Good,' he said.

'Yes, that's where you are. It's only a short trip to get to Excellent. Where are you as a defensive midfielder? And as a centre-back?' Eric thinks he's further ahead as a midfielder than as a defender. We had a long chat about that because I disagree. In the end, I said to him, 'It doesn't matter. If you give 100 per cent wherever you play, it'll go well.'

There are certain things that footballers have to discover on their own.

*

National team captains voted for the Best FIFA Football Coach by choosing their top three. Victor Wanyama picked me first, but Hugo Lloris didn't choose me at all. I told Simon Felstein to tell him that I was absolutely furious when I found out. I still laugh when I remember his sheepish face next time that I saw him.

*

The transfer window is now open. I've already told Daniel that, unless something incredible becomes possible, we don't need anyone and, when we're short of players, we'll turn to the Under-21s. There are loan offers for Harry Winks and Josh Onomah, but I'd prefer to keep them close by. The fans, who understand what we're working towards, aren't demanding lavish spending. It will be good to get Lamela back.

Next up is Chelsea.

*

A story has just broken claiming that I said the following about Guardiola: 'If you arrive in the Premier League and you aren't humble enough, you'll be disappointed.'

I didn't say that. Or I wasn't clear. I was speaking in general terms about how the Premier League is perceived in Europe. I used the fact that English football is often underestimated. People think it's just long balls and there's no quality, but the Premier League has changed considerably in the last decade, with so much foreign influence. Hispanics and Latin Americans may still think that they're a level above, but when they get here, they realise how wrong they are. If you aren't humble when you arrive, you won't make the grade.

I have always been very aware that you can't say that you're coming to England to change the style of football here. It's like saying you're going to Spain to ban siestas and paella. Nobody is above the culture and idiosyncrasies of a country like England. There's no such thing as perfect tactics, the perfect manager or an infallible methodology. Saying that you possess the system that is going to revolutionise everything shows a complete lack of respect. It all depends on the players at your disposal.

I'm lucky in the sense that when I got to England, people wondered who I was and didn't expect anything from me. I soaked up everything: the expectations of the players, referees with a different perception of what is a foul, fans demanding to up the pace, the media obsession with individuals, chairmen not looking to take centre stage.

It's better to come here looking to learn it all.

*

This week we had a game of England v the Rest of the World and I played, of course. If anyone did three nutmegs, the victim of the last one would have to sing as a forfeit. Nobody ended up warbling on this occasion. I got injured while challenging for an aerial ball with Carter-Vickers and tweaked my back. He's a strong guy!

He said, 'Bloody hell, I've injured the gaffer!' I think he was laughing inside.

*

Today is the second recovery day since our last match and the day before we play Chelsea. We will be facing a side that beat us 2–1 at Stamford Bridge in late November. They're ten points ahead of us and deserve to be top of the pile. They went up two gears when they switched to a back-three that nobody has been able to cope with. They've racked up 13 wins on the bounce, but nobody has ever got to 14 in Premier League history.

Let's see where we are. Chelsea are always a good benchmark.

Our starting XI was already decided at the end of the Watford game. We have a powerful group of players (only Lamela is missing) which allows us to play in a number of different ways depending on what the game requires. We're going to use three centre-backs, two very attacking wing-backs and three in the middle of the park.

I decided to mix it up in training. We prepared a few longer-than-usual videos explaining how we wanted to play, how we could avoid the problems from our previous game against them and showing their strengths and weaknesses. We then broke it down further by position: first of all the three centre-backs: Dier, Alderweireld, Vertonghen and also Wanyama who has to mop up in the space at the back and also start the play. Then the full-backs, Rose and Walker, who'll have to offer something constantly. Then the two midfielders, Eriksen and Dembélé, and finally the two forwards, Alli and Kane. They're all fresh and in good shape.

I took the session, as I always do when it's with the starting XI, and it was a tactical affair – I couldn't make it particularly intense having played just two days earlier – in which I explained how we have to attack, how to release the ball and how to press.

*

4 January, matchday. We arrived at the training ground just before midday for a short video session. I wanted to tweak the way we were going to play in the centre of the pitch. That'll be key, I am sure. They have two holding midfielders and we're going to put three players there, including Victor who will also have to help the centre-backs out, as they'll be facing a front-three.

The journey to the stadium was slow and we needed a police escort to make way for us. A slow-moving van was leading us but nobody seemed to want to make way. 'Come on!' some were shouting. We got to White Hart Lane a little later than planned, with just an hour to go until kick-off.

We found out their starting XI while still on the coach. It was the line-up that we expected.

In the dressing room Jesús reminded the players about set-pieces. We put Chelsea's line-up on the board in their usual formation before heading out for the warm-up.

Nobody was nervous. The players were buzzing.

The match got underway.

The first half was even and intense. Chelsea didn't create any clear-cut chances aside from one opportunity where Hugo Lloris showed just how well he's been doing. Their player was through one-on-one, but instead of rushing out, as everyone does or he would've done three years ago, he stayed back, bought himself time, allowing the defender to get back and, at the same time, reducing the angle. If he'd moved away from his goal line too early, they would've scored.

We took the lead in stoppage time on the stroke of half-time, through a wonderful Dele Alli header to finish off a Christian Eriksen cross.

As the referee blew his whistle, Jesús and I headed to the dressing room without saying anything. Miguel had already been there for a few minutes to analyse the footage that our analyst had collated from the stands.

First things first: I drink so much water to relax during games that I inevitably have to go the toilet as soon as the first half ends.

I decided not to use anything from the video. I just told them to keep playing as they were with the same aggression with and without the ball. Jesús showed three set-pieces.

We lost some of our momentum in the second half and they had a chance to equalise, but I felt we didn't need to change anything – sometimes it's best to wait till the storm passes. Our wing-backs were getting into one-on-one situations and we had control of the central channel. We always had an extra man and Victor was everywhere. Despite having dropped our rhythm slightly, we managed to score our second goal, in the 54th minute through Alli again.

I could see that Dembélé was tiring and needed to be replaced, but I didn't want to rush.

I asked my colleagues what they thought, but I remained convinced about the direction in which the game was heading and decided to hold off making the substitution for a bit. Finally Winks went on for

Dembélé in the 74th minute and with him we regained control after a difficult spell. There's so much talk about experience. Some players have so many years and games under their belts, but lack experience or an understanding of the game. Harry Winks plays as if he's been doing so for over ten years.

We won.

During the press conference, I said that it was just one game and three points, and that to win trophies, you need to keep up that level of intensity against all opposition. I praised Jesús, whom I described as my right hand, left hand and eyes, and I also cleared up the Guardiola issue.

Daniel came down to the Manager's Room. He was pleased with our performance. He told us that it was a game that half the world had watched.

We're third, two points behind second-placed Liverpool and seven behind Chelsea.

Today marks my 150th Premier League game.

Tomorrow is a rest day.

*

I'm sitting on the sofa by myself. The echoes from today's game are still running through my head. I'm not drinking any wine.

Jesús has just sent me a message. He says that the press conference was good because I didn't make the win all about me and our tactical decisions.

The chairman also sent me a WhatsApp saying that he can't sleep either from the excitement.

*

After the Chelsea game, I stated that Dele Alli is one of the most important players to have emerged in English football in recent years. Four of his seven goals this season before the turn of the year came in December, and he's already scored four in two games so far this month. On top of that, two of them were in a big game. The statistic that we've seen this morning is remarkable. He's scored more in his first fifty league games than Steven Gerrard, Wayne Rooney and Frank Lampard . . . He may go on to be better than all of them because he has the quality; now he just needs consistency.

There's an urban legend that says that I didn't want to sign him. It's not true. I went to watch a League Cup tie between Milton Keynes Dons and Van Gaal's Manchester United on 26 August 2014. I told Paul Mitchell, who was joining us at Tottenham, that we'd have an early dinner to celebrate his birthday and then we'd go to watch the game because there were two young players that I wanted to see: a full-back and a 17-year-old Dele Alli. MK Dons ran out 4–0 winners and Dele played in midfield in front of the defence. He was fantastic and displayed real ability and personality . . . I left before the end – no need to stay any longer.

We kept tracking him and had the chance to sign him in January 2015. After a game against West Brom, I had a meeting at the training ground with the chairman, Paul, Jesús and John McDermott. We decided to cough up the £5 million, an astronomical figure for a League One player. We loaned him straight back to MK Dons for six months, but asked him to come to train with us twice a week to get to know his new teammates and our way of working. He would get changed in the youth-team dressing room. Everything has an order and a time.

The following pre-season was demanding and I had to draw his attention to certain things, so that he wouldn't get confused and could iron out some aspects of his behaviour. I was strict with him and he started to work hard. Jesús said to him one day in front of me: 'The manager didn't like you at all in your first two weeks here. Now he adores you.'

He started playing in the Premier League, but two games in I called him into my office because I could see that he was struggling despite having scored in his second league game. I showed him some videos of his performances and also training sessions. He wasn't giving 100 per cent. Dele's face said, 'I can't believe I did that.' I said to him, 'It's just as easy to take you out of the team as it was to put you in it.'

Around November, he started to cement a starting berth. He was developing and also making waves with the national team. And he has something else I love and that I mentioned after the CSKA game this season. He is 'naughty', with that streetwise intelligence that can't be taught.

The danger remains, as is often the case, that he'll forget what has got him to this point. I've had to repeat that to him this season. The other risk is whether those around him know how to treat a top-level professional. His WhatsApp photo of a cartoon of a boy surrounded by people who all want a piece of him suggests that he needs to be surrounded by the right people.

He's only 20 years old.

*

We're going to see how the troops are today after a rest day. Our next game is in the FA Cup against Aston Villa on the 8th, which is an opportunity for some of the boys who don't usually play, such as Vorm, Wimmer, Ben Davies, Carter-Vickers and Janssen. We're the team that picked up the best results over the festive period for the third season in a row. I have to admit we were lucky with the fixture schedule this year, but it does still seem to confirm that we always cruise through this part of the year. After the Chelsea game, you might have expected a certain level of euphoria, but we know that we have a jam-packed January and February ahead of us. No time to rest on our laurels.

We're planning to interview candidates for the new chief scout position before today's press conference, where I'll certainly be asked about Lamela who's going to Rome. He has an injury that we thought would clear up in a day or two, but it's been troubling him for two and a half months. He needs a change of scenery it seems.

My throat is hurting a bit. Toni has the flu meaning he didn't come in today and he was missed. He must be really ill to miss training. He didn't feel well on the day of the Chelsea game. Certain things are perceived badly in the world of football and it makes me laugh. Weakness is apparently one of them. Simon Felstein was surprised back at the start when I admitted I'd slept badly or that my neck or back hurt. I prefer to be open in all areas, otherwise it comes back to bite you.

The good thing is that I have been doing exercise. Today I was on the running machine with Miki while watching Manchester United. The diet is punishing me, but I'm certainly losing weight.

*

Luis Enrique has announced that he's leaving Barcelona and *Sport*, among other newspapers, has singled me out as a potential successor. My initial thought is that I must be doing something right in order to be considered. Whether or not it's a true story is another matter. As is whether I'd accept such an approach, based on where I am at present and the club in question. Espanyol was my club, so I would never go to Barcelona.

*

I liked hearing Eric Dier say that if we don't win a trophy with the squad that we have, we'll feel very disappointed in five years' time. That's the attitude of a winner. In the words of Napoleon, 'Great ambition is the passion of a great character. Those endowed with it may perform very good or very bad acts. All depends on the principles which direct them.'

Harry Kane spoke in similar terms: 'Something is happening here. I'd be surprised if any of my teammates would go now. We just need to take that last step, which is to win trophies.'

He said 'trophies'. In the plural.

*

Today, four days after the Chelsea game, we have played the home cup tie against Aston Villa, a big club currently languishing in the Championship. Toni is back after two days laid up in bed. He still looks slightly under the weather, but he wanted to be here because Michel Vorm was starting the game.

It was a tricky game in which we struggled going forward. I brought Alli on for Janssen, which boosted our movement. The Dutchman came here to contribute in many ways and made a promising start to the season, but now the demands of the game here are weighing him down and he's struggling. I'll speak to him tomorrow. He has to offer more in training and in matches. I know that he can.

It was goalless at the interval. I decided to bring on a pacey wide player in the 70th minute (N'Koudou) in place of one of our centre-backs (not young Carter-Vickers, but Alderweireld) because they only had one man up top.

Goal-kick by Vorm in the 71st minute. The ball reaches N'Koudou who crosses it in and on the end of it is . . . our full-back! It was Ben Davies' first goal for Tottenham, what a moment. Luck hasn't been on his side until now. He gets forward, but there have been no sign of goals before today. Ben is an extraordinary guy. He's always ready to

184

train hard and possesses real quality. Son rounded off the scoring ten minutes later to make it 2–0 and we made it through to the fourth round.

*

We've had a full week of training, which doesn't happen often. It's important to enjoy calmer periods. We gave the players time off: Sunday and Monday for those who didn't play against Aston Villa and also today, Tuesday, for those who did. The first important training session ahead of West Brom will be tomorrow. They're always tough opponents and our last two meetings have ended all-square. We haven't actually beaten them at home since 2012.

We've drawn League Two outfit Wycombe Wanderers in the FA Cup fourth round.

Rumours are doing the rounds that both Manchester clubs want our full-backs.

I've lost four kilograms.

*

Since Wednesday, we had only one training session per day for the rest of the week. After about an hour of ball work almost every day, we headed home between three and six o'clock, allowing us to spend more time with our families. Energy levels are being restored and I feel personally refreshed.

*

Saturday 14 January. We beat West Brom 4–0. Our home form has been sensational, with six wins on the spin.

We seem to be on a mission to bid farewell to White Hart Lane by leaving a fitting legacy and reminding everyone of what a difficult place it was for visiting teams. We dominated throughout and our first-half display was up there with the best football we've played this season; we went in at the break two goals to the good, one of which came from Harry Kane, who ended up notching a hat-trick. The only sour note was the injury to Jan Vertonghen, who'll be out for a couple of months. Opportunity knocks for someone else.

We've moved second. We keep progressing. Let's see how far we can go.

*

I gave an interview to Argentinian newspaper *La Nación*. I'm not all that well known in my homeland. I said that I don't need shows of affection from the public to make me feel good about myself. I don't seek popular acclaim; the support of my loved ones, my friends and family, is enough for me. Was I being totally sincere? Pretty much.

I also opened up at one of my press conferences about another key feature of our philosophy: the fact that there's no such thing as perfection, but we always aim for it and will never be happy to settle for less.

*

17 January. Since the beginning of the year . . .
    I've gone 16 days without drinking a glass of wine.
    I've dedicated 16 hours to my health.
    And I've already lost almost five kilograms.

*

With no game until tomorrow, Saturday, we've been able to take advantage of this week to go over concepts that we hadn't touched on since pre-season. We've managed to get a good amount done and the players have been receptive.

The line-up for tomorrow's game was decided in part by a plate of lasagne. We'd agreed to meet the squad at midday today. At 11.30, my staff and I were debating our team selection and there were two players in contention for one spot. The lads filtered in and variously ordered themselves some coffee, juice or a piece of toast. And then one of the aforementioned pair helped himself to some lasagne. Our first reaction was to laugh: who in their right mind would scoff down a plate of lasagne an hour before training? But that was precisely the point: based on this insight into the lasagne-eater's frame of mind, the other guy got the nod for the final place in the starting XI.

We revealed the team, trained and then travelled to Manchester.

*

We were second-best against Manchester City.

Jesús noticed in the warm-up that the team weren't as pumped up as they should've been. City had lost 4–0 to Everton six days earlier, whereas we went into the game on a high. The upshot was that our players did not feel the right amount of tension. Not good.

Off-the-ball play proved to be the difference. They put the squeeze on us, forcing us into errors and making it difficult for us to regain possession. And whoever won the ball back quicker was always going to be able to attack more effectively.

Such was their stranglehold in the middle of the park that we had to make changes. One option would've been to push Dele Alli into a deeper role, while the other, which we plumped for, was to switch from three at the back to four, with Eric Dier – who had started at centre-half – stepping into midfield. By doing so, we managed to slightly curtail the dominance City had enjoyed in the first 25 minutes.

Still, we were lucky to go into half-time at 0–0.

We decided to bring off one of the defenders and Wimmer, having been booked, was the fall guy. But should we introduce another central midfielder or a more attacking player like Son, so that their backline had something to think about? We opted for the latter.

I gave the lads a necessary talking-to: 'I don't care about how we play, our style or our defensive set-up. All that's irrelevant; if we're not more aggressive, it's futile. It's a matter of attitude: either we match their aggression on and off the ball, or this game is as good as lost.'

Son provided us with an outlet for long passes in behind their defence. But a comedy of errors led to City opening the scoring four minutes after the break. Shortly afterwards, they doubled the score-line following a swift counter-attack. Both goals were avoidable and came from the types of moves that we'd flagged up prior to the game. City would've gone on to crush a lesser team, but we responded and reduced the deficit just four minutes later, getting ourselves right back into the game.

I think it was the thought of being on the brink of humiliation that jolted our players into life. As a group, we showed that we won't lie down.

Toby got injured and instead of putting on Ben Davies at left-back, I dropped Wanyama back into defence and introduced Harry Winks, who gave us more control. Suddenly, in the last 20 minutes, we realised that we had the upper hand physically. City had done a lot of sprinting and covered a lot of ground. Our equaliser, in which Winks had a hand, was in part a consequence of the opposition's tired legs and delayed reactions.

2–2. We were happy with the result – it was the most we deserved.

The refereeing was one of the main topics at the post-match press conference, but I always keep in mind that more contact is allowed in England than elsewhere in Europe. The fact that fouls aren't awarded in many instances involving contact explains why there are so many turnovers, and it's the same for both sides. The problem is that we're not able to play with the same defensive intensity in European competitions.

I bumped into Guardiola after the game. 'You've got to tell me all about Monaco,' he said to me.

'What?' I replied, not understanding at first. City are up against them in the next round of the Champions League.

*

After the game, we set off for Barcelona. All of us except Lamela. Vertonghen travelled wearing a protective boot. The poor guy – we went on the same trip this time last year and he was on crutches.

We got to the hotel at 3 a.m. and gave the squad the Sunday off.

I used the day to pick up the car I keep at my house in the city and gave my best tour-guide impression for some of the players. We stopped off at a small shop to buy Spanish ham, then I took them to the Zona Alta (a high-lying, upscale part of town), after which we headed down to Espanyol's training ground, where I pointed out the tower on which Miki used to practically risk his life to film training sessions. Then we returned to the hotel and went for tapas. In the afternoon, Miki and I had agreed to work out together in the hotel gym. While we were pedalling on the exercise bikes, we switched on Chelsea's game against Hull and saw what happened to Ryan Mason.

It was a horrific clash of heads. Seven or eight minutes passed and the kid didn't get up. The commentators were lost for words. In the end he was stretchered off with his eyes closed.

In the evening, we all went for dinner. While we were there, we found out that Ryan had fractured his skull. I'd already left a message with his girlfriend, whom I met when the two of them came round to our place for dinner one day so that Karina could give them some advice about nutrition and diet. John McDermott had been in touch with his dad, who told him that Ryan wants to see us as soon as possible. We'll go to visit him when we get back.

We trained at Montjuïc on Monday morning. Since we'd had such trouble bringing the ball out from the back against City, we devoted a whole hour of the session to that. 'Think about one thing,' I told them. 'Even if you make a mistake passing the ball out, you won't be penalised. You won't concede goals because of it, as there's always someone on hand to cover your back and get a foot in. Or because the opposition still have to put the ball in the net, which is never easy. Playing long balls is worse, because if the opposition win possession and we're in disarray, that's when they can cause the most damage.'

Harry Kane has made the same point, if not in those exact words, in several interviews. And he's done so with conviction: his way of thinking has changed, which is the hardest thing to do.

The squad recorded a video to send to Ryan. After the training session the lads were free to spend the day as they pleased, with an 11 p.m. curfew.

That was Monday. Yesterday, after work on the pitch, I had something to show the players. Since we've been training at the Olympic Stadium, the press team made the most of the opportunity to tweet a video of the long-range strike I scored past Zubizarreta there, in a game against Valencia. The clip included my celebration, in which I pushed my teammates and yelled out *golazo*. I made sure everyone watched it. In the evening, my staff and I went to celebrate Sebas's birthday at Espai Kru.

Today is our last day in Barcelona. We're drinking *mate* in the sun.

*

It is Thursday. Jesús, John, Allan and I went to see Ryan.

We'd heard that he'd perked up a bit, which was good news, but you never know. He made for quite a sight, all swollen. He'd had to go under the knife and have his scalp cut open, and he hadn't been very talkative previously, but we were pleasantly surprised when he spent three-quarters of an hour chatting away completely lucidly with us. He told us that what had happened was a result of the position in which he plays, as a central midfielder who defends balls that come in from wide. This is something that he never used to do before, but which he added to his game under our stewardship.

Ryan always showed himself to be intelligent. Without that, you can't go from the sidelines to being an international in the space of eight months. He overcame his limitations through hard work. He's a warm, humble person. A real role model. I miss him.

Lamela is coming back from Rome today. Depending on how his recovery goes, he could be like a new signing for the second half of the season.

*

28 January. I need to jot down a few observations about the FA Cup tie against Wycombe, of League Two, at White Hart Lane.

We went 2–0 down, before pulling it back to 2–2 thanks in part to three substitutions, which helped us take command. Then Trippier got injured and we had to play the last 25 minutes with ten men. They scored a third, but two goals at the death through Dele Alli and Son Heung-min, in the 89th and 97th minutes, turned it around and handed us a 4–3 win.

Why did we make such heavy weather of it?

They scored from their first chance. Buoyed, they went on to win a penalty. They had a towering centre-forward who made every long ball stick. These sorts of matches are very difficult to control. When you make four or five changes to your starting XI, your coherence suffers, but if the fringe figures don't play in a match like this one, when will they? In these types of situations, the opposition get their tails up if you don't dampen their enthusiasm with an early goal. What's more, dead balls serve as a leveller for lower-league sides because contact, shirt-pulling and little kicks are tolerated more than usual. If you con- stantly applied the rules against such teams, there would be stoppages every minute and the game would be continually interrupted, which isn't the done thing here.

Anyway . . . it was a lot of fun!

*

Today is Tuesday and it's the last day of January. As planned, we have not signed anybody. We round off the month this evening away to Sunderland, who lie bottom of the table. Since beating Chelsea,

Antonio Conte's side have won both of their league games, while we've won one and drawn with City. I wasn't very pleased with the first-half performance against the latter or against Wycombe.

*

Disappointing.

We never reached top gear; we were once again lacking that little something that makes the difference between being champions and missing out, between winning a game and not winning it. In the first half, we weren't ourselves: we offered very little attacking aggression and, correspondingly, zero defensive aggression. We were up against a goal-shy team, but were only managing to win the ball back in our own box. In fact, we recovered possession closer to our goal than in any other match this season. We wasted the first 45 minutes and although we dominated and created chances in the second half, we couldn't take them.

0–0.

We stay second, because Arsenal lost 2–1 to Watford.

It's very much two points dropped.

8.

FEBRUARY

*D*rawn to face Gent in the Europa League last 32 and Championship outfit Fulham in the FA Cup, Tottenham's three league games of the month were headlined by the trip to Anfield to face Liverpool.

After the Sunderland match, we weren't sure whether our flight was going to be able to depart Sunderland or land in London owing to fog. We ended up arriving home at 2 a.m., but that didn't stop us from getting into the training ground bright and early this morning to analyse the game.

The next thing we've got to do is clear: enlist some influential players who are willing to pass on our disillusionment over yesterday's performance, as well as some of the solutions, to the rest. Today I asked Kane, Dembélé and Lloris to come by my office. It's not so much a question of putting pressure on them – the impact of external motivation is only fleeting. Certain players were below par and we're going to give them a wake-up call, but we want the dressing-room leaders to help us go further than that.

We need the lads not just to understand but to take to heart the team's principles and the fact that if we stray from them, our chances of winning are diminished. And the idea that footballers who don't stay true to their essence become much-diminished versions of themselves. Last year, Kane suffered a ten-game scoring drought during which his mind was awash with doubts: 'Maybe I'm moving around too much, maybe I'm wearing myself out, maybe ...' He was consumed by everything the press and his camp were saying. But if Kane didn't run his socks off, if he didn't put himself about and instead simply waited for the ball to reach him, he wouldn't be Kane, or wouldn't get the best of himself. And the same applies to the others.

It's up to the coaching staff to lay out the demands and raise the bar constantly. But it is not enough. The high standards at Barcelona, Real Madrid, Bayern Munich and Juventus are ingrained. They don't sign players to get into the Champions League, but rather to win things. And to keep winning. It's the be-all and end-all. If you don't win, they get rid of you. Arrigo Sacchi spoke about this very subject in a report that was aired on a French channel the other day, which Lloris brought to our attention: a crucial ingredient for success is a club's culture. In other words, the ethos, the rules, deep-seated things that must be respected and which serve as a yardstick.

Not so long ago, finishing fifth was fine and it was good enough just to give one of the big boys a scare. Now we're trying to create those standards that are present at the big clubs. But we know a mentality like the one at the likes of Real Madrid doesn't come about overnight – and nor does the ability to thrive under the pressure of constantly having to win.

What's encouraging is that this team no longer have the same shortcomings as two and a half years ago. And they were really angry about dropping points against Sunderland. That's a good sign.

After that disappointing draw, the following message did the rounds among the four members of the coaching staff on WhatsApp:

'Dogs and wolves are the same, except for one difference: dogs live at home, food and water are provided and they sleep in their owner's bed. Wolves, meanwhile, live on mountains, have to find their own food and somewhere to kip . . . I want a team full of hungry and ambitious wolves.' (Boza Maljkovic)

We also shared it with the players.

*

When things don't go well for you as a player, you can look for a new team or work hard to earn back your place and the coach's trust. Obviously, the first option is more straightforward.

Eric Dier has rediscovered his focus. He's making good decisions again and understanding his limits. We mustn't forget that he's 23 and has only just reached the top.

I recently saw him in the gym doing intense exercise. I went up to him and said: 'Eric is back.'

*

One day when I was in Newell's reserves, I was invited to train with the first team under coach José Yudica. I was 17, young and hungry. Not scared of anybody, cocky even. I was picked to play against the starting line-up that was set to face Rosario Central that weekend in a traditionally heated derby.

Tata Martino, one of the Central team leaders, received a pass and I went in on him hard. He turned around and said to me, 'Kid, I'm going to kill you.'

The Central coach shouted, 'How could you do that to Martino?'

'Sorry, sorry,' I responded.

Tata said, 'I don't want to see you within three metres of me. I'm putting a restraining order on you.' When I was back in the dressing room, getting changed before heading back home and annoyed by my lack of tact, the fitness coach said to me, 'You're going to be in the squad this weekend.'

And that's how I ended up travelling with the first team. That *clásico* was part of a series of fixtures played in Buenos Aires. I made my debut 15 minutes from the end of a game at Vélez. I also got a 15-minute run-out away at Ferro. I kept training with the first team. One day, our centre-back Jorge Pautasso got injured and I started playing alongside Jorge Theiler. We established ourselves as the new centre-back pairing, even after Pautasso returned from his lay-off. That was in mid-to-late 1989. Eight months after my arrival, Bielsa was brought in as coach.

I see myself in every player making his first-team debut. And also in Yudica. Someone has to give you that first opportunity. When they open the door to you, make sure it never shuts again. Young players, when they get their first opportunity, must overcome two sizeable enemies: fear and insecurity.

Ferguson told me that when he took over at United, there was only one first-team player under twenty-four and he thought that was a mistake. 'They say fortune favours the brave.' Maybe other managers think it's easier to win trophies with experienced players, but Sir Alex and I both see that as a 'laugh now, cry later' approach. I understand that this business is geared towards immediate success and it's rare to find someone like Daniel who is willing to take a longer-term view in terms of building a team. Something else is also needed: in order to create your own identity and a winning mentality, you need players who dream of reaching the first team, like Harry Kane or Harry Winks.

And who'll always remember who gave them that first opportunity.

*

We were 2–0 up at home to Aston Villa last season. It's a tight scoreline because it just takes a slice of luck or a moment of magic for the complexion of the game to change drastically. Although we were playing well, Jordan Ayew scored to make it 2–1 and the atmosphere in the stadium turned. You could almost feel the nerves.

Instead of bringing on an experienced defender, I handed a debut to Josh Onomah, an England Under-19 international midfielder. Such decisions can boost confidence levels, which drives everyone forward and, in turn, improves performance.

Someone recently said to me that it must be easier to bring through talented youngsters at Southampton or Tottenham than at Manchester United or Chelsea. 'Why's that?' I asked.

'They are less demanding,' they replied.

'Oh really? And they don't sack managers at Southampton and Tottenham if they lose games?'

*

Academy chief John McDermott told me what Sir Alex Ferguson recommended to Ryan Giggs when he started his career as a coach. 'Arrive early. Speak with the lady that makes the tea. Go to see the people in charge of the laundry and the press team, even if it's just to say hi. When things turn sour, they're the ones who'll always be with you.'

I often head to John's office which is on the same floor as mine, but in another wing of the building at the training ground that I call 'the House'. Just like at home, everything is informal and free-flowing, with him and with everybody else. We share information and ideas. I have great respect for his job and I don't interfere. Sometimes I ask him to send up a few youth players to train with the first team. I know their names. Whenever they train with us, I thank them for their efforts. Sometimes John comes up with any old excuse to bring an academy player to see me, such as George Marsh this week, a tough-tackling holding midfielder – even if it's just for a couple of minutes. They always appreciate the hug as much as I do.

On the first day when we spoke, John asked me what I needed.

I told him, 'First of all the boys have to respect the team, work hard and be honest, good people. Then they have to be smart, fast, physically fit and have good technique and – this one is important – they should come here full of internal motivation and not expect their fathers or the coach to set the level of demand. The message is clear: if you're responsible in your life, you'll also be so on the pitch. If you acquire the right principles off the pitch, you'll apply them in football. That's how we can have faith in you. 'And they have to believe.'

'Believe? What do you mean?' John asked. I explained it means having faith in what we're bringing to the table. And if we don't . . . That is not good news. Howard Wilkinson told John that he calls that stage FIFO: 'Fit in or fuck off'. You can't only be at 99 per cent belief, it needs to be 100 per cent. If you can't manage that, it doesn't mean you're a bad person. It just means you don't fit in here.

That's the theory.

The problem is that a footballer's psychology is directed towards self-defence. They don't want to get too close to their coaches because they don't want to put themselves in a position where they might get hurt. Maybe they think that someone who hugs them today might drop them from the team tomorrow. That can't be negated with a chat or a second hug.

We offer a learning experience that can be applied to football and life, we suggest a way. 'Sell, not yell,' as they say in English. But it doesn't always work which is when you have to mark your territory.

When we arrived, Tottenham used to be a side without any real battling spirit. We had to instil habits on and off the pitch, because there were only very limited training and disciplinary protocols in place. We demanded the squad train consistently and systematically, and we introduced tests to monitor performance in sessions. The players needed to be whipped back into peak shape and injury-prevention practices had to be instituted. Our style requires steadfast commitment and a lot of risk, so it was paramount that some fundamentals be established. Certain big names had got too comfortable – for example, one player who had been at the club for many years no longer came in for training on Mondays – but we gave them the chance to make mistakes and rethink things. It took us four months to approach the desired threshold and prompt a drastic transformation among the players.

All search for identity requires a deep understanding of where you are, a sensible analysis of consequences of any decision, and the courage to lead the club in the direction you want. When you apply all that to every minute of the day, answers and solutions arrive naturally, and the path gets slowly shaped. Some players came on board, others did not – not everyone accepted the changes and there was a lot of tension. In our first season in charge, we took the step not to have the team spend the night at a hotel all together before the League Cup final against Mourinho's Chelsea, because we felt doing so wouldn't help them: the tension created by the transition we were living would have inundated everything. It was best that people just came to play the game.

The day after we lost that match, one of our own players sang the José Mourinho chant to Jésus's face. That is what we had to contend with.

Since our arrival, players had to understand which values were on the up and which were on the down. Tom Carroll went through this process. He made a very good start to pre-season in the United States, but Michael Dawson hit the ball into his face which left him stunned and dizzy. The protocol for head injuries came into play. He had to train on his own, but he wanted to be on the ball and with the group. That frustration caused him to lose respect for Jesús. I made it very clear to him that if anyone caused a fuss with Jesús, the doctor or Miguel, they were also doing so with me, as they were an extension of me. Once that has been explained to the player, if he learns, the matter is forgotten. If not, our relationship reaches breaking point. Danny Rose, Jan Vertonghen, Eric Dier, Moussa Sissoko and a few others have gone through just that. Those who have stayed are those who understand the new rules.

I often talk to Marcelo Bielsa about how times have changed in terms of player development. It's true that there's been a transformation, but it's our responsibility for players to be reacquainted with aspects of the game that are being lost. The boy that plays football today is the same as forty years ago. He feels the same when he touches the ball, even if it isn't made of leather and the pitch is artificial rather than grass. The academy coach has to be a teacher, first and foremost, who transmits those life values and is more focused on the future than the here and now.

Whenever I walk around our magnificent training ground in the afternoon, with all the expertly maintained pitches, I stop to watch training or games involving the boys from eight through to 12. I observe them very carefully: do they react in the same way that we did, would they go without food or sleep to keep playing? The answer is yes. The problem is that their passion for the game dies sooner these days because when a boy dribbles past three players, there are several people queuing up to be his agent and promising him fame and fortune. When the game turns into a profession, you start to lose your desire to play.

I often think about Dele Alli's WhatsApp photo. John says that when the trough is full, the pigs come from all over to feed. The coach used to be the dominant voice, but now the player listens to so many others, especially those who promise the world. On top of that, there's a certain lack of integrity at some clubs regarding which teenagers are chosen and their wage structures.

The paradox is that many of the aspects that curtail a player's enjoyment of the game are, in part, what brought us here in the first place:

we wouldn't earn so much if football didn't generate so much money.

The Argentinian writer José Narosky says that whoever exchanges happiness for money can't exchange money for happiness. In that context, how can we get teenagers and their parents to believe in our way of doing things when other clubs offer higher salaries? That's our battle. If you ask Cameron Carter-Vickers to run into a wall, he'll say, 'Do you want me to do it twice?' But that isn't common.

What type of society are we building where only success, money and material possessions matter? It's certainly not a very spiritual world. John McDermott told me that the main cause of death among 18 to 35-year-olds in the Western world used to be road accidents. Now it's suicide.

The world is confused.

What's in these young players' minds? What makes them so desperate? You have to try to understand them, although that's often rather laborious. Five minutes before the warm-up, when their boots are on and their shin pads and kits are in place, practically all of them take another look at their mobiles. Is it that important to know if you have a new message right at that time? It doesn't make sense. Their heads should be focused on training, improving, putting in the effort and enjoying what they're about to experience. But how can you prevent them from checking their phones if they all do it? When they get back, they do it again. Banning it would create conflict. My job is to make them see that they should approach training and the profession differently.

I was told that John showed the Under-16s and Under-18s one of my recent press conferences in which I spoke about our philosophy. That's also a way of transmitting values. Sometimes I watch those sides play, and the Under-21s as well. But my analysis of them as players won't be complete until I've seen them defend against Harry Kane or break away from Victor Wanyama.

Most will get their chance. Once we've opened the door, our job consists of shaping the environment in which players can channel their energy; we try to give them confidence and allow them to express themselves. But the source of that energy comes from their own motivation; we can't constantly keep up that level of passion all season long or throughout a player's career. That passion has to be accompanied by rationality. We need to shape their way of thinking, so that they want to do what we want them to do.

Breaking into the first team is but the first chapter of many. They must then develop the right mentality in order to stay with us and keep improving. Harry Kane is the perfect example: a player who understood us, took on new habits and is now making the most of each and every one of his qualities.

He was a frustrated guy when I arrived. He struggled to visualise his future at the club, with two or three strikers ahead of him in the pecking order and he was constantly being shipped out on loan. It was doubly exasperating for him as a Tottenham fan. The club then suddenly hired an Argentinian coach and I picked up on his sense of resignation: 'I'm sure this guy will bring in some other big-name striker.' It was a tough few months because we didn't click initially. He was out of form and, at 21, had the habits of a player in his thirties, the type that has been around the block.

Human beings tend to naturally settle and stop doing those small things that are so essential if you want to keep winning. I had several stern conversations with Harry in which I had to make him understand that he had to get ready for whenever the opportunity might arise. Fame and a hefty transfer fee don't pave the way to a starting berth, only hard work. Harry was humble enough to listen and take advice. We put the tools in place for him to improve. The moment finally arrived for him. He played and then played again. By seeing his progress the boys coming up through the ranks realised that we kept our word.

Kane is a warrior now. He already was, but he didn't know he had it in him. I'm not speaking about qualities or traits, but that absolutely essential mental strength to be able to stay in the elite. I believe Harry Kane is the best player in the world in terms of mental strength, willpower and endeavour. He is completely focused on his football. He has a house in Essex but spends the week at another one that he owns closer to the training ground. He's the first person to arrive and the last to leave. He likes to join in when someone with different experiences in football comes to visit it. He enjoys sitting down with us, soaking it all up and also participating in the discussions. At those times it is as though for him nothing else in the world exists. We both enjoy marvellous little football moments when they occur.

*

If I were to move into international management one day, I'd relish the opportunity to coach the England national team. I've heard that I've been considered for the job before, but I don't know if there was any truth in it. I'd be reunited with loads of familiar faces: Harry Kane, Danny Rose, Dele Alli, Eric Dier, Adam Lallana ... Of the last 21 England debutants, 17 have played under me: there's also the likes of Rickie Lambert, Jay Rodriguez, Calum Chambers, Nathaniel Clyne, Luke Shaw and Ryan Mason ... In the last four and a half seasons, 11 regulars in the England squad made their international debuts while under my stewardship.

I remember once telling Lallana how taken aback I was when I first witnessed the mentality of English players up-close – their eagerness and enthusiasm in training, the sparks that fly in 50-50 challenges. Lallana himself was once so angry with a decision during a training match that he blew his top and swore at Miki (who was serving as the referee, as he often does). He subsequently apologised, but I thought to myself, 'I want guys like that in my team.' The English are brave, honest and aggressive, and the good ones want to add to their game.

We see all of those things in the lads at our academy ... until they start getting confused by the stuff I was talking about before.

*

The season continues to present us with exciting challenges. In the Europa League we've been drawn against Gent; we have the potential to go far in this competition. We're through to the FA Cup fifth round, just a few matches away from the final. But we've been giving off mixed messages. Do we have what it takes or not? Are we in it to win? Do we really want it? Are we the wolves or the dogs?

Over the course of this week, we've kept pushing the guys who still have more to give; we've asked the team's main men to try to drive us on from within. And we've also been visited by some old friends: Florin Răducioiu, my former Espanyol teammate, and Dimitar Berbatov, who – after seeing the training ground and getting a glimpse of some details from the new stadium – said that this is a bigger club than Manchester United. Sometimes we place too much stock in big buildings. He told me he'd love to sign for Tottenham again and that if I was looking for a striker, he had been training – he lives between London and Bulgaria – and was ready to go. I don't know whether he was being serious or not. I think he was. It reminded me of one time when we were looking for a goalkeeper at Espanyol. A former pro offered his services and claimed he was still fit because he swam with his daughter twice a week. It's easy to lose sight of how extraordinarily far apart elite sport is.

In the briefing on Friday, I outlined the strengths and weaknesses of Aitor Karanka's Middlesbrough, our upcoming opponents, who are languishing in the lower reaches of the table. I also told the players that they knew as well as I did what had happened in the previous three games (against Wycombe in the FA Cup, and Chelsea and Sunderland in the league), and that I was expecting a different demeanour from each and every one of them.

On Saturday afternoon, Chelsea beat Arsenal 3–1 to move 12 points ahead of us – we're still second.

Ours was the late match that day. It turned out to be a decent display. We controlled the game and created twenty chances against a team who sat very deep. We didn't make the breakthrough in the first half, but Kane scored a penalty in the second. Middlesbrough didn't threaten once . . . until the last minute. We nearly dropped two points.

Following back-to-back draws, we finally got back to winning ways in the league in what was my 100th game in charge of Tottenham. We remain the only side who are still unbeaten at home. Next up, we take on Liverpool at Anfield.

*

Everton's Ross Barkley celebrated a goal against Bournemouth before scoring, after rounding the keeper but before having put the ball in the net. It was their sixth goal and in the 94th minute (6–3 was the final result). Sport gives you grounds to cry and rejoice, but we must never forget that it's our duty to promote good values: you must never disrespect your opponents. You should want to win, to destroy them, but there are lines that can't be crossed.

*

Adam Lallana has told me that he has very fond memories of the dinner that Nicola Cortese organised in his honour after he signed his last contract at Southampton. Adam, his wife, his family and the coaching staff were all there. Lallana had spoken very highly of me to his dad, but we were yet to meet. We enjoyed the meal, accompanied by some fine red wine, and his father, who is a real gentleman, witnessed our great rapport with his own eyes. We both went away with a good impression; it made me better understand why Adam is the way he is. His son is going to be a mascot at Anfield this weekend. By the way, Adam hasn't trained for Liverpool all week, but I'm convinced he's going to come back to haunt us.

*

This period of the season has confirmed certain impressions that we've had about the team for weeks, months even. That we can only compete with the best if we're firing on all cylinders. When we go off the boil, we can get steamrollered, as was the case today at Anfield.

It'd been a while since we'd felt this powerless.

You can get a feel for a match's outcome and what sort of mood our players are in within the opening 50 seconds. Liverpool went into the game defiant, their pride dented after a run of three points from a possible 15, including a loss to Hull last time out. The Reds were sensational, displaying conviction and ambition going forward, and making the most of their quality in central midfield and up front. They could've scored three times in five minutes, when we'd conceded only 16 goals in our previous 24 league games.

We once again succumbed to the backlash from a wounded powerhouse. Mané, Lallana and Wijnaldum all showed us up with their ability, their pace and their mental strength.

Our team structure, the organisation, papers over many cracks when individuals make mistakes. Today was one of those days when taking action can only make things worse, so you're best off doing nothing. You just have to keep calm. What can you do?

The verdict is clear: having been unable to haul in Leicester City last season, it's going to be at least as difficult for us to reel in Chelsea this time round. Not because of Chelsea's level, but rather because we need to give much more.

In the last three seasons, we've won only once away to the top sides, which was against Man City. That stat was doing the rounds in the press today, but we actually analysed it a couple of weeks ago. We've also fallen short in the Champions League. It's the same old story. And after games like today's, we've got to do some deep and honest soul-searching. It'll be painful, but we'll come out of it stronger.

Both attitude and ability matter, but where does one begin and the other end? Who is responsible for the mistakes? Every time they caught us out they got a shot off, and as time passed they made us feel small, breaking us physically and psychologically. The opening 25 minutes made us think that we're not ready to win the title.

I didn't rant and rave at half-time, or gesticulate wildly. I didn't even raise my voice, but I made myself clear: we all knew what was missing. 'Lads,' I said, 'this isn't good enough. This isn't what football's about.'

We came out with a better attitude in the second half, but we were 2–0 down by then (Mané got both goals, incidentally) and all we were able to do was keep them at bay.

Manchester City have leapfrogged us, so we've dropped down to third place, level on points with Arsenal and ten behind Chelsea. It's very tight around us: we're two points ahead of sixth-placed United, while fifth-placed Liverpool are a point away.

*

It's Sunday today and we've got the day off. I took the time to check out some statistics earlier. Unlike what the press have been doing over the last few days, I didn't limit myself to the last three seasons; rather, I delved back ten years in order to get more perspective. And it turns out that the club's struggles against the top sides have been a constant. But that's not all: Tottenham have actually been faring better in these fixtures in recent times than in the past. We're competing increasingly well against the heavyweights; they're no longer putting four or five goals past us, which used to be a common occurrence. We're measuring up better than ever, even though we're still failing to beat them away from home.

Now we've got to lick our wounds, wash the bitter taste out of our mouths, build ourselves up again and talk shop with our leading lights.

We've got a great opportunity to advance in Europe and the FA Cup, with three cup games coming up before we return to Premier League action. I've decided to leave Vincent Janssen behind for our trip to Gent.

Meanwhile, my diet is going well. My weight has stabilised and even though I'm not exercising every day, I'm trying. When I don't make it to the gym, it's because I can't, not because I don't want to.

*

I've just got a message from Jesús, who's been watching the Africa Cup of Nations final. One of the players involved caught his eye. While we continue to search for that extra something to push us over the line and make us win more matches now, we're planning for the future too. They are parallel processes.

What's most important is for everyone at the club to agree that we need to make changes. And then stick by that decision.

*

We lost 1–0 to Gent in the first leg of our Europa League last-32 tie.

*

I asked for some videos to be cut. First I played the squad some footage of us at our best, and then I broke down where we could have done better against Liverpool and Gent.

I reminded them of our rationale, reiterating that we can't afford to work less hard or play with less intensity than the opposition, because that's what defines us as a team. Then I switched the monitor off.

'Do you want to win trophies?' I asked. 'Have you got the same ambition to win that I have? If so, why don't you show it? Not every match can go according to plan, but in my book, it should hurt when that happens. You've got to keep trying, even if things aren't coming off. And you should be big enough to own up to your mistakes. There are some areas on the pitch where you have to tread more carefully, but mistakes are something we have to learn to live with, in fact, we learn from making them. If you're not free to commit them, you curb your creativity.

'Having said that, if you're going to hoof fifty balls upfield from the back every game, I'm not going to be impressed, because that's not what I'm asking of you. Why are you defending so deep when we've specifically asked you not to?

'What do you want? For us to dwell on each aspect of the game and run the same drill a hundred times? I did that as a player; we'd practise a hundred corners the day before matches. I am sure you don't. I am sure you want to be treated like adults – we explain, you listen, we practise, you improve. No rules off the pitch, no impositions, because if I don't trust you to take responsibility and make decisions off the pitch, how can I expect you to do so on it? So, fine, we treat you like adults. But for that to continue, you have to behave like adults.

'I've been here for two and a half years now and the progress we've made together is down to a certain sense of discipline that comes from doing everything collectively and with mutual respect for one another, as well as for the people around us who are here to help. Without that spirit, we'll win nothing. I want more of that.

'And lads, I really hope these things stand you in good stead in football and in life too, in every sense. I hope that one day you realise how wrongly you've been approaching so many things. You'll thank me for it.'

Emotions run very high in football. If you're in trouble, which is how I see it right now, you have to make sure the players know the score, yet reassure them at the same time. You've got to remind them that there's a way out of the situation, but that even if we provide them with the solutions, ultimately it's all up to them. It may just have been me, but they seemed pensive immediately afterwards while they were doing their pre-activation workout before training.

Will any good come of all this, this rehashing of things they already know?

Tomorrow we're away to second-tier Fulham in the FA Cup.

*

We won 3–0 through a Harry Kane hat-trick. We're through to the FA Cup sixth round.

Tomorrow I'm going to play them a clip of the first two minutes of today's match: we bared our teeth, winning three aerial duels in the first 50 seconds. Fulham didn't know what had hit them.

I was asked about Janssen again. I left him on the bench throughout against Fulham, having previously omitted him from the squad

We played a friendly at Camp Nou in 2004. I was part of the Rest of the World team that included a skinny Anderlecht player by the name of Vincent Kompany. I met Johan Cruyff, who coached one of the sides. A brave man and a visionary footballing genius.

I went back to Espanyol in 2004. Here I am with club legend Raúl Tamudo, listening to Miguel Ángel Lotina, the Espanyol coach.

When we won the 2006 Copa del Rey at Espanyol with Walter Pandiani, Martín Posse and Pablo Zabaleta.

Another departure. Another change. An image of a footballer and his family that you rarely see. My farewell dinner at Espanyol in 2006.

The day I was given the gold-and-diamond badge to commemorate my 264 league appearances for Espanyol.

I hung up my boots in 2006 and we went to Bariloche in Argentina. The trip signified a transition from one era to another.

I have taken the family skiing once. We look great, right? But we didn't have a clue how to ski. We shall not be going back!

(*Below*) Gaining experience with the Espanyol Women's team in 2008. We trained on one half of the pitch and the youth team trained on the other. The boys often got distracted by looking at our female players. 'Come on, look somewhere else, guys!' I would say to them.

'Always with the youth academy' epitomises my time at Espanyol. I really like this photo.

We made a promise to climb Montserrat if we kept Espanyol up in my first season as coach.

In Nicola Cortese's private jet on the way to England in January 2013. It was the beginning of my Premier League adventure.

The wooden-arrow challenge and walking on hot coals barefoot.

I had these pictures on the wall in my office at Southampton: the Argentinian Pope, a photo from my first game in charge and a newspaper cutting about what we were doing at the club.

While at Southampton, I decided to wear the tie that Cortese had given me before his departure a few months earlier for the final home game of the season. I asked Miki to take a photo of me to pay tribute to him.

A photo with all of the coaching staff and my colleagues at Southampton after my final match in charge of the team.

After a year in England, we had all gone pale, so as soon as we arrived in Barcelona we went to the pool. Taiel, our dog, came with us.

Meeting Sir Alex Ferguson was one of the greatest professional pleasures that I have experienced. Here I am admiring him alongside Guus Hiddink.

José Mourinho and I have always had a very good relationship. We sent each other messages for a long time, but now that we are direct rivals, we naturally keep a bit more distance.

In Nice with Daniel Levy on the way to Joe Lewis's yacht during the summer when I decided to join Tottenham.

(*Below*) The trip to Argentina with Daniel Levy and the coaching staff brought us closer together. Some of us almost didn't make it back!

In the car with Miguel, Jesús, Toni and Xavier Elaine, our chiropractor and medical expert. We had signed for Tottenham but still lived in Southampton. We were wearing kit from the campaign that had just finished.

Going for a walk and getting away from everything. Sometimes you come across some real gems while clearing your thoughts.

entirely against Gent. After the first of those games, I said: 'He needs to show more.'

*

It is just a matter of minutes since the end of our return clash with Gent, which was played in front of 80,465 people – the biggest crowd in Europa League history. It finished 2–2. We led twice, only to be pegged back on both occasions. The first equaliser was a really ridiculous own goal. Dele Alli was sent off just before half-time for a high tackle.

We were going to change formation, but on being reduced to ten men, we decided to stick with our three at the back and simply attack, attack, attack. We took risks and gave it our best shot. It almost paid off. We held nothing back; our effort, intensity and teamwork were superb.

I never give post-match team talks, but this time I felt the urge to. I told them that I'm proud of how we played with ten men. This is exactly why I get so annoyed when we don't show what we're capable of; I told them that if we performed like this all the time, we'd never lose.

'And one more thing . . .'

Dele Alli was down in the dumps. That's why I told him, in front of the rest, that these things can happen to anyone and that he hadn't let us down: 'You simply made a mistake. There are other players who let us down all week long, from Monday to Sunday; they feature in plenty of matches, but it's like being down to ten men because they're passengers. They, the guys who hide, are the ones who are unforgivable.'

Dele never leaves us in the lurch. Now it's my job to protect him at my press conference.

*

Today, Saturday the 25th, we showed the squad some highlights from the Gent game to press home how well we started and also how dynamism can make up for numerical inferiority. You have to be willing to run risks, but where there's a will, there's a way.

I rounded off by putting on that Robbie Williams song, about loving your life and what you do.

Some of them were singing it as they left the room. Half-mockingly, I think. Bastards.

*

We went for the same starting XI in today's league game against Stoke as against Gent. It was a calculated choice. We were 4–0 up by half-time, with Harry Kane hitting another hat-trick – his third in nine games – inside 23 minutes. No further goals were added in the second half. We're back up to second in the table.

*

Earlier in the week, the press reminded me that Tottenham have won only three trophies in 33 years (an FA Cup and two League Cups) and haven't claimed any silverware since 2008. Then they asked me about what stage we are at in our process.

This was my reply:

'We have pushed the expectations higher, and that is good. But maybe we are not ready [to win trophies]. It's like the stadium: if we want to move today, we are not ready to play there. We need to wait, to put in the foundations. Our chairman is helping with it – new facilities at the training ground, a new stadium to help to be a better team and a bigger club. We are on the way to building one of the best clubs in Europe.

'But we must be patient.'

9.

MARCH

There were only two league games in March (against Everton and Southampton, both at White Hart Lane), while Tottenham also hosted League One side Millwall in the FA Cup sixth round. The papers became rife with rumours about the future of some of the players (including Dier, Rose, Walker and Kane) and of Pochettino himself, after he was seen with the FC Barcelona president.

Jesús has just sent the following diagram in the coaches WhatsApp group. It's a good reminder of the kind of leader I would like to be to the group. And, when in doubt, the kind of path I must follow.

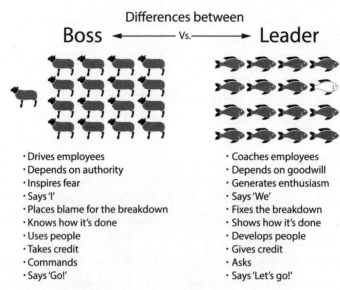

Differences between

Boss ◄——— Vs.——► Leader

· Drives employees	· Coaches employees
· Depends on authority	· Depends on goodwill
· Inspires fear	· Generates enthusiasm
· Says 'I'	· Says 'We'
· Places blame for the breakdown	· Fixes the breakdown
· Knows how it's done	· Shows how it's done
· Uses people	· Develops people
· Takes credit	· Gives credit
· Commands	· Asks
· Says 'Go!'	· Says 'Let's go!'

Speaking of leadership and how to be a coach, Carlo Ancelotti gave a fascinating interview to Gabriele Marcotti for ESPN, which provided food for thought and warrants a few remarks.

The journalist quizzed Ancelotti about a recent comment by Guardiola about deriving more satisfaction from performances than from results. 'The result is an empty thing,' Pep had told NBC Sports, 'The result is [that] I'm happy for the next two days and I get less criticism and more time to improve my team. But what satisfies me the most in my job is to feel emotions, the way we play . . . the process is the reason.'

'Sure, he's right,' Ancelotti replied emphatically.

But does this really reflect the essence of Ancelotti's and Guardiola's thinking, and what our job is all about? Sometimes we change our tune depending on the situation. Like a rich person proclaiming that money can't buy happiness, we tend to fall into the trap of saying that trophies aren't important . . . except when we win them.

Where does enjoyment come into play? For those who climb Everest, suffering and gratification go hand in hand during their ascent. They reach the peak, spend a few minutes there and then climb back down again. It's the same for me: I take pleasure in the journey. I only know of one path to the top of this profession: enjoying your work, being flexible and willing to evolve, and finding time to be alone and think creatively . . . although it's getting increasingly difficult. But we all play to win; anyone who says otherwise is lying.

I hope I don't change my tune when I win trophies. If I do, I'll be a successful coach, but I'll have lost moral authority.

Ancelotti went on to observe that, 'The only thing a manager can't control is the result. When it comes to our clubs, when you reach a certain level, we have almost total control. But this is an unpredictable, low-scoring sport where individual episodes have an outsized influence. And a manager can't really control that. That's the irony though, isn't it? You as a manager are judged on results and not on the work you do and the performance of the team . . . not on the things you can control, but on those you can't.'

Obviously it's a results business and football revolves around the players. But we have a major influence on the decisions they make on the pitch, and that means eventually on the results too. I'd go further still: we're constantly making decisions that affect their lives off the pitch. I wonder how many families I've made happy in my eight years as a coach, and how many I've left frustrated.

Given that responsibility, decisions must be properly thought through. There is a tendency towards rash judgements, of which I was a victim during my playing career. During my first conversation with Daniel, he abruptly asked me, 'What do you think the squad's strengths and weaknesses are?'

'I don't know,' I replied, 'and I won't until I've worked with them for six weeks.' I hadn't arrived with all the answers on a pen drive.

Ancelotti also said that, 'The fact is on matchdays there's very little a manager can do. You do your work during the week . . . As for reading the game and adjusting . . . I don't know. First of all, you don't see the game well from the dugout. When I watch our games back, I spot plenty of things I missed the first time around because I have a different vantage point.'

I strongly disagree with him on this front. I think we have a considerable impact on games. For starters, the image we convey to the players can give them peace of mind. Lots of coaches jump up and down on the touchline screaming out, 'Calm, calm, calm!' Is that really going to enable them to keep their composure?

I've always felt that it's useless yelling at players to tell them to run this way or that; they just look at you and think, 'Why don't you come and do it yourself?' Shouting accomplishes very little, especially if you lose. It's basically total hysteria. Frankly, those sorts of coaches never put themselves in their players' place, because if they did, they'd go bright red with embarrassment.

I've got to admit that I only learnt that over time, though.

The players don't miss anything that goes on in the dugout. During the opening match of my second season at Southampton, away to West Brom, our goalkeeper, Artur Boruc, was about to play the ball out from the back. One of our full-backs was unmarked right out by the touchline, near where I was. I started gesturing to Artur with my hand: 'Pass it here, over here, to the full-back!' Artur went the other way, mishit his kick and the ball went out for a throw-in. I turned to Toni: 'Son of a bitch! What the hell is Boruc doing?'

At half-time, Toni said to me, 'I think Artur knows we were talking about that incident.'

After the final whistle, I made a beeline for Artur and said to him, 'Did you see my reaction?'

He responded, 'Yes, and from that moment on, all I could think when I saw you was "That bastard has been taking the piss . . ."' It's just as well we won (1–0); if we'd have lost, my body language could have been used by the keeper as an excuse to justify his mistakes. Coaches have to take away as many excuses as possible from players, as they are often ready to blame others for their own mistakes.

So it's not a matter of being passionate or showing lots of emotion, but rather of not forgetting that our role is to be the support act to the stars of the show.

I don't know whether or not I'm a good manager. I don't know how you gauge that. If you coach Espanyol and don't win any trophies, does that make you a bad manager? Does winning things make you the best? Frank Rijkaard, Guardiola, Tito Vilanova, Tata and Luis Enrique all won things at Barcelona. But when Messi, Iniesta, Piqué and Busquets are no longer around, it'll probably be somewhat harder.

The complicated challenge with great players like that is to ensure they remain hungry to carry on winning. The glory of victory can become like an addiction; you need good leadership to keep fuelling their competitive juices, but do that and these beasts will work like men possessed to get to experience those magical moments again. If you've never tasted glory, it's impossible to imagine what it's like and external motivation isn't enough – you've got to feel it within you. But how can you, if you can't imagine it? That is the Catch-22 that a manager has to break by creating the right environment and mentality.

That's why it's impossible not to admire serial winners like Federer and Nadal, who never tire of the taste of victory and make all sorts of sacrifices to repeat the feat. Some footballers think that success means having 3 million or 30 million in the bank, being on TV and people wanting your autograph. But money doesn't buy you happiness and the fame is fleeting.

In any case, there are no absolute truths in football, despite the growing ranks of coaches, myself included, who devote hour upon hour to the search for them – studying the science of the game, trying to control everything and sometimes even putting far too many limits in place. We follow one another, steal ideas from each other and develop our own. Still, I think that it'd be ideal if we could strike a balance between current trends and the ways of the past. A few decades ago, football was creative, it was all about playing and having fun, and there weren't many restrictive structures. Perhaps I'm romanticising that era, but I've got infinite respect for the likes of Menotti and Ferguson, walking encyclopaedias whose knowledge and experience, when studied closely, help to remind us what it's all about.

It's a shame I did not have more chances to play against Ferguson's teams, but I'm lucky enough to be around at the same time as, and compete regularly against, many others who inspire me to keep improving. Wenger, Mourinho, Simeone, Guardiola and Conte are just a few of those who are capable of springing surprises at any time, which forces me to try to stay a step ahead. What team will he field? Why is he moving his full-back infield? What's the idea behind that change? There are hundreds of questions that make it such a fantastic challenge.

There's a certain type of manager who is always preoccupied with external noise, for the large part banal things, and suffers whenever he receives criticism. I used to be that way: I'd let lies, or comments that stemmed from a lack of knowledge, affect me. An inaccurate image of me was portrayed in some circles; I suppose there must have been a hidden agenda at work. I ended up paying for unpopular decisions, like my handling of Raúl Tamudo, because there are plenty of people sitting there waiting and hoping you drop the ball. I gradually learnt to take a step back and look at the bigger picture when analysing the team, making better decisions by considering the consequences. You have to show foresight, so that what you say today doesn't impinge on you tomorrow. And, above all, you've got to make sure you have all the information to hand; without it, it's easy to get things wrong, as has happened to me on more than one occasion.

I don't deal with the budget, salaries or new contract negotiations – that's Daniel's domain. But managers don't just decide a team's strategy on the pitch; they are also involved in the travel arrangements, the dietary side, planning the schedule for the season and determining the make-up of the squad. That's why you should acknowledge that every gesture and word leaves its mark – everything you do leaves its own indelible DNA trace on it, however microscopic it may be. Your communication must be spot on to avoid any confusion. And you must be honest. You can't fool a large group of people; you might get away with it for a short while, but not in the long term.

Marcelo Bielsa used to weigh everything up carefully and then tell you what he thought to your face, even if it hurt. On top of that, he somehow seemed to get inside your head: when you'd answer, he'd already know what you were going to say, so he'd have the next question ready. It was as if he'd seen the script for our conversations in advance. That's experience for you.

'A good coach can change a game; a great coach can change a life.' These are the words of legendary basketball coach John Wooden. I second that sentiment.

John McDermott says I'm a diva. He's seen pictures of me from my playing days, with my long hair, and he thinks – rightly so – that I had a considerable ego. A 'humble' diva he has called me more than once, maybe to make the description more . . . palatable. All coaches must go about their business with confidence in their methods. But, like many others, I need people by my side; I enjoy sharing, helping them to grow and giving them a voice. So, in John's book, I'm a diva who gives back, a 'humble diva' if it's not too much of a contradiction in terms. A few times I've explained to him that, when I'm feeling strong and lucid, and I think of something with sufficient conviction, it then comes to pass. He associates that with high self-esteem, but I'm not sure it's about ego; I think it's a gift that helps me to decipher the world.

I don't like seeing myself on television – I laugh at my own English. 'Turn off that TV,' I say after hearing myself for a short while. Thinking about it, if I'm honest, I feel some of the things I've written in this diary do verge on arrogance, on the egotism that can be all-consuming. And the idea of drifting over to the dark side worries me.

John has told me about the huge popularity of showjumping in the United Kingdom in the 1970s. One of the biggest stars was the supremely arrogant Harvey Smith, who once said, 'Put me on a pit pony and I'd still win.' John says that I'm like Smith – that I have the audacity to believe I can handle anything and everything. Coming from him, it must be true. But in any case, my ultimate goal, my 'everything', is more than a picture of myself lifting a trophy for Tottenham.

'No person was ever honoured for what he received. Honour has been the reward for what he gave.'

This quote by former American president Calvin Coolidge was also sent to me by John, Mr Academic.

That's my true dream.

*

I have bought tickets to see Sting next month.

*

It's 30 March today. In football, all you can do in order to win and keep winning is to put all the requisite ingredients together, make the decisions you deem right, surround yourself with the right people and lead the way. The magic lies in the fact at some unspecified moment, which often isn't of your choosing, it will all come together and click into place. And then everything flows naturally.

There can be no doubt that we've clicked.

Let's go back over the last four weeks, including the Barcelona speculation following my encounter with their president, Josep Maria Bartomeu.

The 2nd was my birthday and we celebrated with a small gathering at home. That aside, there was a calm vibe at the training ground. Following two wins in a row in the league and our European elimination, not to mention a fortnight of intense discussions, we were searching for a bit of tranquillity. We decided to do some refresher training – running through the fundamentals of our game, the defensive and attacking hallmarks of our style – and to check on the lads' fitness. We wanted to intersperse work and rest, making the most of the fact that we only had three matches coming up in four weeks. Some of the players have already played over 40 games this season, so tailoring workloads individually is hugely important. In fact, sometimes we put on up to eight different types of training in a single day.

Physical conditioning isn't just about doing sit-ups, jumping or doing weights like in my Newell's days. It's experienced a huge evolution within football. We have six fitness coaches and Jesús systematically coordinates everything by studying the requirements and advising on the type of training and workload based on detailed data for each player. It happens in various cycles, depending on the time of year. When Jesús has a clear idea of what he wants to do, he tells me, but on most occasions he does so without needing to consult me because we know each other so well.

Toby Alderweireld, Jan Vertonghen and Harry Kane all had knocks, but they recovered in time for the Everton game on Sunday 5 March. We had prepared attacking game plans catering for them playing either three or four at the back, which were the two set-ups they'd used up to that point. In the event, Ronald Koeman flooded the middle of the park – fielding a 4-5-1 with five central midfielders, something he'd not done before – in an attempt to stymie our build-up play between the lines, but we controlled the match and displayed variety in our game. We completed more sprints and covered more ground in the opening 45 minutes than in any other first half this season, with Kane's goal coming as a result and putting us at ease. We created loads of chances. Harry scored again, before Lukaku pulled it back to 2–1 with nine minutes to go. What happened next was a catalogue of errors, including one of my own.

In the 90th minute, Dele Alli made it 3–1. I celebrated effusively for a change – excessively so, as if the game were already over, something that I thought I had stamped out. And the team fell asleep, to the extent that Everton went right up the other end and scored. I spent what was left of stoppage time shaking my head. I felt that my celebration had opened the door for my players to switch off.

At the final whistle, all too aware of my lapse, I looked at my staff to see if they had realised. I pulled out my phone and, as I'd expected, there was a message from my wife, who tends to give me her opinion after matches. 'What were you playing at? Did you lose your mind when Dele scored? Never again!' I'd been busted. I was really angry with myself. When I got home, as a diversionary tactic, I told her that the fact she hadn't come to the stadium for a while was clearly a lucky charm, because we've been winning.

Harry remains in excellent form. He's the top striker in the league with 19 goals and has scored 14 times in 12 matches in 2017. And, at 23, he is as enthusiastic as ever: he enjoys training, he prolongs his sessions and he studies elite players, past and present. I WhatsApp him videos of goals or interesting pieces of play by other strikers. At all hours. The last one I sent him was at 11 p.m.

We're engaged in another battle, although we're not talking about it publicly because it's of secondary importance: the chance to finish above Arsenal for the first time in 22 years. After the Everton game, we'd moved six points ahead of them with 11 games to go. We were seven points behind league leaders Chelsea and were hopeful that West Ham could get a result against them the following day. We had to keep believing that catching them was possible, and at the very least be ready to pounce if they slipped up – which didn't happen in the derby at the London Stadium, where they won 2–1.

That Monday, the first of two days off I'd given the squad, I spoke to John McDermott. The Under-16s had suffered a bad loss and I decided to attend their training session – or, rather, to take part in it – as a show of support for the coach and to give the kids a lift. And to demand more of them. They're at an age at which they need to be aware of their responsibilities. I had a great time.

Rumours about Barcelona possibly being interested in me have resurfaced. I was asked in a press conference whether it was flattering to be linked with the Catalan giants. 'I've seen the list of replacements for Luis Enrique and it's about a hundred names,' I replied. 'I know the business; I don't take that as being flattering.' I know there's no smoke without fire, but what else could I say?

I had other matters to worry about, such as my players. Around that time I had a very tricky conversation with one of the key men, whose name I'll keep to myself for the time being. It was our second in the space of two years. I got Jesús to prepare the ground and they spent almost an hour talking. I swooped in to add the finishing touches, although Jesús kept chiming in with phrases like, 'You do this in training, this in games and these are the statistics.' I went down the contract route: 'If you carry on like this, we don't need you.' There ended up being a trigger in a video that we showed him, clearly proving that he reacted conservatively on two occasions in the same match instead of doing what he should've done, which was to move forward. His decision affected him and the team. 'Ah, yes, it's true. I made a mistake,' was his response when he saw it.

He wasn't going to feature against Millwall in the FA Cup the following weekend, but I decided to play him and he was brilliant.

*

Jesús is about to finish watching *House of Cards*, whereas Miki and John are a bit behind. I like asking them which episode they're on. 'Ah, I remember,' is my usual response when they tell me. They then usually walk away because they know I'm going to come out with a, 'Well, after that Peter Russo goes and . . .'

'Nooooo,' they shout, as they distance themselves. That's called a 'spoiler', right?

Francis Underwood has an incredible ability to understand the context and achieve his targets in the most ingenious ways. There's a phrase that we've made our own, one uttered by the character that Kevin Spacey plays about Chief of Staff Linda Vasquez when he beats her for the vice-presidency in an internal battle: 'I've never thought higher of her than I do at this moment. She lost, but she played to win.'

FA Cup fever was rife over the weekend and we had a whole week to prepare for our sixth-round tie, which was our second game of the month. We told the boys that it would be tough because League One

Millwall had knocked out three Premier League sides, although they were at home in all those ties, and would be full of confidence knowing that they had nothing to lose. We couldn't make the same mistake as we did against Wycombe by letting them come into their own at White Hart Lane.

It had been noticeable in training in recent weeks that we'd had enough time to recover and, as a consequence, all the players were extremely focused and in tip-top shape. The wake-up call that I gave them last month had worked as an attempt to rediscover what we're all about and get back to the basics that we were letting slip.

There was a special atmosphere in the stadium for the cup tie against Millwall. It was the last fixture in the competition at White Hart Lane. Both during the warm-up and in the dressing room, I insisted that we couldn't give our opponents as much as a sniff. That's just how it went. We had a very serious approach and were fully focused from the first whistle. Before our first goal (which came on the half-hour mark), Harry Kane picked up another ankle injury. We weren't even ten minutes into the game. That's football.

Son hadn't started recently and I gave him the nod, leaving Eriksen on the bench. But Christian had to warm up from the fifth minute when we saw that Harry couldn't continue. If I had left Son out of the line-up and he had come on for an injured player, he would not have felt the boost of confidence a footballer gets from playing from the start. Often luck plays a part in the outcome of games.

Our 32 efforts on goal yielded six goals, including a Son hat-trick.

Dele Alli once again showed why he's such an ideal partner for any striker. During his first season he played all over, from holding midfielder to winger, but this season he's only played as a forward behind Kane. He's being compared with Lampard, but Dele isn't a midfielder any more, although he may say otherwise. He's a lethal finisher in the box who shows aggression and always looks forward.

After beating Millwall, we are two games away from a trophy.

Following every game, those who haven't played partake in an intense training session at the stadium – three fitness coaches set up a travel gym wherever we go. Those who aren't in the squad do so at the training ground, meaning everyone undergoes a similar level of physical exertion. We give them the following day off whenever we can, even if the game has gone badly.

In this instance, when we went to pick up our cars, we saw Kane again at the training ground. He was with his partner who had come to pick him up and he reiterated the message that he gave everyone after the game: 'It's not as serious as the previous injury, I'll be back soon.' With Kane going to be out for just over a month, it is now down to Dele, Vincent Janssen – against Millwall he scored his first goal from open play this season – and Son to get among the goals. Our worst run of results this season came when Harry was injured. We'll see.

We expect him back for the FA Cup semi-final against Chelsea next month. This season, we lost to them at Stamford Bridge, but we beat them at home. We played different formations in the two games. Chelsea will show us where we stand once again.

The weather started to pick up around halfway through the month. I managed to find an hour and a half to stroll around the park with my wife. How am I not able to do that more often when the benefit is so huge? We'd wanted to do something for so many weeks, but the following always happens when we're free on Sundays: where should we go? Mauri is playing football. If we drive to London, we have to sit through the horrendous traffic. Should we take the Tube? We'll get noticed. You can't just be spontaneous. What about staying home to watch a film? I can't remember when we last went to the cinema or the theatre. Wait, there's football on. And so we spend hours watching football. I'm a right bore for my wife. On the one hand, it's fine because I'm a good catch and I'm not that much of a pain in the neck, but on the other, I'm quite a complicated fellow.

We had another free week leading up to the Southampton game, allowing us to carry on with our collective and individual work without distractions. The whole team went out for dinner on the Thursday. I wanted to pay, but Kane and Alli wouldn't let me and they ended up treating everyone. We were also joined by the chairman and Steve Hitchen – our new chief scout who will gather information on players for the coaching staff and Daniel as part of our new structure.

There was plenty of talk at dinner about Monaco, who'd just knocked Manchester City out of the Champions League. As a way of putting the season in context, we went back over our games against the Monégasques that saw us knocked out of the competition. We dominated at home, although we lost. They let us come on to them by defending very deep and we missed two glaring chances. We were forced into four or five changes in the away match. Injuries punished us and we started some of our less regular players. We had some clear-cut chances at 0–0, we missed a penalty and ended up losing 2–1. We came up against a good team at the worst time for us.

We went over the English sides' results in Europe once again. You can look at it from a different perspective: what type of football is played in England which doesn't allow us to enjoy success abroad? You can't dominate the play in the same way in the Premier League as you can in most European competitions. Here the matches are open and long balls can create uncertainty. The fans demand a fast-paced style with quick transitions. There are so many mistakes because of the rhythm of the matches and the inevitable fatigue that sets in. Not only the style, but also the referees are different in Europe. We need to close the gap between both competitions.

I continue doing a bit of sport myself when I can. We had a game of football tennis the other day. Toni, Lloris and Winks against Miki, Lamela – who says he's feeling better and has been training – and me. We hadn't played in a long time. It's very common in Argentina and we also used to play a lot at Espanyol. Toni claims that I'm a cheat, which is why we always end up bickering. I also tend to feel pain all over my body for days afterwards.

On that same day, we were paid a visit by Eduardo Domínguez, who was the Espanyol fitness coach during my final season, when manager Miguel Ángel Lotina was in charge. Eduardo is actually partly responsible for my retirement. That afternoon we exchanged a few home truths that had gone unsaid back then. I had to eat a lot of shit when others should've taken the blame. I was accused of controlling the dressing room and conspiring against the coach. I found it very tough and plenty of bad words were said about me. I don't often go over that spell in my head, but there is another way to look at it: I am where I am now because I hung up my boots when I did. I turned over a new leaf with Eduardo in what was an essential cathartic exercise.

We sought out solutions to compensate for Kane's absence for the visit of Southampton, our third and final game of the month. When we're in such a situation, our *mate*-filled meetings in the office take on an air of excitement mixed with apprehension, as we try to unpick the best way to maximise our resources. Which approach should we take? What would you do? We discuss and try to visualise the plan.

We had previously played Son as a number 9 against City and he performed brilliantly in that role. Kane is a striker who has great movement and can get a goal from any position. He doesn't possess that explosive burst of pace, but he has a great engine, helps the team and intimidates our opponents. Son is the polar opposite: he's faster, more mobile and better suited to getting in behind and taking players on in one-on-one situations. He brings very different qualities.

The way we build the team doesn't change according to which striker is playing. We're sticking with three at the back because it's the best way to incorporate our most in-form players. Right now Dier, Vertonghen and Alderweireld all have to start and we have to fit them in. This formation gives the wing-backs more space, enhancing one of our most potent attacking forces, and the increased freedom helps Alli explore his talent. Last year we switched to a 3-4-3 while attacking, and although we defended with two centre-backs, our holding midfielder Dier could drop back in to make it a back-three if needed. Now that 3-4-3 has become a constant as a consequence of the players' development, particularly Dier's, who is producing very solid displays at the heart of the defence.

Having Wanyama is a great help in terms of making every piece of the jigsaw fit. He's the perfect player and that's not just because he has played every minute in the league or because our record at White Hart Lane has been remarkable since he came into the team – we've won 12 out of 14 home games and drawn two. He is influential with and without the ball: he's among the top ten Premier League players in terms of ball recoveries, passes made and tackles won. He also makes life easier for our attacking players by filling in the gaps, releasing the ball without overcomplicating matters and he's relentless when it comes to pressing.

We almost put the game to bed in the first half-hour with Eriksen opening the scoring and Alli tucking home a penalty. We could've exerted greater control in the second half, but despite them clawing a goal back, I wasn't fearful about the result. Winks came on for Son for the final 15 minutes and we moved Alli to centre-forward, until bringing Janssen on in the 86th minute.

The 2–1 win left us second heading into the international break, ten points behind Chelsea and nine ahead of Arsenal, although our neighbours have a game in hand on us, while Manchester City and Liverpool are breathing down our necks. We have once again made history by racking up ten consecutive league wins on home soil for the first time.

While en route to the room where our families were waiting for us, I took a moment to look out of one of the windows at the ongoing works at the new stadium. It's like a huge animal gradually coming out of its shell. It's currently silent and slowly stretching out its limbs. The coaching staff were involved in designing the dressing rooms. We were asked what could make them more functional and where certain things could be located.

It reminded us of conversations that we had during the construction of Espanyol's new stadium, meetings that lasted just as long, with the only difference being a smaller budget at the Catalan outfit. We spent a lot of time trying to improve the club's infrastructure. We also asked for a physio room, a gym, a relaxation room, a new kitchen and a small private restaurant for the players at the training ground, but it all had to be built with hardly any funds. The press claimed that we were separating the club from the fans. Respect for infrastructure is one of the biggest differences between England and Spain.

After the game, Karina, the kids and I grabbed our things and headed to Barcelona until the end of the following week. It was about time: during the other breaks I went to the Alps and Argentina without the family.

While I was relaxing in the garden of our flat in Barcelona, I received a link to an interview with Hugo Lloris. 'My destiny is linked to Mauricios,' he said. His contract extension until 2022 and wage structure fit within the club's protocol, as decided by the chairman. It involves a base salary and a good percentage of bonuses. Daniel is the only one who knows how far we can go and why things sometimes don't come off. He has a tough job. In England, for example, the directors don't like players coming to the end of their contracts for fear of them leaving on a free, although it's something that coaches could more often use to motivate them and test a player's mental state.

Toni made the most of the time off to visit his sister who is ill. He's suffering, but he's carrying it on the inside. When a player has a problem, you have to react immediately, understand and explain. When it happens to a member of the coaching staff, you have no option but to keep going.

I went out for dinner in Barcelona with friends two or three times and I bumped into Josep Maria Bartomeu at the restaurant Farga. We've known each other for fifteen years and our children went to the same school. He was actually involved with the construction of the port in Southampton and on occasion we've spoken about our experiences in the city. We gave each other a hug and spent ten minutes discussing tactics, the 3-4-3 that we use and that Barcelona sometimes employ, as well as whether or not Luis Enrique would go with it against Juventus. He offered me tickets in the directors' box for the game.

Despite the rumours, I don't fit the profile that they're looking for (essentially someone who knows the club inside out). As there's been so much talk about it, after the international break I repeated in a press conference that I'm an Espanyol man and going to Barça would be akin to signing for Arsenal, which would be impossible even if Daniel sacked me. I truly value loyalty.

I returned to the Tottenham training ground to discover some bad yet unsurprising news: Lamela is going to have hip surgery. He hasn't played since 25 October and the pain has been continual, even when he seemed to be making a recovery. He decided to head to Rome to be seen by a trusted physio and he came back to training two months later. Before the international break, we spoke about how well he was progressing. Sometimes he'd start training with the warm-up and last until the end; on other occasions, after four or five drills, the discomfort was too much for him to bear. An athlete's body can be unfathomable and, in some cases, extremely vulnerable. In this case, we're going to be without him for the rest of the season.

With just a few days to go until the Burnley game, we have been visited by Stanley Okumbi, the coach of Victor Wanyama's Kenya. We've decided that we have to travel to that marvellous country. It was a welcome distraction as we only had four players in training. The rest were gradually arriving back from international duty, with some of them touching down the day before the match, meaning there was no time to work on tactics. It's difficult to know what sort of state they'll come back in, no matter how many tests we do, which plants a seed of doubt. That's why we're waiting until the day of the game to decide on our line-up.

But all in all, we're happy. Each season contains a moment or two which could be a turning point in terms of the team's response. We all feel that thanks to fewer fixtures, the time spent reviewing our style and the break, March has allowed us to get back on track in terms of attitude, intensity and performance. There's been a resounding and very visible improvement which should be obvious next month.

10.

APRIL

T*he month of truth had arrived. There was nowhere left to hide. It was time to find out who the top players were and if Tottenham really were on the up during the business end of the season. If it all fizzled out in April with six league games and an FA Cup semi-final against Chelsea, there would be nothing to show for all the merits of the Mauricio Pochettino method. People would say that's Tottenham and nobody can do anything to alter that.*

You play football both with and without the ball, which may be stating the obvious. In concrete terms, we wouldn't be much cop if we played passively without battling and pressing. This came to the fore when I was asked a question in my press conference ahead of the Burnley game: 'How would you define Mousa Dembélé?'

'I always tell him: "Mousa, when I write a book, you'll be one of my genius players that I've been lucky enough to meet, alongside Maradona, Ronaldinho, Jay-Jay Okocha and Iván de la Peña."' That was my answer. I also thought that if we'd signed him at 18, he would've become one of the best players in the world. At 28, it's more difficult to remove habits that nobody has previously helped correct.

We've discussed it in depth. When we first met, he said that he knew where he needed to improve, but he didn't. He mistakenly thought, like some others, that you don't need to do much preparation to play football. Having said that, he has improved noticeably over the years, just like a good wine. Vertonghen, who is having the best season of his career at 30, is another good example of this. Mousa missed the first four games of the campaign, but since that point he has become a key cog in the machine. His progress means he is increasingly able to play two games a week and achieve even greater consistency. When he's fit, his powerful profile makes a huge difference.

By the way, he's going to be on the bench at Burnley.

*

I was sure of our starting XI yesterday, but didn't announce it until today. We decided to play with three at the back again and Janssen up front, although he had the flu in Holland and we knew he was not 100 per cent. We asked him to keep going until his energy reserves ran low.

The first half was particularly difficult. We didn't have clear moments of sharp and intelligent possession or create dangerous situations. They were right on our heels and were very compact defensively. We had to change our structure.

Wanyama picked up an injury with not even half an hour on the clock, after taking a blow to the back. He stayed on, but wasn't really in a state to do so.

43rd minute: Dembélé went on for Wanyama.

44th minute: Winks twisted his ankle in what looked like an ugly injury. Sissoko went on in his place. Two of our starting centre-midfielders had to be withdrawn before the first half was up.

We managed to keep our shape during the final minutes of the first half, but I needed to change things around at the interval.

Miki told us that Palace were beating Chelsea at Stamford Bridge – they had kicked off at the same time as us. Cesc opened the scoring, but it was 2–1 to the visitors by the 11th minute. A surprising scoreline.

We went in goalless at the break. I switched Dier from centre-back to midfield. While we crossed the pitch to head to the tunnel, I said to him: 'Eric, play just behind Dembélé in midfield when we attack, and when we defend, drop back in as the third centre-back.'

Back in the dressing room, I explained to the boys how we needed to play. We had to press more without the ball and look to get in behind them out wide through our full-backs, Trippier and Davies, neither of whom began the season as a starter, but they've both come on in leaps and bounds. It's their turn.

We performed much better in the second half. We managed to find the path leading to their penalty area more easily and created danger. We were dragging their defenders from side to side and gaps were starting to open up. Our moment was approaching.

Goooaaall. Dier. The ball was delivered into the penalty area from a corner and it fell on the edge of the six-yard box to Eric who tucked it home. 1–0.

The goal settled us down and our game management was very good. Our opponents started to struggle.

73rd minute. Janssen put in a good shift, but couldn't last any longer. He was replaced by Son who had been in Korea and was jet-lagged.

We instantly carved out an opening. Son played it across goal to Dele who spurned a glorious chance. The ball fell to Dele, who found Son . . . and he scored! 2–0 with 13 minutes to go.

The final whistle was about to be blown. I can't say how, because it isn't allowed, but news reached us that Chelsea were still losing 2–1 and that Manchester United had equalised.

Full-time. We got to the dressing room and the television was on. The match at Stamford Bridge was still going and there were seven minutes of stoppage time. Palace were camped in their own area, but they were holding firm. Final whistle! We were seven points behind Chelsea.

In the press conference, I said: 'If Chelsea drop more points, we'll be there. I always tell the players, "We must show we have learned from last season, that we are intelligent people." We'll see if we have learned. It's true that the Premier League is more competitive this year. But we are in the fight.'

I cracked open a good bottle of Argentinian wine when I got home that evening.

*

Today, 2 April, Érik Lamela had surgery on one of his hips. He'll certainly have an operation on the other one when he can. The fact that he underwent treatment in Barcelona and worked with the Roma medical staff obviously fed the rumour mill, but where's he going to go? Érik has to get back to being a footballer. That's the priority. He may not be able to train for seven or eight months, minimum.

A year and a half ago we could've signed a striker, but we discovered a physical problem and didn't want to take the risk. You end up paying for it in these situations. We missed Lamela, but our strength lies in the team.

Danny Rose also has his troubles. He has been out since January, although he could start training again at the end of this month. I invited him over to mine one evening. There had been talk of a possible transfer and that we were in for Luke Shaw. He sent me a message to ask, 'Is it true?'

My response: 'Why? Are you jealous?' He arrived at seven o'clock and left after ten. We both really opened up, we shared our dreams and spoke about our families. I told him about some of my investments and even gave him advice on what to do with his money. I insisted that he would have my full backing, whatever decision he made about his future.

The team seem to be ticking over on their own accord, but Jesús and his assistants are doing their bit, keeping the group in tip-top shape and tailoring individual training regimes. We're wary of picking up cards and suspensions, so we'll try to use everyone who is available. Our tactical work depends on how much time we have. We have three games this week, having got the first against Burnley out of the way already, despite the fact we didn't have any time to prepare for it. Next up is a battle against a Swansea side scrapping for their lives tomorrow and finally Watford, who are trying to ensure their season doesn't peter out with a whimper.

Three matches lie ahead before we face Chelsea in the FA Cup semi-finals. It would be great to cut the gap at the top further before then. They're at home to Manchester City. Antonio Conte has told his team that we're their only title challengers and that we're going to win all our remaining fixtures, so they simply can't slip up.

*

Whenever you have a congested fixture list ahead of you, everything happens very fast. You can only think about the next game and little else. There's not even time to head to the gym.

On the morning of the Swansea game, we all met up at the airport. John McDermott also travelled with us on this occasion.

The first time my team and I travelled to Wales, one of those things took place that helps everyone understand their role at the club. It was with Southampton and Nicola Cortese was in the travelling party. Jason Puncheon, now of Crystal Palace, asked him about his holiday. I could not believe my ears. I had to make it clear to Jason and Nicola that things didn't work like that. It wasn't appropriate for a player to ask the chairman a personal question, nor was it the time to ask. It all had to go through me.

Winks is facing a spell on the sidelines due to an ankle problem. Wanyama travelled, but we left the decision of his inclusion for after our afternoon nap.

After landing in Cardiff, we got on the coach to Swansea which was when Lloris said that he didn't feel well. When he arrived at the hotel, he had a siesta and woke up feeling better. After the briefing, Hugo told Toni that he was feeling dizzy again, so we left him out. It was the same story for Victor, whose back trouble persisted. It's better to give him more time and for him to be fit for Watford. Jesús observed that our spine was lacking, with Wanyama, Lamela and Kane out, so we decided to play a back-four, with Rose absent too, and Dier in midfield. It was going to be a new test for our young group. We bumped into many familiar faces at Swansea. Nigel Gibbs had been our Under-19 coach and Karl Halabi head of physical performance at the academy. I exchanged hugs with Kyle Naughton, Tom Carroll, Jordi Amat and Gylfi Sigurdsson. I told Gylfi it was a shame that he hadn't stayed because he would have fitted into our style perfectly.

We were fast out of the blocks and carved out two decent chances in the first five minutes. We then took our foot off the gas. Swansea earned a few corners and we seemed to be wasting possession. Swansea broke . . . Goal! Bloody hell! We were only 11 minutes into the game. It was scored by Wayne Routledge, another former Tottenham man. Did we think it would be an easy match?

Swansea, who were fourth from bottom, one place clear of the drop zone, were playing with confidence. They were compact and left us no space to play. We weren't set up well positionally to attack them. We lacked that finesse and cutting edge, which is why we seemed off the pace.

We went in 1–0 down at the break.

'We're going to change formation,' I told them. 'We aren't doing well going forward and we've dropped ten yards deeper defensively for fear of their long balls.'

After giving my instructions, Jesús went over set-pieces and reminded them of the mistakes for their goal, while stressing the importance of positioning. Sometimes half-time gets away from us and recently we've been fined for being late back out on to the pitch, so I made sure this was not the case this time.

All sorts seemed to be going on at Stamford Bridge. Jesús said that Chelsea were 2–1 up, but the game could yet go either way and Manchester City were on the attack.

Swansea defended very deep and we were struggling to get in behind. We lacked precision in our play. We kept trying to unlock the door. We moved certain players around. Sissoko went out to the left before moving centrally. We'd made two changes so far.

Janssen then went on for Sissoko. We moved Eriksen further back and Son lined up close to Janssen. We pushed Eriksen further forward. Son went out to the right, Son dropped back, Son to the left.

We tried a total of five formations. We cracked jokes afterwards about how if any scouts from rival teams had come to watch, they'd have been rather flummoxed and would have needed a whole notebook to explain what was happening.

Their goalkeeper, Fabianski, got injured. He received treatment, but didn't want to come off. He ended up being withdrawn, but was not best pleased. The whole saga lasted seven minutes.

There were two minutes remaining and we were losing. Chelsea were still 2–1 up.

At least we weren't just launching long balls up top. We spread the play, got in between the lines and our movement all over the pitch was excellent. We tried to force an equaliser in keeping with our style.

88th minute, it's in! Eriksen drilled the ball towards goal from just inside the area and Alli stuck his foot out to make it 1–1.

Come on! We were right back in the game and the players grabbed the ball to speed up the restart.

91st minute. GOOOOOAAAAALLLLLL. Son! The ball came through to Janssen on the edge of the box who flicked it on to Son who ran on to finish with a first-time shot. I jumped for joy, what else could I do?

Our goalkeeper, Vorm, picked up an injury from a corner. Alderweireld fell on top of him, seemingly causing damage to his knee and ankle. Toni's facial expression suggested it may rule him out for the remainder of the season.

94th minute. What a pass by Dele Alli! Come on, Eriksen. He bamboozled the defender and broke into the box . . . Incredible! The third goal! The boys all ran straight over to the fans, our amazing travelling fans! They were celebrating, we were celebrating. It was 3–1 after three quick-fire goals in five minutes!

After the final whistle, I went over to show the supporters my appreciation. I just felt like it, although it's not something that I usually do. It was a real pleasure to see them all so happy. Since I took over at Tottenham, we've picked up 53 points from losing positions, and already we have the best record in the league for that this season. We've scored the most and conceded the fewest goals, while also losing the fewest games in the Premier League. And we've racked up more points over the last two campaigns than any other club. The Swansea game was one of the most one-sided this season in terms of possession. At times it was over 80 per cent in our favour. We didn't give up. That's what we're made of and progress is inevitable.

If only we'd done slightly better in a few areas . . .

We greeted Paul Clement, the Swansea manager, whom I wanted to cheer up. They aren't a team that deserve to go down.

My message in the press conference was clear: 'The most important thing is the badge. When you play for Tottenham it is not about the names, it is about the team. This season we are showing that we are a team. I don't care what people say or what people think of the history of the club. This season we are fighting again. We are in a good way.'

*

Kane is fit. The press expected him back at the end of the month. We've won games without him, but our opponents will now have a new problem to face.

*

8 April. Our third match of the week was against Watford at White Hart Lane.

Dele Alli once again notched our first goal. He turns 21 next week and has better statistics than Cristiano Ronaldo had at his age: 26 goals and 14 assists compared with 14 and 13 for the Portuguese star. Another statistic: he's been involved in as many goals (40) as Lampard, Gerrard and Beckham combined at his age and he's the top scoring player (16) under 21 in Europe's top five leagues. Muhammad Ali said about himself, 'Float like a butterfly, sting like a bee,' which I quite like for Dele as it happens.

Dier and Son, with the latter grabbing a brace, rounded off the scoring. It ended 4–0 and the players celebrated the win on the pitch. I waited for them in the technical area, as I almost always do, to give them a hug.

The group is as united as ever.

Chelsea are four points ahead of us and have a game in hand. They are away to Bournemouth later today.

*

Chelsea ran out 3–1 winners. They're seven points clear.

*

9 April. We couldn't go to see Sting; it's been a chaotic week.

*

I have been named on the list of candidates to replace Edgardo Bauza in the Argentina hotseat. A proud moment to see my name on that prestigious list but I am committed to my project here.

*

I'm keeping a close eye on the Borussia Dortmund team-coach attack. I found out on the way home and have now switched the television on. It's a big reality check. Certain thoughts are once again swirling around my head, including memories of a beloved family member whom we've stopped contacting. How often are we guilty of not taking the time out to enjoy fresh air, smell a flower or chat with a friend or family member? Sometimes we're so foolish and arrogant that we get angry over nonsense and create problems where they don't exist. Every day is a preciously decorated chest for us to open and revel in. In our football bubble, value is attached to things that should be underplayed, including victory and defeat. People come up to you and insult you, they want to knock you out, they want to launch objects at you, but it's no more than a game of football!

The lads, or people in general, spend eight hours asleep and eight hours at work every day. Fine. The other eight are to be enjoyed. So why spend them glued to your phone on Twitter or Instagram? We don't communicate, we don't share. Being with someone no longer has the same significance as it used to. One eye is always glancing at a phone.

Maybe I am getting old. Older. So there is a natural tendency to see the past through rose-tinted glasses. I feel our generation (maybe all generations) lives between two worlds, different but equally exciting, sometimes prompting us to ask ourselves, 'Are we losing the essence of what life is all about?'

*

15 April. We were in action before Chelsea once again, with Bournemouth coming to White Hart Lane.

Dembélé, who opened the scoring with a goal from a set-piece that we'd rehearsed, performed very well. Harry Kane was back in the starting line-up and scored our third, becoming the first Tottenham player to score more than 20 league goals in three consecutive seasons since the legendary Jimmy Greaves towards the end of the sixties. We were completely dominant. A Bournemouth side that like to be in possession had never had so little of the ball. We registered 14 shots on target to their one. Son and Janssen also got on the scoresheet in the 4–0 success. We've scored four or more goals on 11 occasions this season and have notched 28 goals in our last eight games. The level of intensity has been remarkable. That's eight wins on the bounce, including five clean sheets. There isn't a single spectator on our books: everyone is committed to their responsibilities.

We're back to within four points of Chelsea who make the trip to Old Trafford tomorrow.

*

We have hardly any injuries, we're carefully calculating our rest periods and are in the best shape we've been in this season. Confidence is very high and the players have made the most of their opportunities, while championing a style that we all believe in. Almost everything is coming off at the moment and I couldn't hide that in the press conference after the Bournemouth game. The club's statistics haven't been this good in half a century. After 32 games three years ago, we were on 54 points. It was 62 last year and it's 71 this time around, trumping our total from last season. If we'd sustained the same points per game average in 2015-16, we'd have won the league ahead of Leicester City.

I did something else in front of the press, which was to remind everyone that what's happening here is down to the team's commitment and hard work combined with our approach. Our starting line-up against Bournemouth included five players that I signed, and six of the seven on the bench were also my recruits. Absolutely everyone has improved. 'Tottenham aren't building in an artificial way. It isn't about putting in more and more money to build a fantastic team,' I told journalists. 'It's a very natural process, ours, with our rules and projections, so, as a consequence, unique in the world.'

And so the FA Cup semi-final against Chelsea, our next game, was effectively already underway.

*

We all sat at home watching Manchester United take on Chelsea. I gave the players the day off and we didn't even exchange messages during the game, although we were all keeping up with the action. The locals in and around Tottenham certainly celebrated when Rashford put United 1–0 up.

The feeling surrounding us now is vastly different from last year. Nobody wanted us to ruin the Leicester fairy tale and there was very negative energy enveloping us last year. Even Ranieri admitted as much on Sky Sports a few days ago: 'The whole world tried to help Leicester.'

We always played after them, for example. The pressure on the youngest Premier League side was huge. Ranieri and his charges deserved the title, but I think that everyone now has a better understanding of what happened to us in that game against Chelsea where it all fizzled out. We were battling against our opponents, the media and football fans alike.

This time it's more balanced and the same conditions are in place for each side. As a team, we're much clearer on what the target is and how to achieve it. All that matters is the next game.

Manchester United scored again! Ander Herrera struck in the 59th minute.

Full-time! United won 2–0, leaving us four points behind Chelsea after the same number of games. There are six league matches remaining.

Jesús just sent me a message. He heard Conte say that Tottenham are the best side in the Premier League right now. He was surprised that the Italian added that his team lacked desire and motivation, and blamed himself. Antonio claimed it wasn't normal for them to be top, having not come into the season as contenders on the back of finishing tenth. When it's not all going to plan, things can be seen in a different light. You can never be entirely sure where a rival coach's words come from or his true intentions, but he seems to think his team are in a tricky situation. They've gone ten games without keeping a clean sheet and so, maybe he's taking the pressure off them.

We have a week to get ready for our semi-final date with Chelsea at Wembley.

It'll be a huge derby.

*

The planets aligned when I scored the winner for Rosario against Central and met the woman who changed my life. But you have to be careful when it comes to derbies. You feel everything more strongly and your senses are sharpened.

I was 18. I had scored the first goal in a *clásico* between Newell's Old

Boys and Rosario Central that we went on to win handsomely 4–0. It was 14 April 1991 and Marcelo Bielsa was our coach.

I opened the scoring and instantly ran towards Newell's fans behind the goal. I climbed up on to the fence where the ultras were and yelled at the top of my voice. As you would expect after a convincing 4–0 victory, we were gods in Rosario that evening. It was crazy. I took Berizzo, Ruffini, Franco and Boldrini back to my flat where we drank beer and ate pizza into the night. We ended up at a nightclub called Arrow and, of course, we had to make a grand entrance. It was around 3 a.m. and we were already quite tired, but still elated. That's where I met my wife, a girl from Misiones who was studying pharmacy in Rosario and had also gone out that night. She wasn't that into football, in fact she preferred rugby. What I didn't yet know was that she'd already set her sights on me a few months earlier, which she told me after we got married.

She was watching the telly with her flatmate who was a huge Newell's fan. We were shown celebrating the Apertura title on a Rosario television channel. I was with Gamboa, who had long, black hair and green eyes. I was blond and also had long hair. They were doing a fun interview with us and Karina's friend told her how much she loved Gamboa. My wife said to her, 'I like the other one, the blond guy.' She didn't even know my name.

Six months later, Newell's team went to the discotheque and headed straight for the VIP room. People saw us go in and it was mayhem, as you'd expect. Women, men, everyone! We made a big impact, not because we were so good-looking, but because we were representing a winning team. I remember that I wanted to dance with her friend, a strikingly tall blonde, and chatted a bit to her, but I then set my eyes on Karina, who I liked more. At that point I was with a non-footballer friend of mine who I grabbed by the arm, sent him in the direction of the blonde girl, and said, 'We're now going to dance as a four.' I'd already told the blonde! For the record, I ended up spending more time chatting to the one that would later become my wife.

I got married a couple of years later, soon after turning 20.

I blame, in part, the Rosario derby.

*

Although Arsenal are our historic rivals, the derby that has defined our progress since I arrived at White Hart Lane has been against Chelsea. It has been the source of frustration and, on occasion, extreme jubilation.

Results weren't going to plan during the first half of my inaugural season here. In fact, there were enough disappointing moments for some to deduce that we were simply going to churn out another underwhelming campaign. Our football wasn't exciting and we weren't capable of keeping up the level required to compete at the top. Exactly halfway through the season on 1 January we welcomed Chelsea to White Hart Lane. They were top and we were seventh, although unbeaten in five games. Just a month earlier they'd comfortably beaten us 3–0 at Stamford Bridge. Harry Kane's tally already stood at 15 goals, but he hadn't scored in a big game. Diego Costa put them ahead, but we kept going and battling. We equalised through Kane. Then we went 2–1 up, 3–1, 4–1. Harry again! 4–2, 5–2. It ended 5–3 against a Chelsea team that went on to win the title.

The result, which moved us up to fifth, made everyone stand up and take note, from supporters to the press, and it was possibly a turning point in my time at the club. Something was happening at Tottenham, so they said. The guy in charge of that group isn't just a crazy Argentinian who speaks bad English.

We faced Mourinho's Chelsea again in early March in the League Cup final. I insisted on the premise of learning from every second that led us to Wembley. Eriksen hit the crossbar before we conceded a goal from a defensive mistake on the stroke of half-time. We didn't manage to get back into the game in the second half and lost 2–0. I said to them, 'Guys, keep this losing feeling with you. Use it and remember it, because if you do and if we get to another final, you won't want to feel it again.' I asked them to stay and watch as Chelsea lifted the cup. Many steps in the right direction were taken that day.

In November of the following season, we drew 0–0 against them at White Hart Lane and in May we had the opportunity to stay hot on the heels of Leicester City. Anything but victory at Stamford Bridge would definitely end our title challenge. We were up against our fears, the world and, of course, it was Chelsea, which ramped up the temperature by quite a few notches. I was surprised that several players in our opponents' ranks declared hatred towards us and love for Leicester, against whom they were playing on the final day at home.

We were battling for the championship, while Chelsea were playing for pride. I understand and value the fact that teams in England give their all in every single game. We have to keep that going, it's a huge positive. Behaviour in the dugout, however, is another matter altogether.

Something that drove Nicola Cortese up the wall was the fact that there were club coaches in the England Under-18s and Under-21s set-up. At Manchester United, Louis van Gaal did not want his assistants to be the England national team's assistants as well. Given the England national team's financial muscle, it doesn't make sense for it not to have its own coaching staff and use club coaches instead, does it? But Chelsea have an assistant who also works for the national team. He should set an example, but he certainly did no such thing that day. The way he looked at us as they piled on the pressure, or the way he came over to our bench to celebrate Chelsea's goals was not right, unnecessary. Incidentally, it was the complete opposite of what Chelsea manager Guus Hiddink was doing. Guus was a real gentleman, while still trying to beat us, despite the tension that arose that evening. When I saw that assistant soon after at our training ground, which the national team was using, I made my feelings very clear to him.

Kane and Son scored for us in the first half. A win would leave us five points behind Leicester with two games left to play. It would be extremely tough, but not impossible. Danny Rose and Willian squared up to each other just before half-time. Sparks were flying and we ended the game with nine yellow cards. 'We aren't 2–0 up. Play as if it were 0–0. We have to win the second half,' I told them in the dressing room.

Cahill capitalised on a defensive error to score and Hazard equalised late on. It ended 2–2 and Leicester City were proclaimed champions without kicking a ball.

Ten minutes after the final whistle in a dressing room where all you could hear was the clickety-clack of studs on the floor, I hugged and shook hands with all the players. 'Don't beat yourselves up over this, you've given your all and I'm very proud of you.' I didn't say much else.

Well, I did. That we had to finish second and keep up the attitude that we showed at Stamford Bridge. We know that didn't happen, but the experience will ensure that next time we're in a similar situation, which may well be this season, we'll try to manage it differently.

*

I'm writing this in the early hours, the night before a game – and not just any match, but an FA Cup semi-final. I can't sleep. Life has floored us again.

The week leading up to the semi-final started off normally. Very much so. We had Sunday off, on Monday we did an introductory session, while two days of hard grind followed on Tuesday and Wednesday. We focused on some fundamentals of our game that we weren't happy with, seeking to adjust our positioning to press better after losing the ball and move the holding midfielders further forward. They're inclined to think that by sitting closer to the defenders they protect the team, but in actual fact that means giving the opposition more space. We'd seen repeated errors on that front, but we hadn't had the opportunity to address them in training.

The players must've thought we were crazy given the intensity we demanded over those two days. We asked them to be aggressive and physical, and to take risks. 'Hold nothing back!' we barked at them. On Thursday we did tactical work, part of which involved playing ten v eleven. The team that was a man down – we were the ones with ten in this scenario and Chelsea the ones with a full complement – had to harry up top. We had to overcome the numerical inferiority through risk: we left ourselves one v one at the back and let the opposition bring the ball out, but then we hunted in packs in certain areas. We knew that Chelsea would look to keep it tight and hit us on the break with long balls, capitalising on any errors we committed.

I'd almost made up my mind on our line-up: Wanyama had recovered well and would start. Son had played an important role in recent matches, chipping in with goals and assists. He seemed so up for it that we knew he'd perform well regardless of where we played him. How would we approach it? 3-4-3, beyond question. The easy thing to do would've been to introduce another defensive midfielder, but . . .

Are we brave? Do we want to play aggressively? Well then, we're going to do that and then some in this match.

I sensed that our lads were feeling strong. There's been real confidence and camaraderie in the air, coursing through their bodies and their minds. We knew that keeping the positivity flowing was important, because everything can change in a flash. In fact, it's a *Sliding Doors* moment. If Chelsea win, it could give them the impetus to go on and claim a league and cup double. If we go through, the confidence boost could help us win one or even two trophies. All that's pure speculation, but it's something we've discussed.

Incidentally, the PFA Premier League Team of the Year was announced: it features four of our players (Walker, Rose, Alli and Kane), as well as four from Chelsea. What I don't really understand is why Dele was only nominated for the Young Player of the Year award and not the main one.

But then, we were rocked by one of those bitter, devastating blows that life serves up sometimes. Jesús and I were heading back in after training and talking about how intense the session had been when we saw the club doctor and two physios running towards the academy pitches. I immediately realised that something serious had happened. I asked Toni and Miki to stay with the first team, while we went over to see what was going on. We came across the lads from the Under-23s, who were traipsing towards the dressing rooms looking distressed.

'What's happened?' I asked.

'There's something wrong with Ugo.' We sprinted over and saw that the doctor was trying to revive Ugo Ehiogu, our Under-23s coach, who'd had a heart attack. An ambulance arrived five minutes later. The paramedics also tried to resuscitate him, before rushing him to hospital. Knowing that he was in good hands, we continued to hold out hope and were in regular contact, but the atmosphere was downbeat. A great many players had worked with him. He was practically part of the first-team set-up, of our family.

At three o'clock the following morning, the phone rang: Ugo had passed away. Aged just 44.

A wave of oppressive, negative energy, of pain, ripped through me. It's so hard to describe. I relived everything that had happened with Dani Jarque.

How easily people disappear and how difficult it is to fill the void they leave. Ugo was taken away in the ambulance and I never saw him again. And I never will. Only memories remain.

*

We changed all of our plans for today, Friday. We trained and showered, and then I sent the lads home.

*

Two different approaches to football collided in the semi-final at Wembley. That was laid bare in the conversation I had with Conte before the match. He came into our dressing room to offer his condolences and we had a wide-ranging chat. Talking to the manager of a club like Chelsea is a good way of confirming how different things are. We're competing in the same league and are based in the same city, but our problems are totally different.

I like the paraphernalia surrounding the FA Cup, with all of us dressed to the nines and the stands full of colour. In England, they certainly know the formula to turn a football match into a unique experience.

Unfortunately, we let in a very early goal, which knocked the stuffing out of us. The mistake wasn't so much bringing down Pedro on the edge of the area, although by that time he was heading away from goal and had three defenders around him, but rather having allowed the long ball beforehand to reach Batshuayi in a metre and a half of space, because we'd worked on those sorts of sequences and the players knew that their move had to finish right there and then. If possession can't be recovered, a foul in midfield breaks up a dangerous counter.

I stayed calm and remained standing after the goal. In fact, I spent three-quarters of the game on my feet in the technical area.

We came back into it and equalised through Kane. Then, just before the break, Chelsea scored again through a harsh penalty, leaving us having to regroup a second time. We made a few positional tweaks at half-time and reminded some of the players that they had to do more.

We equalised again after the interval, through Dele, during a 20–25 minute spell in which we played some of our best football of the season. We had them right up against the wall; in fact I think it's

242

the most comprehensively one of my teams have dominated another in my four years in England. We passed the ball around well, pinned Chelsea back very deep and forced them to go long even more than they'd planned. Trippier was sensational, containing Marcos Alonso, one of their biggest threats, who ended up frustrated because he wasn't able to get forward. I appealed to the fans to make more noise.

But then we conceded a third goal, which came from Chelsea's only corner, after they had crossed the halfway line for practically the first time since the interval. We gambled after that, only for them to settle the contest with a fourth and final goal, a long-range screamer from Matić.

We played better than Chelsea, but it was one of those games that we just weren't destined to win, whatever we did. It was almost irrelevant whether or not we started Son, as we'd debated, or whether we went with three or four at the back: we conceded from a free-kick, a penalty, a second ball from a corner that we failed to deal with and a 40-yard strike that whizzed into the top corner. They scored four times from five attempts on target; we had 66 per cent possession, 11 corners to their one, and I don't know how many shots . . .

There's not much more we could've done.

We went away with genuine pride at having given it a go and having stayed true to our principles. Nobody can accuse us of shrinking away or not playing to win. I know that the result is what will be remembered, but can anyone guarantee that we'd have won playing any other way? It's true that we were missing something, something we simply don't have. We deserved more, but at this level, deserving it isn't always enough.

I understand the supporters starting to leave five minutes before the final whistle. Although I don't know how fair it is to us, they viewed the match within a wider context: a record seventh straight FA Cup semi-final defeat, and a fourth against Chelsea. In any case, it's the first under me, but I share their ambition. Just playing well won't cut it.

Now we've got to move on and look ahead. We've got Crystal Palace in four days' time.

We're still in the title race.

*

Sunday was a day off, but I had a couple of meetings. Back at home, I put the TV on with the sound off and watched Real Madrid v Barcelona out of the corner of my eye. Sitting there on the sofa, with no audience or obligations, Ugo came back to the forefront of my thoughts. It is almost incomprensible that he is gone for ever. On Monday, everyone was still distraught, and some psychologists came in to offer support, especially to the academy kids. I took the reserve team out for dinner. Every person is a world unto himself, every group is a different universe, and every moment calls for different words to be said. In this instance, there was a need to get the positive energy flowing again.

While at Espanyol, shortly after I was appointed coach, I experienced an electric moment that transformed the atmosphere. We were struggling to haul the team out of the mire. During a game that we were losing, I was about to bring off De la Peña because he was on a booking and was in danger of getting sent off. I decided to keep him on in the end, and we wound up drawing. Back in the dressing room, De la Peña said to me, 'We're going to stay up.' We were a long way from safety, but something had got into him – a fit of madness, a surge of optimism and faith. It infected his teammates, as well as the fans. We all believed him. And we stayed up.

Sometimes our group could do with a dash of madness. But it's got to come from them, not from us.

Two days after the cup semi-final, the players were asking us about their holidays and whether we were going to go off on tour right after the end of the league season. My mind turned back to the Newcastle game. I was a footballer too, so I understand them: after a match, your attention shifts to what's coming next. They see what they can squeeze out; I did the same as a player. That's not to say I wasn't focused on the next game – it's just that I wanted to know everything in advance, to have everything mapped out. I saw everything from a different angle.

But as a coach, it's tough to swallow. These things piss me off, but I don't let on to the players. I guess if they ever read this diary, they will know! We spend all year reiterating that they've got to be invested in what they're playing for because that will bring better performances out of them. But it is not always easy for them to act accordingly.

It's Wednesday morning right now. It's going to be a long day: we're playing tonight. We've got three London derbies in a row: away to Crystal Palace, at home to Arsenal and away to West Ham. Then we face Manchester United. Chelsea won yesterday to move seven points clear, so it's win or bust for us against Palace, who beat the league leaders the other day.

*

We were made to fight hard to overcome a disciplined, defensive Crystal Palace.

At half-time we switched our system and took off the two holding midfielders, Dembélé due to injury and Wanyama because he was on a yellow card. Son and Sissoko came on tasked with giving us more width, and Eriksen dropped deeper alongside Eric Dier in central midfield. We were supremely dominant; truth be told, we were helped by Palace having had a day's less rest than us. They only managed one shot on target in the second half.

With just over 12 minutes to go, Christian Eriksen smashed home from outside the box to hand us the three points.

We showed character and mental strength.

Chelsea's lead is back down to four points.

*

Danny Rose has had another setback in his recovery from a knee-ligament injury and needs surgery. He'll be out for another four months, meaning he'll miss the rest of the season and pre-season.

I had to speak out to counter some comments made by Xavi Hernández on a television programme, although some friends of his subsequently denied he'd ever said them. They were about Manchester City and their supposed interest in Dele Alli, suggesting that City were lining up a big bid.

I'll always remember facing Xavi in a derby with Espanyol, which Barcelona unfairly won from the spot after it looked to me as though he'd dived in the box. After the match he claimed that Raúl Baena, a youngster who'd just broken into our team, had admitted that it was a penalty. There are lines you shouldn't cross.

Thierry Henry came to the training ground to film an interview with Harry Kane for Sky Sports and we spent some time with him. I reminded him how, when my staff and I arrived, people used to say to us, 'We've lost twice in a row to West Ham.'

'Bloody hell, if we're fearing West Ham, we may as well pack up and go home,' I'd reply.

Now it's a similar story with Arsenal. It's been repeated a thousand times that we could finish above them in the league for the first time in 22 years. Kane joined in our conversation and told Henry, 'Maybe it's something that excites the fans, but we've got bigger fish to fry.'

The last North London derby at White Hart Lane is fast approaching. Memories are flooding back of Espanyol's 3–2 win over Valencia in the final fixture at Sarrià. Like that year, the stadium is playing its part: we want to go the whole season unbeaten at home.

*

We were at the training ground at 10.30 on Sunday morning.

'Shall we do a bit of running on the treadmill?' I asked Miki.

We ended up power walking, only occasionally breaking into a jog, but we still worked up a sweat. We showered and then the players started to arrive. I sat on my couch while they had breakfast. By that point, we'd decided on the team: Dembélé was carrying a knock, so we'd leave him on the bench. The players' expressions and choice of food didn't tell us anything new, so we started with Lloris, Davies, Alderweireld, Vertonghen, Trippier, Wanyama, Dier, Dele, Eriksen, Son and Kane.

I knew there'd be speculation over the reasons why I left Walker out of the starting XI, but we felt that Trippier was the right pick for the match. He didn't have a great start to the season but he got into gear when his opportunity came. His form dipped again over the Christmas period, but after that he kept upping his game, despite not being a regular starter. And sometimes, however much you put it off, you have to take the plunge and give a player a chance at another's expense.

Leaving out a regular always wounds them, creating a rift between them and the coaching staff that can be very difficult to heal. A while back, we benched one of our three best players. He's usually a nailed-on starter, one of the first names on my team sheet. His face hardened when he found out. Three weeks later, his agent showed up wanting to talk to us.

These days, footballers lack perspective and demand immediate answers. Ultimately Trippier forced his way into contention and he's been one of the team's standout players every time he's played. Like Ben Davies, he hasn't been daunted by having to battle a high-profile international for a place in the side.

We later reconvened to travel to the stadium together on the coach; I was one of the first to arrive. We switched the TV on because Everton v Chelsea kicked off a couple of hours before our game (4.30). We averted the usual bickering between Harry Kane and Dele Alli over whose music should be played; they let Toni choose for a while. Complaints ensued because, even though he put on stuff the lads listen to, he slipped in the odd Spanish song too and they weren't about to let it slide.

Once we got to the ground, though, we didn't turn on the television in the dressing room and none of the players asked me about the Chelsea score.

White Hart Lane was packed. There was a mixture of apprehension and a party atmosphere in the stands; the fans were in full voice and you could see the anticipation on their faces. Chelsea had beaten Everton, but there was still a huge amount at stake. When the match got underway, the tension had spilled on to the pitch. Our players were a bit off and were making lots of poor decisions. But we didn't see it as a bad thing: we took it as a mark of respect for Arsenal, even though they were 14 points behind us.

A lot has been made of Arsène Wenger's switch to three at the back after 20 years playing with a four-man defence. We analysed ways in which we could get the better of their system and so at different points during the match we used three or four at the back, as well as variously playing with two centre-backs and three holding midfielders, pushing the full-backs right up the pitch to become wingers, or tucking them in as auxiliary midfielders.

Toni, Miki, Jesús and I still believe that less can be more, that the slightest detail or decision can be crucial to getting an advantage. Miki asked our video analyst to prepare something on the team's movement when we had the ball. Ben Davies was finding himself free, but Son and Alli were playing through the middle too much.

Back in the dressing room, with the score 0–0 at half-time, my staff and I talked things over among ourselves for seven minutes, as usual, before putting our game plan for the second half to the players. We moved Son from the left to the right, while Eriksen shifted infield. Ben Davies gaped at me: 'What about me?' I'd only written ten names on the whiteboard and he was the odd one out.

'You're going to play as a wing-back, with Dele ahead of you. You're going to make a very important contribution, that's why I don't even need to include you on there,' I said. We laughed.

This is how we broke the deadlock. Dele was popping up in the middle and then on the right. Ben got possession, but had no one to link up with down his flank. Then Dele drifted over to the left. So much for sticking to his position! We exchanged glances in the dugout: 'Fine, he can do what he wants.' The ball went out for a throw-in. Trippier, who's very intelligent tactically, grabbed it and quickly threw a long one to Kane. That's where things opened up. The ball made its way to Dele, who was bursting into the area up the right. He played it to Eriksen, who did well to jink past a couple of defenders and unleash a close-range strike. The keeper could only parry it as far as Dele, who turned the rebound into the empty net. My staff and I shared a group hug on the touchline.

Two minutes later, Kane drove into the box, was brought down and picked himself up to convert the penalty, his fifth goal in as many league appearances against Arsenal.

There are people who don't like some of our goal celebrations, especially those special handshakes when the players' hands seem to take on a life of their own. I love them. Those types of things create bonds between the players; the physical contact brings them closer. It's communication, coordination and football rolled into one. It hones their concentration and imagination, which is also an important ingredient in a team's success. At Newell's we used to celebrate like crazy; we'd scream out 'Goooaaalll' and jump up on to the metal fence. We weren't very subtle.

With a minute to go, the television cameras started zooming in on me, as usual. I saw them, but paid them no heed, as if they weren't there. Before I used to be more self-conscious about them, but now they're just part of the scenery.

2–0.

I went over to Wenger. 'I'm full of respect and admiration for you,' I told him. He shook my hand and then walked away; he wasn't in the mood to talk, which I understand. It hurts to lose, all the more so when you're being asked to prove your worth after 20 years of doing so much for a club. He deserves to be judged on far more than a single result or season.

Toni hung around with me to salute the players before we all headed down the tunnel. You've got to enjoy such occasions, because they're over before you know it. He was waiting for Hugo, whom I bear-hugged. The magic normally fades within five minutes of returning to the dressing room, because my thoughts will turn to the press or the next match.

The celebrations lasted longer this time round, however. It was a moment for the players and the coaching staff to savour together, shutting out the rest of the world. After that, I exchanged greetings with Wenger's assistants, who joined mine for a chat and a glass of wine, and then I went off to my press conference. Jesús later told me that we ran 10 kilometres more than Arsenal.

We're four points off Chelsea. We're not looking over our shoulders (Arsenal are 17 points behind us); rather, we're looking ahead. There are four games to go and one more point would clinch second place, guaranteeing that we finish above City, Liverpool and United. We've won nine on the bounce and all of our league matches in April. We've got used to it, but what we're doing isn't normal.

We left the stadium. Waiting for us, in the shadow of the new ground, was a taxi: the players had taken the coach back to the training ground to pick up their cars. There was something different about the Tottenham supporters we saw as we rode past them; they had a spring in their step and a smile on their faces. Full of pride, they were singing and walking along side by side. The streets belonged to them: the Arsenal fans were nowhere to be seen.

This emotion is what football is all about and no, it wasn't just an ordinary game.

And no, nothing happens by chance.

11.

MAY

I n May the season reached its climax and several cycles came to an end. A Tottenham side that nobody expected to finish in the top four battled it out for the championship with Chelsea, and, if they picked up four points, would match the tally with which Leicester won the title the previous year (81). It was also the culmination of collective and individual goals, while White Hart Lane's doors were closed for ever. And Pochettino had the chance to put to bed the Newcastle game from the previous campaign in another final-day fixture away to a relegated club.

I've just started to read *Leadership*, Sir Alex Ferguson's latest book. We've sent each other the odd text message since that lunch back in May 2016 and I hope that I'll be able to sit down with him again soon. He may even pay us a visit at the training ground.

I said to Simon Felstein, 'I'm having lunch with Sir Alex.' As I had my own press conference to attend, I suggested mentioning it to avoid any misunderstandings. Louis van Gaal was walking a tightrope at

Old Trafford and our meeting had nothing to do with his future or mine. Simon convinced me not to broach the topic but, to pre-empt any reaction to the meeting, I could reveal that I'd reached a verbal agreement with the club on a new five-year contract, which is what I did. 'You'll be photographed with Sir Alex,' Simon said to me.

'I imagine so,' I replied.

I'll always remember each and every detail from those hours of conversation. It was a dream come true. I felt like a teenage footballer all over again, listening to a knowledgeable coach. I sent the photos that we took of us together to everyone. John McDermott commented that I seemed to be in a trance. He called me a 'hero worshipper'.

I knew many details from Ferguson's career and admired him for the way that he turned United into a successful team, while creating something different in world football. But when I met him, what impressed me most was not so much the CV, but his energy and aura. His character, his charisma engulfs you. I'd love to keep calling on his advice.

He spoke to me about how he had to restructure everything when he arrived at United. He did so in keeping with his own philosophy, even though they finished 11th two years out of three, followed by 13th, sixth, second and only after that did he achieve league success. His Manchester United side were like the Tottenham team that I inherited when I took over, and the chat reassured me about following my own path. 'You play two games each matchday,' he told me. 'The first is in the press. Never lose it.' We're slightly different in this regard, but I did take note.

And at the end of the meal there was, as I thought there would be, a fight to pay the bill. I wanted to do it, and so did Sir Alex. But he had planned this beforehand so he proposed a solution. 'I will ask you a question,' he said. I smiled. 'If you get it right, you pay. If not, I pay.' I suspected that he must have thought of something hard to get so that I would have to admit defeat. But I accepted the challenge.

'Deal,' I responded.

'Final of the 1930 World Cup. Argentina v Uruguay. The result was 4–2.'

'Yes, go on.'

'Who scored the goals for Argentina?'

This time I laughed loudly. 'Carlos Peucelle and Guillermo Stábile,' I answered.

Ferguson started clapping and shaking his head. 'Well done, well done . . .' I proceeded to pay.

Photos from our meeting were published the following day, while I was still on cloud nine. 'Bloody hell, I was with Sir Alex!'

Why aren't there more Fergusons? Because football is like an express train without any stops. It's almost impossible to find someone in charge who is willing to be involved in taking unpopular measures. Sir Alex always says, 'Many times you have to make decisions that screw you over emotionally, that won't be understood and you won't be able to explain.' I agree. Managers live in a perpetual state of solitude, even when surrounded by people at all hours. Everybody seems to know better. I often joke with the chairman: 'It's easy to coach a team: put on Sky Sports, listen to what the pundits say, run a poll in any newspaper that you have access to and at five or six o'clock, when you have all that information, decide who should get a new contract, who has to play, who makes the starting line-up, who is to be sold . . .'

*

After beating Arsenal, Daniel and I celebrated the fact that we were going to finish above our historic rivals for the first time in over two decades. It wasn't our aim, but you have to stop and enjoy the good moments, even if only briefly.

Two hours later, articles started to crop up about an alleged row between Kyle Walker and me.

I've never had a fight with anyone during my three years at Tottenham. I may not have shared the same view as certain players, but nothing more.

Here are the facts: Walker had just played back-to-back games for the national team. Our first match after his return was against Burnley on the Saturday. Kieran Trippier had been doing well in training for a few months and got the nod, meaning Walker was on the bench. We played Swansea on the Wednesday and Walker started. Trippier came back into the team to face Watford on the Saturday and was named man of the match. We won all three fixtures and were happy to have two regular starters competing for a place, with both players looking fresh for the final stretch of the campaign.

Walker came to my office after the Watford game.

'Gaffer, I've been at Tottenham for nine years. I've thought about it and my heart isn't here any more. Nor is my head. I've given all I have to give. I wanted to tell you before I tell my agent that I want to leave this summer.'

'Kyle, you have to stay professional. There's a month and a half of the season to go. We're battling for the Premier League and FA Cup. We have to be focused and finish the campaign strongly.'

'OK, gaffer. But it's already decided.'

'Well, that doesn't just depend on you or me. It depends on the club, above all. You've disappointed me because you've decided to tell me that you want to leave when there is a month and bit left in the competition . . . You could've sucked it up, kept quiet, trained, played and helped the team when not picked . . . And at the end of the season you could've come and told me.'

Miguel was present. I always try to ensure there are witnesses during private conversations. I considered it to be an alarming lack of respect for his teammates. It's also a slap in the face for the club that turned him into a professional.

None of that could be explained to the public at the time; I had to bite my tongue. From that point, the rumours started to proliferate. They clearly suggested that Walker was on the market. We'll see how possible negotiations with other clubs proceed over the summer.

It's that time when agents look to secure transfers and improved contracts for their clients, which is lawful, but I'm not one to feed rumours. I don't read that type of content in the press. If I did, I'd find out we'd signed 200 players and sold 200 others, not to mention the number of managers that could've replaced me. Someone should put all the names together and calculate the percentage of accuracy. Having said that, rumours are an important part of the business, since they effectively put the player on the market, help feed his ego and give other clubs ideas ('What if it's true and we can sign him?'). You just have to understand it and not let it get under your skin.

It is a sign of success too. One thing that doesn't often get pointed out is that supposedly twenty players out of our twenty-five-man squad are coveted by other clubs, despite the fact that we aren't a selling club any more. We sell on the players that we don't want. Daniel has more experience now and no longer restricts the process to cold and mathematical analysis. I also see things differently compared with three years ago. I understand the club better and know that not everything consists of instilling basic performance-linked principles.

It's May and the decisions that we make at this stage will affect the whole of next season. We don't need to change many players. Those who go will be the ones who want to play more or whose motivation differs from the club's.

And those who arrive ... Will they fit in? The pitch at Wembley, where we will play our home games next season, is five metres longer and one metre wider than at White Hart Lane. It's great for playing expansive football, but it requires a bigger physical effort. We have to look for more athletic players who are quick both going forward and defensively, and maybe others who have a trick or two in their locker and use their pace out wide as there is more space. It would be great to improve the team in those areas.

The new players have to be affordable, whether that means they have problems with their current clubs or are entering the last year of their contracts if they ply their trade in the Premier League. If someone wanting to come in demands high wages, we'd have to give the others a salary increase as well, and that simply can't happen. Daniel is a tough negotiator and hasn't made many friends in the process. When you dive into the market, they're waiting for you. As we can't sign the very best, the next level is young players who need to be nurtured. The demands are higher and higher. If the team's level drops, even marginally, we'll fall behind.

So for all those reasons the most feasible option could be to ensure we have good back-ups in every position and improve what we already have even more.

Our club has been linked to major players who are looking for an escape route from their current employers. Some of them called us. I have had a good relationship with Álvaro Morata, who phoned me when he was at Real Madrid B and I was at Espanyol. He wanted to ask me how he could impress José Mourinho, who was in charge of the first team back then. He could see that we also worked with young players and asked me for advice. His agent has been in touch with several Premier League clubs even before the season is over, but a transfer is out of the question for us, partly because he himself does not see how he can take over from Harry Kane. That is the problem we will face this summer – it is so hard to improve on our regular players.

Marcus Edwards, our little Messi, the guy who could conquer the world, will be another prickly subject. We've set very high standards which not everyone will reach, but he certainly could. But will he? Does he want to? He's already played for and trained with the first team. He, in tandem with the club, will have to decide which path to take his career and if he feels the process we offer is the right one for him – we think it is. But we live in an era in which it is very difficult for clubs to deal with youth players who have lots of talent – the money other clubs sometimes offer for youngsters who have not even made their first-team debuts can make you dizzy.

To sum up, it'll be a busy summer.

Anything can happen, but we are ready for anything.

*

During a conference that I attended to renew my UEFA Pro Licence, Arrigo Sacchi, another extraordinary thinker whom I admire, spoke to us about the effort required to win the ball back. 'What do we coach? Feet or brains?' he asked us. He insisted that a high press is more about the desire to carry it out than the players' physical capacity. Attackers find it harder than others to understand how crucial their role is when you lose possession. Christian Eriksen may well be the exception to that.

When we're on the ball, his link-up work with Dele Alli has worked brilliantly. We have two mobile number 10s who interchange positions, not only between themselves, but also with those who break forward and burst into the area or move from central areas out wide. Both understand how flexible the system is. If necessary, Christian drops deep to help the team build the play from the back in our half.

We call him 'Golazo', because he scores so many spectacular goals in training. He isn't the type who needs people or the press to show him how loved he is. He isn't after external recognition. He's remarkably calm, and I'd occasionally like him to be a tad more fired up. At Espanyol I had a player who was scared of contact and decided to do kickboxing to get over it. Christian isn't scared, but he could make better use of his physique by earning more free-kicks near the box. That's the next area where he could evolve.

He's rounding off a very good season, having racked up 11 goals and 16 assists. His goal against Crystal Palace saved us and he'll start at West Ham. We have to keep the pressure on Chelsea, although it'll be difficult to catch them. They're four points ahead with four games left.

*

It can be so hard to be a manager sometimes. Especially when you come to a crossroads and have to choose a route.

It's been an unpleasant week. I haven't really been able to enjoy the win over Arsenal, with the Walker stories flying around. I've been rather subdued. My pre-match press conference ahead of the West Ham game was tough. I was asked many questions that weren't easy to answer.

'Has Walker trained as normal?'

'Why wouldn't he?' I replied.

'Is Walker happy at Tottenham?'

What was I supposed to do? Tell the press about our conversation? At that time?

'Don't you think it's strange that the player hasn't come out to deny the alleged row with you?' a journalist asked. If someone doesn't want to leave, he'll certainly come out and deny the story, right? I am convinced that his people are leaking stories to the press. So should I be the person to deal with the matter publicly? If I were the club owner, would I want to support the manager or give off the impression that if Walker leaves, it's purely down to the boss?

The whole topic was discussed internally, and whether it was a co-incidence or not, a tabloid newspaper devoted four pages to the team the following day, with two about my influence and two on the new stadium.

Such conflicts prevent you from being completely free when it comes to making decisions. No manager controls all the media, every player or the club as a whole. Choosing the starting line-ups allows you to show your authority, but it's often conditional. How can you leave a regular on the bench without it causing adverse repercussions?

After mulling it over, we decided to start Walker against West Ham because we wanted to keep rotating, but what if the decision affected the team?

We didn't play well against West Ham from the get-go. We tried several things, but none of them came off. We deserved to lose 1–0 and that hurt. We were not at our best. After nine straight wins, the defeat paves the way for our rivals, who won their game. They're now seven points ahead with nine left to play for.

We gave everyone two days off and I travelled to Barcelona on that same morning. When I'm back, I'll need to get them to regain their focus and make it clear that the season isn't over.

*

I couldn't get the game out of my head while in Barcelona. Was that faltering attitude at the end of last season rearing its ugly head once again? It's as if the campaign came to an end after the Arsenal match. I was convinced that, as a group, we were in a different place and wouldn't stumble over the same rock. On Monday, when I got back, I spoke to the players in the usual place, the sofas at the restaurant. But I didn't hide my disgust and was rather cold. I didn't feel as though it was the time for hugs or kisses. I heard that many players got worried. 'What's up with him?'

I didn't go to the first session of the week. The rest of the coaching staff were also distant in calculated measure. It was going to be a very long week.

I didn't go on the second day either. Jesús was aggressive towards them. He didn't let a single one of them off the hook. He pushed and pushed.

'Maybe Poch wants to leave the club? There are rumours about Inter . . .' was the talk at mealtimes. Alarm bells were ringing, thanks to a meeting that I had with Piero Ausilio, the Italian club's sporting director whom I've known since they loaned Coutinho to Espanyol.

I arranged separate chats with the club captains, all of whom were visibly worried. 'Are you OK? You seem irritated and far away. Do you want to leave?' The reactions were rather eye-opening. The more experienced players didn't need much of an explanation about where I was coming from and didn't look to shift the blame, but remained concerned. 'What can we do to make you feel better?' they asked. Jesús told me that was the price to pay for the way I work. 'In general, you treat them like a father would and you get 150 per cent out of them. The day that you treat them like a manager should, they take offence.'

I decided to take training on the final two days before the Manchester United clash. I asked Jesús what we should do. 'What does it matter? The group is asking you to be there,' he responded. So on Thursday I went through some tactics and defensive organisation with two groups and on Friday we did some set-piece work. We had the idea of practising a corner routine from the left and a different one from the right. We did so ten times or more, but didn't score many goals. In any case, the intensity was there and we were satisfied, although we didn't openly show it.

We spent the week in negotiations over holidays, another sensitive subject that is also a distraction. At this stage, everyone battles for their own thing and the collective unit suffers. Last year we gave the suspended players holidays before the Euros and some of the others took that badly. They do need a break, of course. We've reached an agreement whereby every international player will have a minimum holiday allocation because the national teams finish the season on different days. There is one condition that hinges on the number of points that we pick up in our final three games. Each additional point above a minimum threshold will equal an extra day's holiday.

On Friday Son received his Player of the Month award and I was presented with mine for Manager of the Month. Six wins, 16 goals scored and just one conceded are the figures that justify the decision to give me the accolade that I'd previously obtained in February 2016. I don't want to appear ungrateful, but I don't really like such awards, first of all because they don't reflect reality. Managers don't make decisions based on the month. It could be replaced by the Team of the Month for the side with the best results, the most goals scored and fewest conceded. A player can receive recognition for four wonderful weeks, but managers don't compete under the same conditions. We aren't all driving the same car, which is why those who don't have much, but manage to get a great deal out of their players, are extraordinarily valuable. It's the same with the Manager of the Year: there should be one award for the champions and another that bears in mind the various squads.

The press conference ahead of the Manchester United match was relaxed. There was plenty of talk about the stadium, with it being the final game at the old White Hart Lane. I felt like responding to Conte who'd said earlier in the week that we'd started the season with an advantage over Chelsea because I've been with the squad for three years and know the league, unlike him. I just didn't understand what he was getting at. But in the end I decided it was not a battle worthwhile picking up. This time.

I then announced the squad list.

*

Players put on a heap of cologne before taking to the pitch these days. We're all, 'Come on, come on, come on!' and they're all pshht pshht pshht. The dressing room smells of humidity, the air is thick and dense, at least the aroma of Deep Heat from yesteryear has disappeared. I always have a shower before the match which is when I decide if I'm going to wear a tracksuit or a suit.

When I head out into the tunnel, I lose all sense of what's happening around me. I don't hear anything else. My head is filled with silence and I'm completely focused on the game. It doesn't matter if there are 90,000 or 300 people in attendance or whether it's at Wembley or White Hart Lane. It feels just like when I played in the field alone as a kid.

*

The match went as we expected. Manchester United attempted to stop us by marking us man-to-man and chasing us down all over the pitch, but we knew they'd do that and were ready. We used the move that we'd practised yesterday for our first corner . . . and we scored! This time it came off. The second goal was also from a set-piece.

We had one change left towards the end. 'Let's bring Sissoko on for Eriksen,' I said to Jesús who started to look for the player.

'He isn't around.'

'What do you mean?'

'He isn't warming up and he isn't on the bench.'

259

Sissoko suddenly appeared from the dressing room, having just thrown up. 'Let's put N'Koudou on,' I concluded.

We showed great intensity once again and created dozens of chances. We covered more ground than them, five miles to be precise. We've exhibited the right attitude in two recent performances, either side of a bloody disaster. The 2–1 scoreline didn't reflect our superiority, but it did ensure that we ended the league campaign unbeaten on home soil and we clinched second place with two games to spare.

It was time for our White Hart Lane farewell party.

There were no celebrations last year linked to qualifying for the Champions League, finishing third or our best ever Premier League finish. Zilch. On this occasion, everything came together for a fitting family celebration at home.

There was a pitch invasion as we headed to the dressing room. We had to wait for it to be cleared before kicking off the ceremony with a host of club legends. It was spectacular. When they were all on the pitch, it was time for my entrance.

We went on a lap of honour with our families and took some photos with all the staff.

It was a truly star-studded affair, with club legends past and present in attendance.

It was press conference time and I invited Miki and Toni up there with Jesús and me.

We headed back to the dressing room. Daniel asked me to head up to the boardroom to see all the directors and the daughter of Joe Lewis. Afterwards, we went back to the dressing room where Sebastiano cracked open a bottle of wine to celebrate.

I really enjoyed what happened next. The fans had all left and I went onto the pitch with my family and the coaching staff to go for one last walk and to take a few private photos. I relished the solitude and peace. All that was left from the celebration and the match was an echo. The game reminded me of when Espanyol played Valencia on the last game ever in Sarria. The silence at White Hart Lane brought back memories of the night when my wife, son and I visited the remains at the old Espanyol ground.

As was the case then, I didn't take anything from the Lane away with me. You can't keep the smell or the sounds ... The feelings can't be locked away in a box. What's the point of having a seat from the stadium at home? It's better to keep those things with you, in your head.

We were going to the dressing room when Donna-Maria Cullen, one of our directors, came out and said that Daniel and his family were also en route to see us on the pitch. Surrounded by the shell of an empty stadium, Daniel said something to me that I hadn't heard him say in three years. He used to spend time worrying about whether certain players wanted to leave or were happy. Now he understands more than ever the relative importance of the individual in this Tottenham – the engine is the team.

It was late when we all went home on an emotion-filled day. That's all part of football, too.

*

We beat Leicester City 6–1 away to seal our 12th win in 13 games. Harry Kane scored four of them and looks set to win the race for the Premier League's Golden Boot ahead of Romelu Lukaku. In recent matches, the players have been seeking out Kane to help him score as many goals as possible and clinch that individual accolade.

Son scored our other two goals at King Power Stadium.

We've racked up 32 wins, ten draws and ten defeats in all competitions.

Our final fixture is in three days' time away to already-relegated Hull.

*

This was the line-up: Lloris; Trippier, Alderweireld, Vertonghen, Davies; Wanyama, Dier; Son, Alli, Eriksen; and Kane.

Twelve months ago, the soundtrack of 'Rafa Benítez, we want you to stay!' echoed around the Newcastle stadium throughout the game. We were expecting the same tune today, but with Marco Silva replacing Rafa.

We recorded a resounding 7–1 victory against Hull. Harry Kane bagged a hat-trick.

We've finished second on 84 points, three more than title-winning Leicester managed last season. We're in sensational shape, both physically and mentally. People said that my teams faltered in the second half of the campaign, but no longer. We have that flexibility which means that when opponents pick up our team sheet and look at our XI, they can't be sure how we're going to play. During games, we can easily switch to whatever we fancy with the help of a couple of instructions.

It's a shame that a silly goal cost Hugo the Golden Glove.

The league is over: we've been everything that we're able to be.

That ill-fated match at Newcastle has also finally been put to bed. In the end it wasn't (and it was) down to me. It was (and it wasn't) down to the players. To sum up, it was nobody's fault. It's simply that that's where we were then and this is where we are now.

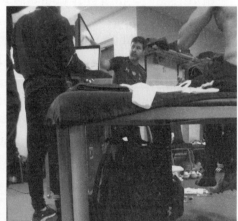

*

The chairman had told us that if we reached the FA Cup final, the visit to Hong Kong, where we're scheduled to play a friendly before the holidays would be off. It wasn't to be. The upcoming three-day trip gives us a chance to wind down.

As soon as we landed, I messaged Karina; it must've been 6 a.m. in England: 'Have you seen what happened in Manchester?' Jesús is usually the one who switches his phone on before anyone else. On the plane, he'd already told us, 'There's been an attack, twenty fatalities.'

How fragile we are. The overwhelming feeling is that you aren't safe anywhere. No one should change the way they live their everyday lives, but precautions are more necessary than ever. In any case, the level of security at the club is at its maximum.

I increasingly prefer to stay away from crowded events. I avoid going to London, but that isn't necessarily linked to security. In a perfect world, I'd live in Barcelona in my house and, if anything, I'd take the train to play football. If I could walk there, even better. I sometimes feel that little universe would make me happy. I've enjoyed my travels, but I find myself losing that need to see the world, having been doing so since I was 14. Spending so much time lugging a suitcase around, sitting in airports and staying at hotels feels as if you're not living life.

And you have to live.

*

I'm in my hotel room in Hong Kong, having just arrived from the airport. When I arrived, I lay down on the bed without taking off my team tracksuit. Next time I go to the training ground, I'll be given a new one: it'll have that fresh smell and that wonderful feeling associated with the start of the season.

Before that, we have a plethora of commitments to see to here. The group is doing well. We all would've gone our separate ways without this mini tour, which serves as a farewell and rounds off the season. Intensity levels will finally drop, we will eat together and go out in groups. It all counts. Victories are achieved by reaching the top, being plunged into hell together and getting back to the top once more.

A snapshot of the campaign shows that we haven't been good enough to win titles, but the feature film shows that we're progressing.

There's one thing that we're going to have to stress to get ahead of the rest. Every side undergoes similar preparation physically, medically, nutritionally and tactically, with varying levels of creativity. There's plenty of room for improvement in the mental side of things. Eric Dier is the perfect example: he's just told me it's a shame that the season is over now, when he feels he has all the answers and is a physical force. What changed? It's all in his head.

If I had to choose a moment from the last twelve months, it would be our opening Champions League fixture. It was this squad's first taste of action in the competition that everyone longs to compete in. I'm always the last person to head out on to the pitch; I'm not the type to rush. That day, however, I said to Jesús, Miki and Toni: 'Let's get out there quickly because I don't want to miss the Champions League anthem.' We were behind the players, ready to head out there and listen to it on the pitch. We looked at one another and tried to contain our laughter. Perhaps the positive emotional peak of the campaign.

What changed from that point onwards? Defeats taught us, challenged us. The team learnt how to win more than before and were more convinced of victory than ever. To keep going, we just had to make everyone as ambitious as we were.

The curtain is coming down for the players, they will go off on holidays, but we're already on to the next mission. I won't be able to stop answering my phone. It's impossible to completely disconnect. I'll send messages to a few players, but keeping your distance can be beneficial. They may feel fearful that we won't see each other again. Even though . . . maybe it is only wishful thinking on my part..

If we didn't go further this year and didn't win anything, it's because it wasn't our time. I'm motivated to try it all again. We're all moving up to the next level.

Does anyone doubt that something big is about to happen at Tottenham Hotspur?

After all, to dare is to do.

POCHETTINO IN OTHER WORDS

Iván de la Peña

Mauricio and I crossed paths for the first time when I was still playing at Espanyol, and he arrived in the winter transfer window during a very difficult situation. I am one of those people who thinks that leaders are born not made, and Mauricio has always been a leader. He showed it from the first minute. I remember a group conversation with him at the first game he had at Montjuïc where he wanted to convince the group that we were more than capable, had the talent and the ability to correct the complicated situation we found ourselves in, and that what we had to have was belief in ourselves. But more than what he said, it was the way he said it that grabbed the group of players so much.

From the day of his arrival I had a great feeling about him. We saw each other every day, went out to supper together and spent hours through the night talking about football and how we could win the next game. Our families got on very well. Mauricio was not just a teammate, he was and still is a friend.

Later on, as coach, he made us believe in what had seemed impossible, namely saving ourselves from relegation earlier than any of us would have dreamed. We were bottom of the table at that time. I was trying to get over a calf injury but he put us all to work. He made us believe in the path he wanted us to take because it would make us better players, better people and a better group. Training sessions were much more professional and very clear. And you saw in yourself every day that you were better physically, and that tactically the team did what he asked of them. What's more – it was working well.

In March 2009 on the 27th weekend of the season we were losing 3–1 and were down to ten men. According to what Mauricio told me later the referee said to him, 'Either you take de la Peña off or I will send him off.' He thought about replacing me but in the very next play I scored to make it 3–2 and we later drew level with a goal from Nene. We earned a draw from a game that just didn't seem possible. At the

271

end of the game I said, 'You will think I am mad but we are going to save ourselves.' And that message came from what I saw on a daily basis, things that the fans don't see. Today Mauricio says those words helped him achieve confidence in the squad. From that moment we all believed it was going to happen.

That season I scored twice against Barcelona at the Camp Nou and we beat them. I was just coming back from a long injury of about six to eight weeks, and he told me to go and play and enjoy myself, although it probably wasn't going to be very enjoyable! Us rock bottom, them top. But we got the type of luck that you need at the most opportune of moments. Obviously we were ecstatic but when you are bottom of the pile, you still have a long way to go before you can achieve your objective; we had to win the next game, and the one after that and another one. For that you had to keep calm, which is what Mauricio did.

I would have liked to have played more games under him, but the last two years I spent most of the time injured. In my last match he gave me the chance to say my goodbyes to the fans and to the stadium, and for gestures like that I love him like a brother.

One thing I will tell you though is that he is a bandit when it comes to playing football-tennis. And I've told him as much!

I recently came to see him in London and noticed that he continues to have the same leadership qualities that I first saw in him in our first group chat at Montjuïc. And that helps him achieve the best possible results because his pupils have blind faith in everything he says. For me he is one of the top five coaches working in the world today.

Jordi Amat

I was playing in the second team, Espanyol B, in the third tier at the time. Pochettino saw two or three of our games. One day he came over to Álvaro Vázquez and me, and said, 'You aren't a third-division player. I'll register you with the first team and you'll come up with me.' I also remember that he gave me the number 5. He said to me, 'It's time for someone else to wear the number 5 shirt,' which had been his. I was thrilled about that.

I made my debut at 17 and he explained how he'd made his debut under Bielsa, also aged 17. He said, 'Stay calm and play your game. You've fought for and dreamt about this, so it'll go well.' That's what he said in the week leading up to my debut. Knowing that he'd also made his debut at 17 gave me so much confidence and reassurance for whenever the moment would arrive.

I also remember that my second game was at the Bernabéu. Someone got injured and I had to come on. He told me to mark Sergio Ramos at corners. I looked at him with the face of a . . . well, scared 17-year-old . . . And he said to me, 'You're right, mark Kaká instead.' There wasn't exactly anyone easy to mark.

He made Álvaro Vázquez do some type of taekwondo or something similar because he didn't feel comfortable with the physical side of the game and that's what football is about. And so he had lessons and took it seriously.

I'll always remember Mauricio's sincerity and direct approach. I think that's very important. It's really difficult to find people in the football world who always say it as it is, but he's one of the few. A couple of months later he said to me, 'Look, Jordi. You're young and you need to play.' I was 18. So we arranged a loan deal to Rayo Vallecano, which went very well, and I then went on to sign for Swansea. I owe him lots.

Adam Lallana

When Fonte said there was a rumour about Pochettino, I had to look him up on Google. It was when it was made official that we met for the first time. We had four or five captains at our club, so José Fonte, Kelvin Davies, maybe Morgan Schneiderlin, Ricky Lambert and I went to the stadium to meet him with Nicola Cortese, who arranged it. It was January and snowing. We must have been waiting a while in the board room, and then Mauricio eventually came in with Toni and Miki. I'll never forget, Mauricio came in and he was in a suit and he looked amazing and he had a fragrance on, overdid it a bit, but I was impressed. Straight away. His staff weren't in a suit so they looked more informal, they were in jeans and a shirt or whatever. Great impression straight away, and a hug. Jesús was the interpreter because his English was the best out of the bunch.

He took us in his second week to a training camp in Barcelona and we stayed in a hotel in the mountains. There was nothing going on there. We got a taxi one afternoon to Barcelona and the boss took us for tapas and jamon. It was nice to be in his environment within the first few weeks. We trained on Barcelona's training pitch, and he got us bonding and explained how he wanted us to play. He kept saying 'press, press, press'.

I remember we'd had a lot of tactical stuff without the ball. How do we set up from the opponent's goal-kick if they play short? Who runs there? And where does the midfield move and where do the back-four slide? If they play back to the keeper, who runs through to the keeper? Someone always has to run through to the keeper to keep him under pressure, and the best thing about it was being told what to do, so you knew what you were doing was right. That was something I'd never really experienced before as a player.

But the manager wasn't stupid. He didn't change everything. And then that summer, the next pre-season, we went to Peralada for a training

camp. It was a basic hotel, nothing fancy, pitches, pool, double sessions, and getting us fit.

He treated us like adults. He said that the four or five captains had to get together every now and again if he wanted to get a message across to the group. There were no strict rules. We had no fear, even playing away at United. 'It doesn't matter the result as long as we give our all.'

The word 'brave' was used a lot. I remember one conversation I had with him on a Friday before we played Liverpool. He said to me, 'How would you rather play tomorrow? Would you rather sit off them at goal-kicks and let them have the ball or would you rather go man for man?' I had a think for about 20 seconds and then said, 'No, we'll go man for man and then press them high.' He gave me a slap on the back and said, 'Good, good.' We beat Liverpool and Chelsea at home, which were two massive results for us in staying up that season. But when we were playing well, he would never be full of praise. He would always want more.

When he first came in I was injured and when I came back he used to take me off during games, even at the start of the next season. A lot of people were asking me, 'Why are you coming off in games, is it bothering you? . . . You need to speak to the manager, or family, or agent.' But I had too much respect to say to him, 'Why are you bringing me off?' I knew he would have a reason. So I just kept doing what I was told. I trusted him that much.

Sometimes he would join in the games, but he was a cheat. He was never in the middle. He would be like, stop, stop, stop, it is a fault, but he was the one fouling! He does mention his past sometimes. He sent me a clip the other day of the Spurs team reacting to that goal that he scored with Espanyol in the league against Valencia at the Olympic stadium when he curled it into the top corner. Obviously, the Owen penalty in the 2002 World Cup came up few times – he will never accept it, but he did foul Owen! [*laughs*].

He broke the news about my England call-up to me. He got me in the office. He told me on my own actually. Ricky Lambert got called up first and next it was me. I think he did it with a joke, you know. It was a very proud moment.

There was a conversation I will always remember when I spoke to him about the captaincy. We were sat down for about two hours on the pitch after training, sitting on the grass. It was a nice day, it was April. It's difficult to recall the whole chat, we literally spoke for about two hours – it probably took longer because Jesús was translating – and that's when I spoke about my Spanish surname and my family origin. That conversation got very deep and I started talking to him about the chairman ringing me after games. That was unsettling me, the pressure, maybe I was not ready for all of it, I was not being myself. The calls from Cortese stopped. A couple of months later my dad met him and the boss treated him like a king.

It was quite strange towards the end of the season because we were safe, we were tenth and we finished eighth. But no one knew what direction the club was going. There were rumours that the club wanted to be sold, about players leaving, and no one came out and gave Mauricio a plan for the future. I remember I was in his office more than ever speaking about it all. 'I didn't want to leave, I didn't want this to end, but we've got to,' I was telling him, and he really had nothing to say. He said he couldn't see himself being here because nobody was giving him a direction or plan, so the writing was on the wall that we would end up going our separate ways. I knew of the Liverpool interest and even though he ended up going to Tottenham, it wasn't possible for me to follow him. He'd only just walked through the door and my direction was different, and we both just respected that fact and that maybe our relationship would be different if I worked for him again.

We decided to go for a meal; it was at the end of the season just before I went off to the World Cup. He'd left the club, but I hadn't yet. I signed for Liverpool after the World Cup. It was me, Mauricio, Jesús, Miki, Toni and Javi, the physio. We were speaking about our times together. He recounted his meeting with Daniel Levy, and I was telling him about their squad and who I thought he'd like and who I thought he wouldn't like.

When we said goodbye, I was upset.

I'd love to work with him again. In the meantime I'm enjoying his success and I'm sure he's enjoying mine as well.

We are in touch, we talk about results, how the family is . . . I'd be lying to say I don't support his teams. I wanted Tottenham to win the league. For that Chelsea game, it was 2–2, and me and Henderson – Henderson is an adopted Spurs fan as well because I tell him all the time about Mauricio – were watching it and we were off our chairs. He's done brilliantly since he has been there.

He always says to me, 'Why do you always up your game against me?' But I don't particularly. Whenever we play his teams I know it's going to be an intense game because Tottenham and Liverpool play in very similar ways. The last game we played must have been good to watch for a neutral. Lots of chances, White Hart Lane early in the season, 1–1, Milner and Rose, just great quality everywhere. It was intense and that's just the way that football should be played. Sometimes if I am close to the technical area or taking a throw-in near him I catch his eye, and I just have to look away or I end up laughing.

Luke Shaw

When he gave me the first hug, I thought, 'Who is this guy? What is he doing?' He didn't speak English and training was a little bit weird in comparison to how it was done before. So I was . . . 'What's going on?'

He used to make me a drink in the morning. I didn't eat badly, but he used to think that my diet wasn't good. So he made me a smoothie each morning made of spinach, loads of fruit and vegetables. He never told me what it was . . . he told me at the end . . . I used to go into his office and he'd let me sit in his seat. That's how much he loved me. He was like, 'No one ever sits there but me, but you can sit there.' It was like a family thing. I'd sit there and he'd have my drink ready for me. Sometimes it was before training and sometimes it was after. Sometimes I'd go in the back way if I was late, and he'd send someone to get me. Or if I was leaving, you have to walk past his office, and I'd hear [makes knocking sound on desk], and he'd be knocking on the window.

He used to call me his son. That's how good our relationship was. I've had lots of ups and downs, but when I was with Pochettino it was only ever up, up, up.

I remember him saying one day, 'You can be the best, but you just have to believe in yourself.' And I think at that point he was the one who changed my mentality. He made me feel that I was the best. He'd show me clips of my games and say, 'You could do this better.' Not in a horrible way. Not I could have done better, but I should have done better, because he knows I can be better.

He was always pushing me. I was the only player who he'd bring back in the afternoon. I'd come back at five o'clock with just him and Jesús. I never complained because I loved working under him. I'd come back, do some runs, and then he and I would play football-tennis for about an hour. And it was so competitive. Because he never wants to lose. And he cheats as well. He would have his assistant manager as referee, but anything that was borderline in or out . . . the decision was always in favour of Poch.

He'd let me go in his changing room before or after games. If the team had a bad game he would ask, 'What's wrong with everyone? Is the team down? Do they need more days off?' He was talking to me like that and I was only 17. He always used to say, 'Just play. Play how you want to play. Feel free.' The whole team did and that's why we were flying.

He wanted to be the first to tell me about my first call-up for England. Again the knock on the window and he told me in a really weird way and I said, 'You're joking!' and he said, 'No, I got the call and they want you for England.' I think I sort of knew that I was in the England squad. But when he called me in and gave me a massive hug it did feel like a family bond to see how happy he was.

The hardest thing for me was when I told him I was leaving. I've never seen a sadder face than when I told him. He was devastated, disappointed. I spent many hours in his office that week. He wasn't begging me but he really wanted me to stay. Because the club was building and we had such good players.

He kept asking me, 'Do you want to leave?' Even on the training pitch he'd say, 'Just think about it. It's not the right time. I need you to stay and help me build this club.' I'd say, 'I'm still thinking about it. There's a lot of things going on in my head.'

I could have left the year before but he convinced me to stay. The football and life was so good. I think that's what made me the person I am because he and his staff were so good to me.

So anyway I eventually went in and said, 'I want to leave,' and he said, 'Really?' And then he said, 'No. You're not.' And then we had a massive conversation about why I wanted to go and it was quite hard.

Part of me was thinking, 'Pochettino has done so much for me.' So inside I wanted to stay with him because he was such a key part of my development. I didn't want to let go of that. We were so close. I used to go to dinner with him. The first time he was staying at a hotel. And he told me to go to the hotel. So I went and had dinner with the four coaches. Only one of them spoke English, the other three couldn't speak English at all. So I went there and they were all talking away and laughing and I didn't have a clue . . . It felt sort of weird to go to dinner with the manager. It was more than once. It was nice and it gradually got better because he could speak more English. So it was nicer. We had so many laughs together.

I think with Southampton he achieved the impossible. We were one of the best footballing teams in the league. The bit I don't get is how Southampton fans do not like him after what he did. I think it's because he wasn't there for too long. But we were a team fighting relegation and he changed our game and our mentality. If he goes somewhere else he's going to fly wherever he goes. He could go anywhere.

I do hope that I can play for him again one day. And I think he really wants me to play under him again.

We exchanged messages when he saw me with the Manchester United shirt, but not many because he was really disappointed in me. He's said to me since that I broke his heart.

But he spoke with me when I broke my leg. Obviously I was in a really emotional place. It was the day or the day after. He called me on my phone. I had been flying, the timing was so bad. He was thinking of anything he could say that would be nice for me to hear. I was crying and he was sad too.

Jay Rodriguez

He definitely made me feel different about the game. Things like the dart task we did during pre-season. You have to push against the dart with your neck and you feel that it is going to go through your neck, but he says if you push forward and believe that you are going to break it, you will. And then we had to walk on hot stones. He used to say that the mind is very powerful and if you believe you can do it then you can. It was little things like that that started to change the way we were thinking.

I remember I scored two against Cardiff and then a ball came towards me. But I was static and if I'd moved forward I would have got a hat-trick. The following week he told me that he needed to show me something and he asked me why I stood still. It's always in your mind that two's not enough, three's not enough, you've got to keep going.

You don't want to cross him or, more like, you don't want to disappoint him. When you went on the pitch you wanted to die for him. I think it's because he connects with people.

Every game we played under him we believed we were going to win, unless we were unlucky. You feel invincible.

And as a person he gave me that belief, he always believed in me. That's something I still have to this day.

With my injury it was very sad, and he was almost as sad as I was, and through that period he was there for me. I remember at half-time he was so sad, and I was nearly crying. It was very difficult. He just said 'Come on, it's OK,' basically to reassure me and then afterwards, 'Don't worry, you will come back strong.'

Probably the first time I played against him was this winter [2016]. It was strange. We got beaten and beaten badly actually [4–1 at home]. It wasn't enjoyable but it was nice to see him afterwards. After the game I spoke to Jesús, Miguel and Toni, and we keep in touch and send messages to each other. Sometimes he will send me a clip of myself in training just as an encouragement to keep on going. He's still a big part of me, he still gives me confidence. He still believes in me.

If he became England manager . . . I think we'd win everything. [*laughs*].

I think he is the best.

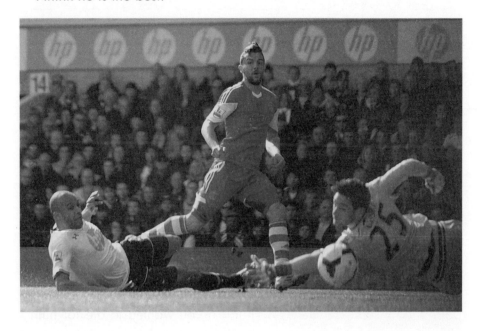

Hugo Lloris

I remember him as a player, with Argentina in the World Cup, with Paris Saint-Germain and Bordeaux, and I always had a great image of him. The way he played, his face, his attitude . . . he was a winner and I can see the same face today, with shorter hair. I remember when he signed for Paris everyone was questioning who this player from Espanyol was, forgetting he was an Argentinian international.

I have a great relationship with him as a man and, of course, as a professional. I never thought I would have such admiration for one of my managers. I respect my managers, but I don't want to cross the line. My manager is my boss and I don't want to be his friend but with him everything is natural.

It's difficult to explain how grateful I am to Mauricio. It was a bad time for me at Tottenham. I was very disappointed with the way the club was going. I left Lyon and I went to Tottenham, and for the first year I had some problems with the manager [André Villas-Boas]. When I signed for Tottenham I wanted to bring skill to help the club to fight for the top four, and I realised that it was not fully working – we were not progressing. In fact, quite the opposite. The second year I thought, 'What is this club?' We sold Bale and we bought eight players or something . . . but had no philosophy. I thought I would have to leave because I was losing my passion, my love for football, for the game. And when I met Mauricio he reawakened that in me. His way of understanding the game is just exactly why I love it – aggression on the pitch from everybody to recover the ball, but wanting to build from the back and share the ball around when we have it.

Even my wife told me that my face changed, she recognised me again, the player I was in Lyon and in Nice. In football and in life you meet some people that are very important. Mauricio is a massive step forward for me in my career. He is fresh, positive, not selfish, he thinks about the team. He doesn't particularly like the spotlight – he has a lot of humility.

You can be a leader without shouting and he is the perfect example of this. OK, sometimes he shouts but it doesn't happen a lot. Unlike when he was a player, as a manager he keeps a lot inside. That's why after the game he does not like to talk to the players. Even in a bad way or good way he doesn't like it. He prefers to save his energy.

It was not easy at the start. I heard a lot from the other players saying, 'It's too difficult, it's crazy the way we work, I've never done this before in my career, blah blah blah.' I was worried. I thought by the weekend the players would be dead. But then Jesús, who was in charge of fitness, said, 'Don't worry, you will see.' I remember one day we beat Arsenal 2–1 at home. We were 1–0 down and played 95 minutes high intensity, pressing. A few days after he said to me and a few other players, 'This is why we work so hard because we are going to play every game the same way.' Now we were ready to run, to fight, to compete in every game. We changed our mentality. When a manager asks you to do something, you do it, but it's better when he explains to you why you should do it.

Everything is recorded, in the gym and on the pitch. I was not too sure about that at the start. In fact, before I did not really like to go to the gym. But now I understand it. Even the recording. When you train, you give everything. You cannot hide. I get it. This is the way to see if your players are involved or not, to know your players better because maybe they are acting one way to your face and then doing something different behind your back. He judges a lot by body language.

After three months we were struggling but there were two key games where we started to change, when we started to put young players onto the pitch. They were more determined than the senior ones, showed more desire, more passion, and from that day it felt like players were fighting for him. Away to Aston Villa we were 1–0 down and we won 2–1 in the last minute. Same against Hull City. They were crucial moments, especially for the younger guys.

When he arrived he tried to find two or three players who would help him show the rest of the squad the right way. And in the second season more and more players bought into his philosophy. And the ones who were a bit more selfish and not prepared to be part of the collective started to leave. That's how he made a strong squad ready to fight for each other.

I felt he handed me authority. 'I will build a team around you and we will be competitive and we will fight with the top teams of this league,' he told me. And it happened.

It's clever how he does it. Nothing is compulsory. He always gives the options to the players. He likes to see players sharing moments. I remember before that players used to put their boots on and, one by one, they used to come out onto the pitch. He changed everything. He said that you have to come onto the pitch together. If you are the first to put your boots on, you should wait for the other players. It's about giving responsibility to all the players about how they act.

When he gives a talk on the pitch then he likes the players to be very close to him. Little things, little details, but very, very important. It's not about football, it's more about human relations.

I heard an interview with Arrigo Sacchi and it was like I was listening to Mauricio Pochettino. Football is not about tactics, it's about spirit, passion and desire. It's not about things like 4-4-2. That may be the way you line up but then there is a lot of movement in the game. I think he likes to know his players, the people he has in front of him before he gets to know the footballer. Football is about ideas but players must believe in the concept and the philosophy.

The defeat against Newcastle was probably his worst day as a manager. I sat on the plane coming home after the game. He didn't understand why some of the players had finished the season that way. He was very disappointed with some. He needed five days to digest the defeat. We fought all season not to finish that way. It meant we finished behind Arsenal after losing the last two games. He felt players were on holidays before the end of the season. When I came back from the Euros, I was in a different frame of mind – we had a good tournament. But he was still suffering. It was hard to see him so down.

I have learned a lot from him. I am from France and we are different in many senses, but from day one everything I like about football came from him. That's why I am still here. I like Tottenham's football and I like them as people too.

I am very committed to the club but even more to my manager. If he leaves, it will put everything into question, everything. If today I feel so well it's thanks to him and Toni, my goalkeeping coach. I have faith in them, I believe in them and to be happy at Tottenham I need them.

Harry Kane

When I found out he was going to be manager I was quite excited because I knew I was going to have the opportunity to play if I did well, like young players did at Southampton. I was about 20 years old, so obviously there were quite a few strikers ahead of me at the time; I was finding it difficult to get into the team. When we first met he was very easy to talk to. You could tell straight away he was very respectful and he wanted to get to know everyone, all the players, all the young ones as well. Sometimes when a manager comes he just wants to know the leaders. The first chat was just kind of meeting him as a group and saying hello and it wasn't too in-depth. I wanted to do my talking and show him my personality on the pitch.

We went to Seattle. Then Chicago. Probably one of my favourite pre-season trips. But it was tough. That pre-season I came back from holiday and I thought I was in OK shape. We had our body fat test done and I was the highest in the team, something like 18 per cent! I didn't really want to believe it. I was like, 'Aargh! This is wrong!' He had his own little drills, his own fitness test – it's called the Gacons. It's like a run that gets progressively harder. We did a lot of them in pre-season. A lot of tactical and shape work because obviously he wanted to instil own philosophy.

I learnt a lot in that short time. Certain movements, for instance. He was a defender himself so he knows what the striker should be doing to gain an edge. Sometimes we did one-on-ones with him, Miki or Jesús training with the strikers, sometimes we were in a group, just movements around the box, or trying to get in behind. He wants to play that high intensity, he wants runners in behind . . . I knew straight away that if I wanted to play in his team I would have to learn that quickly and adapt. He likes to film everything, so if he thinks something isn't right in training he will show me on the clips.

As expected he was not afraid to give the younger players a

chance. He wanted everyone on the same page, working in the same direction. It is difficult to do what he's done in such a short amount of time.

I remember one early conversation. I was doing well in the Europa League at the start of his first Spurs season, but I wasn't getting into the Premier League team for one reason or another, and I remember getting quite frustrated. So I went to see him and he explained to me that I wasn't doing enough. He said that my body fat was high, I wasn't trying as hard as I could, and that was it! Maybe other managers would try to beat around the bush and try to keep players happy but he was just straight up. He said, 'You need to do this and this and that's why you're not in the squad.' And it just hit me. This is what I've got to do. So I took that on board and I've been doing OK since.

In one of the first competitive games we played – AEL away in Cyprus, a Europa League qualifier – we were expected to win. We were 1–0 down at half-time, and he told us to 'show some *cojones*'. He was really passionate and let it all out. To a lot of the players it was just a Europa League qualifier but from day one, that half-time he set the tone: he wants to win every game, he wants to win every moment and every challenge. He was so passionate. We won the game 2–1. But that doesn't happen often at half-times.

I have not been to his place for a meal. Actually, I should invite him round to meet my daughter. He'll have to come round one day. I'll have a barbecue and we'll spend some time together. Because he's a family man I feel comfortable with him. Maybe with some managers you wouldn't feel comfortable doing that but he's a friend.

Sometimes I will just come in and go to the gaffer's office to say hello to him. If we've been off for maybe a couple of days or been away on international break, he might start asking about your personal life – how's the kids, how's the Mrs – and then maybe we'll start talking about the game, certain things in the game that we can do better.

He has told me 'You can be the best striker in the world.' We have a joke about it now and then and, of course, when I hear him say it in the media I know he's just trying to give me confidence. But yeah, he'll text me the next day to show me what he's said publicly and then he'll say, 'But we need to work harder and we need to do more.'

Dele Alli

I didn't know he was coming to the MK Dons v Manchester United game. When I heard, someone said he'd come to see Danny Welbeck. But as soon as I heard that Tottenham wanted me to come, in the last few days before the January transfer window closed, he was the main reason why I signed here. I was a youngster and I knew he wasn't afraid to play youngsters. There aren't many managers that do that. I came to have a look around the training ground but I think he was in Spain, so he wasn't here when I signed. I didn't see him till I came back for pre-season.

It was really hard and I didn't know what he thought of me. The first proper one-on-one, it was with Jesús. They were speaking in Spanish and then Jesús said to me 'He didn't like you . . .' or similar. The boss was staring me in the eye to see how I reacted. I was speechless! He paused for like a second, and he said '. . . but now he loves you.'

When you're on the bench you can see him getting up and shouting and saying loads of . . . I don't know what he's saying! I've had to take

Spanish lessons to try to learn what he's saying! He's helping me with it as well. He tries to speak to me in Spanish as much as he can. I've wanted to learn for a long time and now it's a good opportunity to do so.

The season before last, there was a bit in the media about me, when everyone was saying I was losing my temper. He pulled me into his office and talked about himself as a player, and showed me some clips of him on YouTube, very aggressive. [*laughs*]. He's scored some goals as well, and told me I need to watch and have a look at some so I can improve my finishing. He's better than everyone! [*laughs*]. He jokes about it. But you can see he's still got it when he gets involved in training. He was a half-decent player at least.

In his chats, he insists we all have to want it, there are no excuses for being tired and stuff. He does push everyone all the time.

At Palace, I scored a goal and I think I made it 2–1 in the last ten minutes. I watched the goal back and I saw that he had run all the way down the line and was involved in the hug. I had not realised.

Do I upset him? Me? Yeah, all the time. [*laughs*]. A few weeks ago we were doing some shape work and I was a bit annoyed, not at him but just with some stuff. I was walking in and looking at the floor and he told me to lift my head up and smile. Later, he pulled me into his office and talked to me about how if I'm not being happy and positive it can have an effect on everyone. I didn't realise how much.

We had Monaco away in the Europa League on the day before the England squad was announced and I didn't think I was going to make my debut in the squad. He called me over and said to me, 'How would you feel about playing for England Under-19s?' At the time I was Under-20 so I said, 'I don't think I can, I'm too old.' And he said, 'They've called me and you're allowed to play for them next week.' I was like, 'Oh yeah, OK, I'll play for England whatever age group,' and then he just looked at me and I thought that was it, I was about to walk away. And then he said, 'Actually, I spoke to the manager [Roy Hodgson] and you're going to play for the first team.' I didn't know what to believe, I didn't know if he was trying to wind me up or not. But I was happy to share that moment with him. We had a little cuddle after! [*laughs*]. And I said 'thank you' because, obviously, I owe a lot of that to him.

Victor Wanyama

We were doing pre-season in Spain with Southampton. I thought I was fit. I arrived about 5 p.m. and thought I would have some dinner, go to bed and then go to training in the morning. But they said no, you've got to get changed, and then I went to do some running and the following day I was so tired. I thought I was fit but I ended up training with the keeper. And after training Pochettino came to me and said it's a different level now so you have to catch up.

At Southampton there was a game when we were not playing well. And he came in and was very angry. He said, 'I need you guys to go out there and take risks. Get out of your comfort zone.' It was an away game against United. We won 1–0. It changed our mentality.

When I arrived at Spurs, he took me to one side and he said, 'Have you seen your little brother?' and I said, 'I don't have a little brother,' and then he showed me a video and it was me when I started at Southampton.

Before the Liverpool game in October, after drawing against West Brom and Bournemouth, he told us we had dropped four points and that against Liverpool we could improve. He showed us a video. From then on everyone played better. He then played a song. It was about life and how you have to take care of your friends. Always smile and be happy.

Harry Winks

First time I had a chat with him I was 17 or 18. I came in in the summer with my dad and I signed a professional contract with John McDermott. The gaffer had just signed for Spurs and he had come in to have a little look around the building. I was in the room waiting to sign and he walked in. He said he had watched my clips and told John McDermott to sign me up straight away but I think he was joking, to be honest. He never really sat down and said, 'Right Harry, here is a plan,' it was more like 'Work hard, just keep working hard', showing me by giving me more opportunities to train and travel with the first team.

My debut was against Partizan Belgrade. I think he brought me on for the last five minutes or so, and for me being a lifelong Spurs fan it was incredible. He put his arm around me, walked me up to the pitch and said to me, 'Just go out there and enjoy it.' I was going on for Paulinho. He said, 'Work hard, be strong, enjoy it and ease into the game and you'll just grow into it.' I remember it just as a blur.

The match against West Ham was the first time that me and the gaffer actually had a bit of an emotional moment. It was after the game in the dressing room, I was still buzzing after scoring, on cloud nine, and I remember I was about to get into the shower, I had my towel around me and Toni told me to come into the coaches' dressing room. All the coaches were in there – I think they had a glass of wine – and I remember just walking in with my towel on and the gaffer said, 'I just want to say well done, congratulations.' And he gave me a hug. There were no tears or anything. A few papers said there were tears – there weren't, it was just a really emotional moment. I said to all the coaches that I appreciated it and thanked them for all the belief and their hard work and how they'd improved me.

He calls me into the office sometimes. When we beat Everton he called me in and showed me some clips, including the assist I got for Dele's goal. We had a little joke about the fact that I didn't know what to do with the ball, who to play it to. He was almost saying, 'Harry, what are you doing, why are you crossing it?' It was the 88th minute, we were 2–1 up but luckily it paid off. You could see by his reaction that he was delighted that I did not think like him at that point.

We have cameramen and camerawomen that walk around filming. They film everything. They film our pre-activation work, all our gym. We did a recovery session a few months ago. We went down to the pool and did ice baths, some were doing swimming and jogging in the pool and the others were doing core, and he brought the cameras down there and filmed us in the pool as well.

Before a game, when we are getting dressed and before the warm-up, he is quiet, he won't speak to us at all. If it's a home game, he'll be in his dressing room. He'll stay out of the way, let us prepare. When the boys come back from the warm-up and are getting ready for the last two or three minutes before kick-off, he'll come in and that's when he'll really start to get us going. He'll be shouting, 'Come on boys, first minute let's get into them, front foot, let's be solid, let's be brave, enjoy it.' He's massive on enjoying the game. He just reiterates the things that we know we need to do, helps us get focused and gets the boys in the right frame of mind.

At half-time his interventions are sometimes necessary. Like when we played Monaco in the Champions League. I think in the first half we were getting a lot of the ball in our half but they were on top of us and getting a lot of shots off. And in the dressing room he changed the formation and we went from a 4-2-3-1 to a diamond. He made a few points. He often brings in a screen so at half-time he can show us clips of the first half, and can tell us, 'Come out wide here, come narrow here,' information like that. If we are doing really well, he'll just reiterate that we need to go out there and stay positive and not get complacent.

He's massive on the mental side of things. Physically we are in great shape, he knows that. Technically we are up there as one of the best teams in the Premiership and he knows that too. It's mentality that separates us from the rest. He showed clips of us earlier in the season, against Man City, when we were on the front foot, in their faces, not letting them play so all of a sudden the momentum of the game was

in our hands and that's what he wants. In the first five minutes almost bully the opposition, make them scared so they are on the back foot. All that is done with the mind as well as with the feet.

Eric Dier

I was bought as a centre-back but ended up playing as a right-back. I made my debut at Sporting as a right-back, so it wasn't new to me. I grew up in Portugal and it's quite easy for me to adapt to things. The methodology here is very similar to the way football is played in Portugal. If I'd come here to an English manager it would probably have been a lot harder for me. One of the things that helped me decide to come was that Spurs had a foreign manager.

I'd only arrived the week before so I was surprised he let me play against West Ham. I scored and did well. I thought, 'Yes, he trusts me.'

I'm fluent in Portuguese but it's funny. When he speaks to me he speaks in Spanish and I reply in English, although if I'm in the office we all speak in English.

I'm a completely different person now to when I arrived. Physically, mentally. I play at a different intensity. I was aggressive at moments but he keeps pushing that aggression and it's much more focused now.

Danny Rose

The season before he came I didn't have a particularly good season and there was talk about me moving on and I was interested in doing so. He was officially appointed in May and then sometime in June, when I was off, my agent told me that Mauricio would like to see me. I spent about an hour in his office and the first thing he told me was that he didn't want me to move on. He had seen me play and he thought that I could be one of the best. He said that if I didn't believe that, then there was no point in my being here. If I followed his philosophy and bought into his ideas, he added, he would make me one of Europe's best left-backs as well as an England player. Two and a half years down the line he has improved my game massively and before I was injured I was England's left-back. He was true to his word and staying was the best decision I ever made.

It took a while to get to grips with how Mauricio wants to play, how hard he wants you to train. Even small things like arriving late he finds very disrespectful and it was hard to understand at the start.

Every morning he goes around shaking everybody's hand and you can see when he's doing that that he's looking into your eyes to see how you are that day. Within a few seconds of speaking to you, he knows if you're going to do well.

We got beaten in one game earlier in his tenure but I thought I played well. The next day I went into his office and he had 26 video clips showing everything I did wrong.

Before this I used to think you had to have older experienced players to challenge at the top of the league. He has proved me and everybody else wrong.

I now have a relationship with a manager that I have never had before. He'll text me sometimes saying, 'Watch this player,' or 'What do you think of this player?' But we also speak about a lot of things away from football – about family, and investments. People ask me when

I do interviews who is my best friend at the club and automatically I think of players, but when I sit down and think about it, I would say the best friend I have at the club is my manager.

He always says you need to have a clear mind so you can give 100 per cent, and whatever small problem you may have, be it with your family or your friends, he wants to help you. I'm the sort of person who likes to keep myself to myself. But recently my uncle passed away and the manager was the first person I called. He was at home on his day off, and he got into his car straight away and came to see me. The manager and his staff all helped me get through it. The manager asked for my dad's number so that he could contact the family.

I went to his house two weeks ago. He has a nice collection of red wine and he gave me a bottle form Argentina. He explained so much about the wine, where and how you plant the vines, what grape to use, and how you look after them how the grapes turn out according to how you treat them. Very much like a football team.

Daniel Levy

At Tottenham, we have always tried to develop players and make them superstars rather than buy superstars. Our fans have a real link with homegrown players and so you have got to try to find a coach who actually believes in that philosophy. A lot of coaches say they do but when it comes to it, when they're working, they are not interested in the young players. They prefer to buy players. I've always been striving to find that coach.

When I looked at Mauricio at Southampton, two things stuck out for me. One was that he seemed to have the ability to develop players and he did a fantastic job there. The second one was how loyal he was to the club – he never criticised the players when things weren't going right and remained very humble. That's quite unique and it's very hard to do in front of the media when you have just lost a game. You probably want to kill one or two players, but he never did. That's how it should be. The telling-offs have to be in private. I wanted somebody who believes in the way I think we ought to operate so that's why I went for Mauricio.

There had been a change in the chairmanship at Southampton and he wasn't totally happy. We also knew he had a buy-out clause in his contract. Having said that, Mauricio is an incredibly loyal person and this was also key in why we wanted him as manager. Regardless of what was in his contract, I don't think he would have left Southampton if there hadn't been personal circumstances that allowed him to do that.

I didn't contact him directly. It was through a third party to his lawyer but he wasn't prepared to come to us mid-season or anything like that, it was only at the end of the season that he agreed to meet. He came to my house and we had a good meeting. We chatted for a couple of hours; his English wasn't as good as it is now. At that time he was a lot more reserved too. In Europe, the relationship between

the coach and the president is very different to the ones we establish here. I'm not the type of person who feels I'm up here and everyone else is below me – it's very much everyone at the same level and I'll talk to anyone at this club. Anyone can come and talk to me. That's the relationship I want with my coach and I think it's taken Mauricio a bit of time to understand that. Yes, I am the chairman, but he can have a very close relationship with me, which is probably different to how he perceives other presidents.

Jesús Perez was also there at the meeting and it was important as sometimes he would have to translate. Jesús is fantastic, very bright, very loyal and I think they're a great pair. And obviously he's got two other coaches as well that he brought in as part of it. We had a couple of meetings. I think with Mauricio it's very much about feeling, that is important to him, much more so than anything to do with the contract, money or anything like that. He was also intrigued because it was Tottenham, a big club, with a historical following in Argentina.

Mauricio says to me that I took a gamble on him because, with all due respect to Southampton, the expectations there are less than they are at Tottenham and he wasn't a big name. Most fans want names, but I have sometimes done the name bit and it hasn't necessarily worked.

The public perception is that managers always want more players and the chairman never wants to spend money. Actually the contrast with Mauricio is quite interesting. If I left it totally to Mauricio, we'd probably just have 11 players! I respect the fact he is definitely not the type of manager who wants to spend money. I know some fans and the media think we have to spend, spend, spend, but every time Tottenham has done a big transfer, generally speaking, those players haven't been the best performing players. It's been those players we bought below the radar for not a lot of money who gave us better performances.

I've never put him under pressure because I am a great believer that all we can do is our best. I know other directors put coaches under pressure if they do not reach targets, finish in the top four or the top five, or whatever. I've never ever had that conversation with him. It's not necessary. We just want to be the best we possibly can be and that's all we can do.

I remember having a conversation with Mauricio quite early on when we weren't doing very well and the style of football was a bit different to what I expected. At Southampton it was quite fast-forward football and at the start here it didn't feel as though that was what we were getting. I was a little bit concerned. He said, 'Don't worry, it will take time and the big thing is the fitness of the players.' He was trying to build them up and to get footballers to *his* level of fitness, often a different level than most people would think. The work ethic of the team took time to be established. He's here at seven o'clock in the morning, often here at seven o'clock at night. He's totally dedicated to winning and he's totally bought into the project.

His ability to talk to all the staff and the link between the academy and the first team is so important. Most managers focus on the first team. They say they love the academy but . . . do they do anything about it? Mauricio often goes round to the academy, he watches some of the matches, he's very integrated with the staff. John McDermott, who is the head of our academy, is always in Mauricio's office. It's one club. Very much like a family club; everybody knows everybody. We don't have a massive infrastructure or big layers of management all over the place and you can get decisions made at this club very, very quickly.

We're both striving for the same thing, that's perfection. He's a perfectionist on the field and I'm a perfectionist off the field. You look at the training facility, probably the best in the world, a fantastic place and environment to work in and the new stadium too. We're building a lodge which will be a 45-bedroom accommodation for the players. When he gets them doing double sessions he can force them to rest. All I can do is give him the very best resources the club can afford and then it's up to him to make the best of them. We're very integrated, so he knows exactly what we're doing in terms of physical facilities and he is involved in suggesting changes and improvements. I see him most days, and we often text each other at night.

I will go and see Mauricio after a game for five minutes. Most of the time I'm saying well done, not much more. There will be times when things don't go well and the kind of bond we are creating means you stick together then. We are strong. I'm very careful what I say because that is his area, not mine. I will often say to him that was a great game, player X or player Y played great in my opinion. But I will never be critical. If he opens up to me and asks what do I think about a player or an ex-player, I'll give an opinion, but really that is his remit.

I don't go into the changing rooms – that is his area. It's his job to motivate and to give guidance to the players. When he needs me I will always be there for him. I'm quite a reserved person. I don't like the limelight, so the idea of me standing in front of the players and giving them a speech is not going to happen. In the almost 17 years that I have been chairman I may have done it three or four times. I went down to congratulate everyone when we got into the Champions League and also when we failed to get to the Champions League after struggling against West Ham due to food poisoning. The players see me at the training ground all the time, my door is always open, so occasionally one or two of them might come to see me about something or they see me with Mauricio having breakfast, or lunch, and they always come over. It really is a family environment.

Signings are a collective decision. Let's say we decide we want to buy a player . . . a defender. Mauricio would be talking to the recruiting department, they would come up with some names; myself, Mauricio and one or two people in the recruiting department would sit down very informally and we'd talk about the options; then the recruitment department and myself would work to understand what is and isn't possible. You can have these names but maybe they're not possible, for one reason or another. Then the recruitment team would go back to Mauricio and say that of the six names, three of them are possible, and then we'd probably have a discussion about the pros and cons of each, such as the type of individual they are, whether old or young, what impact would he have on other positions in the team, does he only play in one position, and money may be relevant, lots of different things. Then Mauricio would decide if he wants player X or player Y or he may say, 'I'm happy with either,' and that's when I really go to work. My job is to deliver what he wants. We can't always have what we want but we certainly try our very best.

We haven't really discussed the money that is available. It's not a secret, it will eventually be between Mauricio and me. We wouldn't go public on it. Mauricio is very aware that firstly we have got a huge capital project that we are embarking upon. For two seasons we have been competing for the title but it's unlikely that we can improve our starting XI without spending a huge sum of money and actually I don't think that either I or Mauricio want to be in that model. It's a huge responsibility, we're a big club but it's run as a proper club, we are self-sufficient. If we make a £60-million investment in a player, that means somebody else is going to be affected in our starting XI, and if we make a mistake, it's very costly. If you look at some stats, particularly for the 2016–17 season – the best defensive record, scored more goals than any other team, best goal difference in our history, youngest squad in the Premier League – you realise we can only aim to improve the squad overall.

I have always said to him that I want him to be a partner, that when he signed a contract for five years – which was a massive commitment for the club – it was on the basis that we were really going to commit to each other. I want Mauricio to be the Alex Ferguson of Tottenham Hotspur and he has the most fantastic opportunity to be that. I have confidence that he can do it. We're so aligned in where we want to be.

I'd be surprised if there wasn't interest in Mauricio from other clubs because it means we are doing well. He's never given me any indication that he'd like to leave. He loves the project and he once sent me a picture of Bill Nicholson – our most famous manager from years ago – holding the fronts of the gates of the stadium. They are very historical gates and we're keeping them at the new stadium. I replied, 'One day it is going to be you,' because that really is what I aspire to. I would love nothing more than Mauricio still to be our manager in ten to 15 years' time. I think to really build success you need time, you need longevity. It's easy to go and become a manager at Real Madrid, for instance. It's a fantastic club, don't get me wrong, but winning at Tottenham Hotspur is far greater than winning at Real Madrid, and he agrees.

Mauricio wants this sense of achievement, this recognition, to be the main guy. And at this club, he can be the main guy. At some other clubs, the president is the main guy but that's not how it is here. I'm so low key, I want him to be the main guy. Him.

Sometimes it's nice to be given something when you are not expecting it like the Bentley I gave him as a sign of appreciation. And it's really weird, we went away for two days in France and we had a wine-tasting experience – we were obviously talking about players as well – and we came back and he bought me a gift and I bought him a gift and it was the same bottle of wine, a dessert wine we'd enjoyed! Isn't that incredible?

APPENDIX 1

2016–17 RESULTS

Date	Competition	Results and goals	League position	Wins	Draws	Losses
13-8-16	Premier League, Game 1 1 point	Everton 1–1 Tottenham Hotspur '5 *Barkley*; '59 Lamela	11	0	1	0
20-8-16	Premier League, Game 2 4 points	Tottenham Hotspur 1–0 Crystal Palace '82 Wanyama	7	1	1	0
27-8-16	Premier League, Game 3 5 points	Tottenham Hotspur 1–1 Liverpool '43 *Milner (penalty)*; '72 Rose	6	1	2	0
10-9-16	Premier League, Game 4 8 points	Stoke City 0–4 Tottenham Hotspur '41, '56 Son; '59 Dele Alli; '70 Kane	5	2	2	0
14-9-16	Champions League Group Stage, Game 1	Tottenham Hotspur 1–2 Monaco '15 *Bernardo Silva*; '31 *Lemar*; '45 Alderweireld		2	2	1
18-9-16	Premier League, Game 5 11 points	Tottenham Hotspur 1–0 Sunderland '59 Kane	3	3	2	1

Date	Competition	Results and goals	League position	Wins	Draws	Losses
21-9-16	League Cup 3rd round	Tottenham Hotspur 5–0 Gillingham '31, '48 Eriksen; '51 Janssen; '65 Onomah; '68 Lamela		4	2	1
24-9-16	Premier League, Game 6 14 points	Middlesbrough 1–2 Tottenham Hotspur '7, '23 Son; '65 Gibson	2	5	2	1
27-9-16	Champions League Group Stage, Game 2	CSKA Moscow 0–1 Tottenham Hotspur '71 Son		6	2	1
2-10-16	Premier League, Game 7 17 points	Tottenham Hotspur 2–0 Manchester City '9 Kolarov (own goal); '37 Dele Alli	2	7	2	1
15-10-16	Premier League, Game 8 18 points	West Bromwich Albion 1–1 Tottenham Hotspur '82 Chadli; '89 Dele Alli	3	7	3	1
18-10-16	Champions League Group Stage, Game 3	Bayer Leverkusen 0–0 Tottenham Hotspur		7	4	1
22-10-16	Premier League, Game 9 19 points	Bournemouth 0–0 Tottenham Hotspur	5	7	5	1

Date	Competition	Results and goals	League position	Wins	Draws	Losses
25-10-16	League Cup, quarter-finals	Liverpool 2–1 Tottenham Hotspur '9, '64 *Sturridge*; '76 Janssen (penalty)		7	5	2
29-10-16	Premier League, Game 10 20 points	Tottenham Hotspur 1–1 Leicester City '44 Janssen (penalty); '48 *Musa*	5	7	6	2
2-11-16	Champions League Group Stage, Game 4	Tottenham Hotspur 0–1 Bayer Leverkusen '65 *Kampl*		7	6	3
6-11-16	Premier League, Game 11 21 points	Arsenal 1–1 Tottenham Hotspur '42 *Wimmer (own goal)*; '51 Kane (penalty)	5	7	7	3
19-11-16	Premier League, Game 12 24 points	Tottenham Hotspur 3–2 West Ham United '24 *Antonio*; '51 Winks; '68 *Lanzini (penalty)*; '89, '91 Kane (penalty)	5	8	7	3
22-11-16	Champions League Group Stage, Game 5	Monaco 2–1 Tottenham Hotspur '48 *Sidibé*; '52 Kane (penalty); '53 *Lemar*		8	7	4

Date	Competition	Results and goals	League position	Wins	Draws	Losses
26-11-16	Premier League, Game 13 24 points	Chelsea 2–1 Tottenham Hotspur '11 Eriksen; '45 *Pedro*; '51 *Moses*	5	8	7	5
3-12-16	Premier League, Game 14 27 points	Tottenham Hotspur 5–0 Swansea '39 Kane (penalty); '46 Son; '49 Kane; '70, '92 Eriksen	5	9	7	5
7-12-16	Champions League Group Stage, Game 6	Tottenham Hotspur 3–1 CSKA Moscow '33 *Dzagoev*; '38 Dele Alli; '46 Kane; '77 *Akinfeev* (own goal)		10	7	5
11-12-16	Premier League, Game 15 27 points	Manchester United 1–0 Tottenham Hotspur '29 *Mkhitaryan*	5	10	7	6
14-12-16	Premier League, Game 16 30 points	Tottenham Hotspur 3–0 Hull City '14, '63 Eriksen; '73 Wanyama	5	11	7	6
18-12-16	Premier League, Game 17 33 points	Tottenham Hotspur 2–1 Burnley '21 *Barnes*; '27 Dele Alli; '71 Rose	5	12	7	6

Date	Competition	Results and goals	League position	Wins	Draws	Losses
28-12-16	Premier League, Game 18 36 points	Southampton 1–4 Tottenham Hotspur '2 *Van Dijk*; '19 Dele Alli; '52 Kane; '85 Son; '87 Dele Alli	5	13	7	6
1-1-17	Premier League, Game 19 39 points	Watford 1–4 Tottenham Hotspur '27, '33 Kane; '41, '46 Dele Alli; '91 *Kaboul*	5	14	7	6
4-1-17	Premier League, Game 20 42 points	Tottenham Hotspur 2–0 Chelsea '46, '54 Dele Alli	3	15	7	6
8-1-17	FA Cup, 3rd Round	Tottenham Hotspur 2–0 Aston Villa '71 Davies; '80 Son		16	7	6
14-1-17	Premier League, Game 21 45 points	Tottenham Hotspur 4–0 West Bromwich Albion '12, '77, '82 Kane; '26 *McAuley* (own goal)	2	17	7	6
21-1-17	Premier League, Game 22 46 points	Manchester City 2–2 Tottenham Hotspur '49 *Sané*; '54 *De Bruyne*; '58 Dele Alli; '77 Son	3	17	8	6

Date	Competition	Results and goals	League position	Wins	Draws	Losses
28-1-17	FA Cup, 4th Round	Tottenham Hotspur 4–3 Wycombe Wanderers '23, '36 *Hayes* (penalty); '60 Son; '64 Janssen (penalty); '83 *Thompson*; '89 Dele Alli; '90 Son		18	8	6
31-1-17	Premier League, Game 23 47 points	Sunderland 0–0 Tottenham Hotspur	2	18	9	6
4-2-17	Premier League, Game 24 50 points	Tottenham Hotspur 1–0 Middlesbrough '50 Kane (penalty)	2	19	9	6
11-2-17	Premier League, Game 25 50 points	Liverpool 2–0 Tottenham Hotspur '16, '18 *Mané*	3	19	9	7
16-2-17	Europa League, round of 16	Gent 1–0 Tottenham Hotspur '59 *Perbet*		19	9	8
19-2-17	FA Cup, quarter-finals	Fulham 0–3 Tottenham Hotspur '16, '51, '73 Kane		20	9	8

Date	Competition	Results and goals	League position	Wins	Draws	Losses
23-2-17	Europa League, round of 16	Tottenham Hotspur 2–2 Gent '10 Eriksen; '20 Kane (own goal); '61 Wanyama; '82 *Perbet*		20	10	8
26-2-17	Premier League, Game 26 53 points	Tottenham Hotspur 4–0 Stoke City '14, '32, '37 Kane; '45 Dele Alli	2	21	10	8
5-3-17	Premier League, Game 27 56 points	Tottenham Hotspur 3–2 Everton '20, '56 Kane; '81 *Lukaku*; '90 Dele Alli; '90 *Valencia*	2	22	10	8
12-3-17	FA Cup, quarter-finals	Tottenham Hotspur 6–0 Millwall '31 Eriksen; '41, '54 Son; '72 Dele Alli; '79 Janssen; '90 Son		23	10	8
19-3-17	Premier League, Game 29	Tottenham Hotspur 2–1 Southampton '14 Eriksen; '33 Alli (penalty); '52 *Ward-Prowse*	2	24	10	8

Date	Competition	Results and goals	League position	Wins	Draws	Losses
1-4-17	Premier League, Game 30	Burnley 0–2 Tottenham Hotspur '66 Dier; '77 Son	2	25	10	8
5-4-17	Premier League, Game 31	Swansea 1–3 Tottenham Hotspur '11 *Routledge*; '88 Dele Alli; '90 Son; '90 Eriksen	2	26	10	8
8-4-17	Premier League, Game 32	Tottenham Hotspur 4–0 Watford '33 Dele Alli; '39 Dier; '44, '55 Son	2	27	10	8
15-4-17	Premier League, Game 33	Tottenham Hotspur 4–0 Bournemouth '16 Dembélé; '19 Son; '48 Kane; '90 Janssen	2	28	10	8
22-4-17	FA Cup, semi-finals	Chelsea 4–2 Tottenham Hotspur '5 *Willian*; '18 Kane; '43 *Willian* (penalty); '52 Dele Alli; '75 *Hazard*; '80 *Matic*		28	10	9
26-4-17	Premier League, Game 28 (postponed)	Crystal Palace 0–1 Tottenham Hotspur '78 Eriksen	2	29	10	9

Date	Competition	Results and goals	League position	Wins	Draws	Losses
30-4-17	Premier League, Game 35	Tottenham Hotspur 2–0 Arsenal '55 Dele Alli; '58 Kane (penalty)	2	30	10	9
5-5-17	Premier League, Game 36	West Ham United 1–0 Tottenham Hotspur '65 *Lanzini*	2	30	10	10
14-5-17	Premier League, Game 37	Tottenham Hotspur 2–1 Manchester United '6 Wanyama; '48 Kane; '71 *Rooney*	2	31	10	10
18-5-17	Premier League, Game 34 (postponed)	Leicester City 1–6 Tottenham Hotspur '25, '63, '89, '90 Kane; '36, '71 Son; '60 *Chilwell*	2	32	10	10
21-5-17	Premier League, Game 38	Hull City 1–7 Tottenham Hotspur '11, '13, '72 Kane; '45 Dele Alli; '66 *Clucas*; '69 Wanyama; '84 Davies; '87 Alderweireld	2	33	10	10

APPENDIX 2

SEASON-BY-SEASON COMPARISON

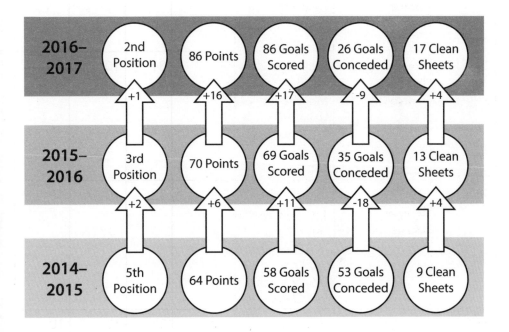

2016–2017	2nd Position	86 Points	86 Goals Scored	26 Goals Conceded	17 Clean Sheets
	+1	+16	+17	-9	+4
2015–2016	3rd Position	70 Points	69 Goals Scored	35 Goals Conceded	13 Clean Sheets
	+2	+6	+11	-18	+4
2014–2015	5th Position	64 Points	58 Goals Scored	53 Goals Conceded	9 Clean Sheets

ACKNOWLEDGEMENTS

Sometimes we lose perspective. When Orion suggested a book about Mauricio Pochettino, I could not believe I had not thought of it myself. It made a lot of sense. I had followed his career very closely at Espanyol, the club I have supported since I was a kid. I had seen him work with the youngsters in a very emotional period for the club, and had heard many times from him and his staff what they were trying to do. They were exciting times – a young coach full of energy wanting to change the recent history of our Espanyol. While at Southampton and Tottenham, we kept in touch. Then Mark Rusher, a big Spurs fan working for Orion at the time, suggested his name – and it was good timing. Instead of telling the story of a coach who had succeeded at a legendary club, or of a couple of players the like of which we had rarely seen before, this was the account of a manager on the up in a team in the ascendant, applying what he had learnt in Argentina and Spain to create the necessary will to win things. So I approached Mauricio with the idea, but it was Karina Grippaldi, his wife, who actually told him to get involved. So he did!

I have to thank Mauricio for the huge amount of time he found for me and for allowing me to roam the training ground regularly, and to Karina for opening the doors of their house and their photo albums, as well as for that deep fascinating chat that included young Sebas and Mauri. I know I disturbed them during the summer as they mixed relaxation with checking the accuracy of what I was writing. Jesús Pérez was ever present and always sanguine, listening and making me understand the intricacies of the job of a manager and his assistants. Many mornings Miki d'Agostino drove me to the training ground, and he always had a fascinating story to tell. Toni Jiménez seemed a bit embarrassed and shy to tell me about his admiration for Pochettino, but that also gave me a huge insight into what kind of bonds Mauricio creates. Susan Bowdidge, Mauricio's secretary, was a welcoming smile every Monday at his office. Simon Felstein couldn't have been more helpful and understood and supported the project from day one.

All the players, friends, directors and coaches I spoke to offered new insights into Pochettino's world. From Hugo Lloris (who even rang twice to give me more anecdotes) to Harry Kane, Dele Alli, Danny Rose, Daniel Levy, Ramon Planas, Alejandro E. Alonso, John McDermott, Paul Mitchell, Jordi Amat, Victor Wanyama, Harry Winks, Les Reed, Jay Rodriguez, Luke Shaw, Adam Lallana and Eric Dier. Bill Beswick helped me understand the psychology of managers and directed my confused thinking once again.

I keep saying this but repetition does not make it less true. It is such a privilege that a company such as Orion and Alan Samson, the publisher of the Weidenfeld & Nicolson imprint, give me the support and confidence that is needed to keep writing books, even though I never thought I had more than one in me. David Luxton is the perfect foil and good to bounce ideas off. Paul Murphy exudes the calmness and vision that is so necessary to give the book the editorial touches that make it what it is.

And of course, I have to thank my team. Without them, this would be much less fun: Maribel Herruzo, the perfect companion, organiser, researcher and so many more things; William Glasswell and his encouraging words while proofreading; Miguel García with his contagious good humour and accurate comments; Marc Joss and Hugo Steckelmacher, the best translators in the business; Peter Lockyer, who is always there when needed; and Brent Wilks, who made sure the rest of the company worked while we were all in another land. From which we have just come back.

DEJÉ LA PUERTA ABIERTA UN AÑO;
LA NECESIDAD DE INTIMIDAD ME PIDE
QUE LA VUELVA A CERRAR.
   CORRE EL VIENTO; PERO ME DA QUE
POR EL CAMINO NOS HEMOS CONOCIDO
UN POCO MÁS.

I left the door open for a year. The need for intimacy is demanding that I close it again – the wind is blowing in.

But I feel that over the course of this journey, we have got to know each other a bit more.